CHRISTIAN IMPERIAL FEMINISM

NORTH AMERICAN RELIGIONS

Series Editors: Tracy Fessenden (Arizona State University), Laura Levitt (Temple University), and David Harrington Watt (Haverford College)

Since its inception, the North American Religions book series has steadily disseminated gracefully written, pathbreaking explorations of religion in North America. Books in the series move among the discourses of ethnographic, textual, and historical analysis and across a range of topics, including sound, story, food, nature, healing, crime, and pilgrimage. In so doing they bring religion into view as a style and form of belonging, a set of tools for living with and in relations of power, a mode of cultural production and reproduction, and a vast repertory of the imagination. Whatever their focus, books in the series remain attentive to the shifting and contingent ways in which religious phenomena are named, organized, and contested. They bring fluency in the best of contemporary theoretical and historical scholarship to bear on the study of religion in North America. The series focuses primarily, but not exclusively, on religion in the United States in the twentieth and twenty-first centuries.

Books in the series

Ava Chamberlain, *The Notorious Elizabeth Tuttle: Marriage, Murder, and Madness in the Family of Jonathan Edwards*

Terry Rey and Alex Stepick, *Crossing the Water and Keeping the Faith: Haitian Religion in Miami*

Isaac Weiner, *Religion Out Loud: Religious Sound, Public Space, and American Pluralism*

Hillary Kaell, *Walking Where Jesus Walked: American Christians and Holy Land Pilgrimage*

Brett Hendrickson, *Border Medicine: A Transcultural History of Mexican American Curanderismo*

Jodi Eichler-Levine, *Suffer the Little Children: Uses of the Past in Jewish and African American Children's Literature*

Annie Blazer, *Playing for God: Evangelical Women and the Unintended Consequences of Sports Ministry*

Elizabeth Pérez, *Religion in the Kitchen: Cooking, Talking, and the Making of Black Atlantic Traditions*

Kerry Mitchell, *Spirituality and the State: Managing Nature and Experience in America's National Parks*

Finbarr Curtis, *The Production of American Religious Freedom*

M. Cooper Harriss, *Ralph Ellison's Invisible Theology*

Ari Y. Kelman, *Shout to the Lord: Making Worship Music in Evangelical America*

Joshua Dubler and Isaac Weiner, *Religion, Law, USA*

Shari Rabin, *Jews on the Frontier: Religion and Mobility in Nineteenth-Century America*

Elizabeth Fenton, *Old Canaan in a New World: Native Americans and the Lost Tribes of Israel*

Alyssa Maldonado-Estrada, *Lifeblood of the Parish: Men and Catholic Devotion in Williamsburg, Brooklyn*

Caleb Iyer Elfenbein, *Fear in Our Hearts: What Islamophobia Tells Us about America*

Rachel B. Gross, *Beyond the Synagogue: Jewish Nostalgia as Religious Practice*

Jenna Supp-Montgomerie, *When the Medium Was the Mission: The Atlantic Telegraph and the Religious Origins of Network Culture*

Philippa Koch, *The Course of God's Providence: Religion, Health, and the Body in Early America*

Jennifer Scheper Hughes, *The Church of the Dead: The Epidemic of 1576 and the Birth of Christianity in the Americas*

Tisa Wenger and Sylvester A. Johnson, *Religion and US Empire: Critical New Histories*

Deborah Dash Moore, *Vernacular Religion: Collected Essays of Leonard Norman Primiano*

Laura Yares, *Jewish Sunday Schools: Teaching Religion in Nineteenth-Century America*

Katrina Daly Thompson, *Muslims on the Margins: Creating Queer Religious Community in North America*

Jonathan H. Ebel, *From Dust They Came: Government Camps and the Religion of Reform in New Deal California*

Gale L. Kenny, *Christian Imperial Feminism: White Protestant Women and the Consecration of Empire*

Christian Imperial Feminism

White Protestant Women and the Consecration of Empire

Gale L. Kenny

NEW YORK UNIVERSITY PRESS
New York

NEW YORK UNIVERSITY PRESS
New York
www.nyupress.org

© 2024 by New York University
All rights reserved

Please contact the Library of Congress for Cataloging-in-Publication data.
ISBN: 9781479825516 (hardback)
ISBN: 9781479825530 (paperback)
ISBN: 9781479825554 (library ebook)
ISBN: 9781479825547 (consumer ebook)

This book is printed on acid-free paper, and its binding materials are chosen for strength and durability. We strive to use environmentally responsible suppliers and materials to the greatest extent possible in publishing our books.

Manufactured in the United States of America

10 9 8 7 6 5 4 3 2 1

Also available as an ebook

For Jacqueline Schmitt

CONTENTS

Abbreviations — xi

Introduction: Consecrating Empire — 1

1. Christian Imperial Feminism and Mission Study — 19

2. Performing Christian Imperial Feminism in Missionary Pageants — 51

3. Learning to Cooperate by Cooperating — 80

4. Christian Americanization and the Tri-Faith Movement — 105

5. The Spiritual Feelings and Religious Politics of Interracial Cooperation — 138

6. Christian Citizens, World Citizens — 168

Conclusion: Christianity and Women's Rights — 199

Acknowledgments — 205

Notes — 209

Bibliography — 239

Index — 255

About the Author — 269

ABBREVIATIONS

CWCRR—Church Woman's Committee on Race Relations
CWHM—Council of Women for Home Missions
FCC—Federal Council of Churches
FWBFM—Federation of Woman's Boards of Foreign Missions
NCCCW—National Conference on the Cause and Cure of War
NCCJ—National Conference of Christians and Jews
UCCW—United Council of Church Women
UMS—United Mission Study

Introduction

Consecrating Empire

"Needed—A Racial Cartography." In this 1940 *Church Woman* article, Leila Avery Rothenburger proposed a map of the Western Hemisphere that would replace national borders with different swaths of color indicating "the racial elements that must be harmonized in goodwill." This hemispheric map of "racial elements" would prompt White Americans to categorize people in terms of race rather than nationality. It would also enable White Americans to recognize that "the white man" belonged to "the smallest color group in this hemisphere, as he is in all the world." Rothenburger explained that once White Americans realized their minority status and acknowledged their dismal record when it came to viewing Black and "Indian" people in the United States as equals, they would be confronted with an alarming question: How could White Americans "say much to the rest of the world about the brotherhood of man?"[1]

Rothenburger's proposed map reflected one of many exercises intended to move White Protestant churchwomen to combat racism in their local communities and in the world. Rothenburger herself had experienced the spiritually transformative effects of interracial cooperation in her own life. The White churchwoman had worked as a public school teacher before marrying her husband, a Disciples of Christ minister, and settling in Indianapolis. She had been in the women's foreign missionary movement and the YWCA, and, in 1930, she joined the "Interracial Seminar on Wheels," a group of Black and White Protestants who toured Black schools and churches across the US South to investigate segregation and to model interracial cooperation. She shared much in common with the mostly White organized Protestant women reading her article in the *Church Woman*. They likely nodded along as they read Rothenburger's familiar instructions that women needed to study national and global racial groups and "racial attitudes" if they were to foster an interracial spiritual community. In their own ecumenical churchwomen's councils, they had likely participated in interracial cooperation projects meant to foster "inter-racial understanding." As Rothenburger argued, these programs had helped "steady the Christian constituency" amid rampant "race hatred." Those programs had also prepared Protestants to take the lead in managing social and race relations more generally. In her conclusion, Rothenburger pointed to the recent Interfaith Conference on Unemployment that called on churches and "their informed laymen" to address racial discrimination in relation to employment, education, housing, and other matters. Rothenburger agreed with one minor adjustment: "the best laymen we know are the laywomen," she wrote, "and the imperative is theirs."[2]

Rothenburger believed White Protestant woman were uniquely positioned and called by God to study race and racism and to participate in interracial cooperation activities with Black churchwomen. Their qualifications stemmed from their missionary past. In mission study classes in the early 1900s, White Protestant women had produced a gendered missionary ethnology that classified and ranked human differences in the service of their evangelical objective to create a pleasingly cosmopolitan and well-ordered kingdom of God.[3] They believed without question that their brand of Protestantism created the conditions for a Christian imperial feminism that called for the emancipation of women from "ethnic religions." They also believed that the birthing of a diverse yet united global kingdom of God depended on the work of an international cast of women. Still, by the time Rothenburger was writing in the early 1940s, the means for creating the kingdom of God had changed. Most White women's missionary societies had been shuttered and their missions had been transformed from straightforward evangelism into a more diffuse campaign to Christianize racial and international relations. Within the United States, churchwomen sought to Christianize social relations as they extended their Christian imperial feminist project to local "Christian Americanization" and interracial cooperation programs. Importantly, these missionary-inspired projects also subjected earlier White Protestant women's missionary history and motives to critique. As White and Black churchwomen established the United Council of Church Women (UCCW) in 1941, they would build on those criticisms as they refashioned Christian imperial feminism into a Christian racial liberalism. Like Rothenburger, they would point to Protestant Christianity's racial progress to justify Protestant women's gendered moral authority to set the terms of the racial order.[4]

Instead of presenting this history as a story of gradual progress as White Protestants recognized and repented for the error of their racist ways, this book instead argues that White Protestant missionary women's Christian imperial feminism persisted in churchwomen's cosmopolitan practices. Through analysis of their missionary literature and cosmopolitan practices, I show how White Protestant women formed their identity and defined their religious activism through the racial, religious, and gendered hierarchies of the missionary movement's imperialism. They did this not only by positioning themselves as the rescuers of "heathen" women, but also by identifying and analyzing the intersecting "problems" of race, empire, and women's rights and seeking to resolve them through their cosmopolitan Christianity.[5]

By focusing on White-led ecumenical women's organizations, both missionary and post-missionary, the book also provides a critical account of ecumenical Protestantism in the first half of the twentieth century. Historians of American religion have tended to contrast racially liberal, anti-imperialist, and religiously tolerant White ecumenical Protestants with conservative White evangelicals.[6] In contrast, I show how ecumenical Protestants, and especially White ecumenical Protestant women, paired their budding criticisms of White supremacy and western imperialism with their own Christian imperial feminist designs for their local communities, the nation, and the world. Organized Protestant women replaced a once vaulted "Christian civilization" with a cosmopolitan Christianity of racial liberalism, internationalism, and women's rights that they claimed to be universally desirable and singularly modern. Further, studies of ecumenical Protestantism overwhelmingly downplay the role of women in this movement. When they do note the existence of ecumenical women, historians find that they had little interest in a budding second-wave feminist movement.[7] Such assessments disregard other modes of feminine authority developed by missionary women-turned-churchwomen. By tracking Christian imperial feminism from its well-known missionary origins in the early 1900s through its integration into the politics of liberal Protestants in the 1940s, we see how organized Protestant churchwomen contributed to ecumenical Protestantism and how their sustained commitment to a particular form of women's rights contributed to ongoing "liberal dilemmas" concerning multiculturalism, religion, and women's rights.[8]

Christian imperial feminism took shape initially in the missionary literature circulated in the White women's missionary movement that began in earnest in the 1870s. Following the Civil War, White Protestant women in the northern United States formed separate foreign and home missionary societies from the existing male-led missions boards. Funded primarily through women's donations and membership dues, these societies grew into a national network of organized Protestant women, and in most cases, local, state, and national women's missionary societies functioned as laywomen's domain within otherwise male-dominated institutions.[9] Thousands of White women who would not work as missionaries themselves participated in the home and foreign missionary movements by reading missionary magazines, attending monthly missionary society meetings, putting on missionary pageants, and praying and raising money for the cause. By the early 1900s, the leaders of the Methodist, Baptist, Presbyterian, Congregationalist, Episcopal, Disciples of Christ, and other smaller denominational women's mission boards began to work together, as did their male counterparts, in what became known as the ecumenical movement. Organized Protestant women formed the Council of Women for Home Missions and the Federation of Woman's Boards of Foreign Missions. These related closely with the male-led and New York–based Federal Council of Churches, the Home Missions Council, and the Foreign Missions Conference, and with other collaborative agencies like the YMCA and YWCA. At the local level, Protestant clergy, laymen, and laywomen set up interdenominational church federations that often included a women's council. Although several Black denominations joined these ecumenical bodies, the leadership was almost exclusively White men and women. After two decades of increasing cooperation, in 1941, the women's missionary Council and Federation merged with other Protestant women's organizations to establish the UCCW, now known as Church Women United.[10]

Historians typically have differentiated these theologically and politically liberal "ecumenical" White Protestants from more theologically and politically conservative "evangelicals," a term with its own fraught history.[11] Yet these distinctions grew more heightened *after* the period covered in this book. The ecumenical organizations listed above often included individuals who might be considered evangelicals or conservatives even as they shared a common desire with liberals to enhance White Protestants' power and influence by forming interdenominational organizations.[12] By the 1940s and 1950s, however, the ecumenical Federal Council had endorsed the progressive economic policies of FDR's New Deal, Black civil rights, and the liberal internationalism represented in the new United Nations. Ecumenical Protestants' support for women's ordination, the ERA, and in many cases abortion rights and gay rights also aligned them with political liberals.[13] As historian Gene Zubovich argues, these stances led more politically conservative White Protestants to break away from many of these ecumenical projects.[14] Those conservative evangelicals also engaged with "the world" through their missions, humanitarian work, and foreign policy interests, but they often positioned themselves against the ecumenical theology and liberal internationalism of the Protestants discussed in this book.[15] These contrasting ideas of American power and human rights are certainly important, but a focus on those later twentieth-century debates can obscure a more complex analysis of the ecumenical movement's own imperial designs.

The early ecumenical movement was an imperial formation even as its participants came to criticize western imperialism and even support anticolonial movements. In the early 1900s, White Protestants created ecumenical organizations for practical reasons of efficiency related to their social programs in the United States and their foreign and home missionary operations. Rather than examining missions in isolation from other endeavors, this book examines them as part of a whole. The ecumenical movement also reflected a developing theological imperative to unify all Christians in one united and universal church, albeit defined in distinctly White Protestant terms. Ecumenical advocates of a new Christian world order believed a (Euro-American Protestant) Christianity would replace western imperialism, defeat the forces of secularism, and bind the world's peoples into a diverse, equitable, and orderly world community that abided by their own liberal Protestant mores. This ecumenical-imperial plan for a Christian world order existed alongside another reason for ecumenical organizing: Protestants sought to bridge denominational boundaries to maintain their moral authority amid Black migration to northern cities and European immigration. Ecumenical Protestants created "Christian Americanization" programs aimed at immigrants in the 1920s and supported "interracial cooperation" with Black Protestants. Analyses of the practical workings of both exemplify how White Protestant women interpreted them less as a departure from Protestant missions and more as a new front of missions that sought to "Christianize" social relations. White Protestants, and particularly White Protestant women, claimed the responsibility of setting the terms of religious and racial inclusion. When those outside of the White ecumenical Protestant fold contested their power, Protestants responded in different ways, sometimes insisting that Christianity alone could peacefully mediate differences, while in other cases criticisms led to a reinterpretation of Christian mores. A focus on the Christian imperial feminism of organized Protestant women foregrounds the ecumenical movement's imperial ambitions and connects its global vision to how White Protestants sought to manage religious and other human differences in the United States.[16]

Missionary and ecumenical organizations were the means through which White Protestant women enacted their racial, religious, and gender identity. I often describe my subjects as "White ecumenical Protestants" and "organized Protestant women" to denote the centrality of institutions to how they understood themselves. Missionary societies and churchwomen's councils unified White women across denominations through a shared commitment to Christian imperial feminism and a related religio-racial identity.[17] Building on the work of scholars of religion, race, and gender, I argue that Whiteness, womanhood, and Protestantism were not separate identities but co-constituted and interdependent and shaped through contrasts with the "degraded womanhood" of "ethnic religions," with Black women, and with organized Catholic and Jewish women. In some cases, particularly following the formation of the UCCW, I use the term "organized Protestant women" to include Black churchwomen and other non-White Protestants in this collective. Black churchwomen were also organized as they mobilized around missions, temperance, and racial justice in the late 1800s, and their own religio-racial gender identity developed in the circumstances of Jim Crow segregation, a missionary interest in Africa, Black educational institutions (often funded in part by White northerners), and racial uplift work in Black women's clubs and church organizations.[18] Black people were often marginalized in White-led ecumenical organizations. But Black women's political skills forged in Black women's organizations and in the YWCA would enable them to play an instrumental role in reshaping White women's Christian imperial feminism in the 1930s and 1940s and in many cases to join their White colleagues in advocating for and managing a Christian world order.

Empire, Missionaries, and Christian Imperial Feminism

For the past several decades, scholars have engaged in a multifaceted analysis of US empire and settler colonialism that often takes religion into consideration. Imperialism can be broadly defined as a system of governance in which a state or polity exerts control over a territory and subordinated—and often racially or religiously differentiated—population. In the context of the United States, scholars have debated whether the United States is a nation-state, settler colony, empire, or all the above. Addressing these conversations, Paul Kramer noted that in addition to analyzing the "formal empire" of US territorial colonies, empire itself can be a category of analysis, "something to think with more than to think about." The "imperial," Kramer writes, "refers to a dimension of power" in which "regimes of spatial ordering, and modes of exceptionalizing difference enable and produce relations of hierarchy, discipline, dispossession, extraction, and exploitation."[19] In this vein, scholars have shown how overlapping hierarchies of race, gender, and religion were potent tools for justifying imperial ventures and ordering colonial governance. The knowledge produced through the imperial project discursively reinforced and deepened those hierarchies as it shaped an imperial culture in the United States.[20]

White Protestant missionaries' letters and reports, meeting minutes, and publications have provided a rich archive for tracking imperialism before and after the pivotal date of 1898 that has tended to mark the beginning of formal empire. Writing about the first half of the 1800s, Emily Conroy-Krutz identified US Protestant missionaries' reliance on imperialism to access distant populations while also noting that they contrasted their own benevolent and hierarchical "Christian imperialism" with what they often saw as the corrupt imperialism of Britain and the United States.[21] As part of their efforts to spread a superior Christian civilization, these nineteenth-century White Protestants articulated and disseminated "hierarchies of heathenism," and as work by Derek Chang, Kathryn Gin Lum, and others shows, those religio-racial missionary categories informed the terms of race, religion, and citizenship for racialized people within the United States as well. Because of their enthusiasm for the missionary cause and their effective organizations, White Protestant missionary women played a central role in popularizing the Orientalist and racist tropes of missionary literature to a wide audience. They produced what Joan Jacobs Brumberg calls a "missionary ethnology" focused particularly on the status of women and the abuses of patriarchal "ethnic religions."[22]

The complicated personal dynamics between White missionaries and their would-be converts could lead individual missionaries to be openly critical of racial, class, and imperial power inequalities and the complicity and even violence of the Protestant missionary movement as an abettor of empire. Many of the missionary women and churchwomen discussed in this book voiced sharp critiques of White supremacy and imperial projects. Yet in spite of individual women's protests, as historian Mary Renda observes, "imperial logics shaped the missionary endeavor" and few disputed "the conceit that white-dominated Christianity, with its culturally specific notions of decorum, had something uniquely liberating to offer around the world."[23] When White Protestant women condemned racism and imperialism, they did so on their own terms which usually differed from how Black and colonized people imagined their own freedom. Moreover, missions-supporting women deepened the missionary movement's imperial logics, naturalized them through making them part of their religious practice, and disseminated them more widely. As Christian imperial feminists, White Protestant women advanced a vision of a Christian empire that often but not always overlapped with US global hegemony. They aimed to "emancipate" women while at the same time also promoting the cosmopolitan knowledge of the missionary movement as a resource for education, self-improvement, and cultural refinement for its middle-class White participants.[24] Protestant women created an appealing and modern Christian cosmopolitanism that linked the hierarchical power dynamics of White women's rescue fantasies of liberating religiously oppressed women to their seemingly more egalitarian vision of a Protestant and transnational community of women.[25]

Christian imperial feminism can be understood as one of many feminisms in the twentieth century. Working with the idea of "imperial feminism" developed by scholars of gender, race, and the British empire, I define Christian imperial feminism in three ways.[26] First, Christian imperial feminism refers to White Protestant women's belief that only their brand of Protestant Christianity could produce the religious, social, and political circumstances that would enable a woman's emancipation. This normative Protestant feminism relied on and advanced a set of assumptions, particularly that racialized "ethnic religions" could not be reformed, as women's subordination was a fundamental part of their core texts. Christian imperial feminism also produced a universal idea of "womanhood" that presumed that all people identified as "women" shared the same fundamental desire to be "emancipated." Second, Christian imperial feminism describes White Protestant women's understanding of themselves as Christian feminists. Mission study textbooks engrossed missionary supporters in a gendered study of comparative religion that resulted in feminist interpretations of the Bible and Christian history from those imperial comparisons. Further, as was the case more generally in the late nineteenth century, women's separate missionary societies cultivated a sense of White Protestant women's moral authority and citizenship. Third, I argue that Christian imperial feminism made the matter of empire and human difference into an object of study of particular importance to Protestant women. Writing about the imperial project of religious studies, David Chidester notes that for these theorists, "the empire was both opportunity and obstacle, simultaneously a context for theorizing and a problem to be theorized."[27] The same was true for White Protestant women who saw western imperialism as a modernizing force that enabled the creation of a global Christianity, yet who also saw imperialism as inferior to a supposedly more equitable ecumenical Christianity. In this sense, Christian imperial feminism also captures White Protestant women's vision of a multiracial and even multicultural Christian feminist alternative to existing global arrangements of politics and power.

The work of organized Protestant women to disseminate these ideas in their churches and local communities offers insights into the multidimensional role of religion in shaping postwar racial liberalism.[28] While many White ecumenical Protestants became strongly invested in the civil rights movement and anticolonial movements, we should also attend to how they maintained the imperial logics of the missionary movement within their own efforts to rethink race relations and internationalism. White Protestant women's Christian imperialism joined other interwar Protestant programs that laid the groundwork for the postwar racial break, a shift that Howard Winant and others define as the Cold War–era shift from one form of White supremacy to a racial liberalism mobilized in part to support American global power.[29]

In all three aspects of Christian imperial feminism, White women tethered their moral, social, and political authority to their expertise in managing difference. Their authority and identity as White women were formed by how they related themselves to non-Christian women in need of rescue and emancipation. They debated what aspects of human life constituted "culture" and what was "religion," and what preferable and aestheticized "racial" and "national" elements would enhance White Protestants' Christianity and what elements needed to be reformed. In this sense, the work done in women's mission study classes and pageants as well as in their Christian Americanization programs and interracial committees was not unlike what scholars of critical secularism studies have defined as the objectives of secularism. By secularism, I mean not the absence of religion, but what scholars define as the means for governing religion. We can, then, see how White Protestant women's work to define permissible religious beliefs, emotions, and practices contributed to a largely Protestant-informed normative secularism in the United States. At the same time, they engaged in the very work of secularism when they distinguished their Christian organizations and religious goals from, for example, those of "secular" women's clubs. Rather than debate whether these Protestant women's brand of feminism was religious or secular, this book instead presents a more complicated picture.[30] Whether or not these churchwomen were "feminists" in the second-wave sense of the term, it is unarguable that they sought to exercise their power as women through managing race and religion.[31] The identities of White Protestant women and, in time, their Black colleagues as "churchwomen" were shaped by the management practices they created and deployed to categorize and order the people living in their communities, the nation, and the world.

Archival Absences and Cosmopolitan Practices

This volume began as a different book. Interested in the connections between missionaries and humanitarianism, I began with the archives of the White Disciples of Christ missionary named Emory Ross who, after two decades in Liberia and the Belgian Congo, became involved in various philanthropic and humanitarian agencies focused on African American and African education. While working with Ross's substantial archive housed in the Missionary Research Library at Union Theological Seminary, I was intrigued by the contents one folder dedicated to Ross's wife and frequent collaborator, Myrta Ross. Myrta Ross attended the same college as Emory, had worked at the same Disciples-funded Black industrial school in Alabama, and had edited the interdenominational mission newspaper when Emory headed the Congo Protestant Council.[32] When they returned to the United States in the 1930s, Emory Ross moved into administrative work for the Foreign Missions Conference and the controversial Phelps-Stokes Fund, and Myrta served on several women's committees and spent two (mostly unpaid) decades as the staff officer and public relations officer for the United Council of Church Women. She was also politically active, and she joined Black churchwoman Anna Arnold Hedgeman in testifying before a congressional committee on behalf of the Fair Employment Practices Committee in the 1940s. One of the Rosses' granddaughters generously sent me copies of Myrta's "Ross Ramblings" that provided more insights into her life in New York City, her partnership with Emory, and her own career. While this book is not about Myrta Ross, it is in many ways inspired by her and the challenging legacies of that generation of White Protestant women.

Very few of this book's Protestant women—White or Black—have personal archival papers stored in a library depository. I have often had to rely on brief obituaries in newspapers and sometimes Ancestry.com records to uncover details about their lives or, in the case of married women, their given names. But these women can be found in institutional records and publications. Both married and single women served as officers of women's missionary societies and local churchwomen's councils. They wrote reports, took minutes, prepared liturgies, and organized countless conferences where Protestant women gathered to attend panels, discuss topics in roundtables, and, often, to be entertained by a pageant and to participate in woman-led prayer services. Women also edited missionary magazines and wrote articles for those periodicals and for the UCCW's *Church Woman*. A few wrote longer mission study textbooks commissioned annually by missionary women's Central Committee on the United Study of Foreign Missions as well. Baptist Helen Barrett Montgomery, for example, not only wrote six United Mission Study textbooks, but she also prepared pamphlets providing suggestions on pedagogical techniques local groups could use to teach the textbook, a metacommentary that revealed a great deal about her own interpretation of Christian imperial feminism.

Working with this varied archive, I reconstruct the cosmopolitan practices that served as the means for describing, visualizing, and experiencing White women's vision of the empire of Christ. In a broad sense, it addresses the fact that Protestants *have* practices even though they are often defined (and define themselves) around belief. Despite longstanding efforts by scholars to describe and analyze White American Protestants' practices, and the importance of materiality, embodiment, and sensory experiences to those practices, generative discussions of how to study and define "practice" more often arise in studies of Catholics, Jews, and other groups as scholars try to break from the mold of a belief-centered and Protestant definition of religion. This is perhaps even more striking when considering White ecumenical Protestants as scholars has focused primarily on interpreting the disembodied theological and political writings of male theologians and Federal Council leaders rather than the ecumenical rituals often created and performed by women. As we will see in the analysis of White women's mission study classes and pageants, racialized and gendered bodies were integral to Christian imperial feminism. They also factored intensively into the White-led but often interracial rituals of committee meetings and conferences and in the cosmopolitan aesthetics and sensual spiritual experiences of the World Day of Prayer, World Community Day, and Race Relations Sunday.[33]

For White and Black women, Protestant womanhood was continuously created in missionary literature and in these practices. To paraphrase Alyssa Maldonado-Estrada's assessment of Catholic masculinity, femininity is not "inherently tied to or emergent" from female bodies but is "made and imagined" through practices.[34] White churchwomen adapted nineteenth-century Protestant gender norms that emphasized White women's innate piety and sympathy into a universalist and what they considered modern Protestant gender ideology that positioned women as effective organizers who were skilled in the art of cooperation. Additionally, women-led prayer services, like the World Day of Prayer, asserted women's spiritual authority to address complex questions of social disorder, class divisiveness, racism, and war. Churchwomen also viewed political activism as a religious practice when they sought to educate and mobilize voters on behalf of Prohibition, of course, but also for foreign policy, immigration, and civil rights issues they saw as enshrining their cosmopolitan Christianity in the law. Organized Protestant women created a Protestant femininity as they routinely described their mission study programs, pageants, meetings, prayer services, and political activism as women's church work in contradistinction to Protestant men's work as ministers and theologians. White missionary women and later churchwomen also developed a sentimental politics that connected their political activism and more traditional religious practices. As an "intimate public," they drew on a common repertoire of emotions through which Protestant women embodied their gender through their religious feelings about race.[35] Through these practices, Protestant women consecrated their vision of empire and consecrated themselves to serving God by helping to bring about order in God's diverse kingdom.

The archival sources for this book included published materials such as mission study textbooks and "how to use" handbooks that included metacommentary on the text as well as recommended pedagogical exercises like debates, dramatic skits, and pageants. Working with Birgit Meyer's idea of "sensational religion," I show how these missionary practices established cosmopolitan aesthetics and structures of feeling related to diversity that became a script for White churchwomen's practices in later decades.[36] When White and Black women (and sometimes Asian American women) formed interracial organizations, White women often described these experiences as spiritually charged, while Black women more often reported feelings of frustration with their

White colleagues' often patronizing attitudes. Rather than assuming a practice is "religious," I interrogate when and how churchwomen defined their practices as such. I also address churchwomen's intentions for these practices. Practices might be intended as devotional, pleasurable, educational, or disciplinary, or some combination of those things, and they discussed how the individual experience related to different constructions of collective identity.

In some cases, churchwomen used outward-facing practices to raise money, to educate the public, and to demonstrate their moral stance on political and policy questions. In addition to voter education and mobilization, they connected personal piety to social and political action in ways meant to make structural inequalities visible. For example, the physical presence of churchwomen meeting in public spaces was one way that they used their practices to shape public opinion. Historian Betty Livingston Adams argues that interracial groups of churchwomen "challenged prevailing discourses on race, space, and religion" and that theirs was "a program of applied theology and religious education."[37] As women with social power in their communities, their practices were different from disruptive protests and instead used their class, religious, and racial position to their advantage. By hosting interracial teas, missionary lectures, or an evening prayer service followed by a reception, churchwomen enacted a Protestant femininity that built on and reinvented the Christian imperial feminism formulated in the White women's missionary movement.

The Scope of the Book

The book begins with two chapters set in the White women's missionary movement of the early twentieth century. Chapter 1, "Christian Imperial Feminism and Mission Study," discusses how White foreign missionary leaders created the ecumenical United Mission Study (UMS) program as a polemical response to other competing turn-of-the-century cosmopolitanisms, both secular and spiritual. I focus especially on the White Baptist missionary leader Helen Barrett Montgomery who authored six UMS textbooks and who used them as a site to work out her definition of Christian feminism. Montgomery expounded on these ideas during the Jubilee Tour in 1910–1911, and even though Montgomery and her fellow White missionary leaders addressed a few segregated Black audiences, her writing and speeches racialized Christian imperial feminism as White. The second chapter, "Performing Christian Imperial Feminism in Missionary Pageants," takes a closer look at the missionary pageants Montgomery and others wrote for local groups to use in their mission study classes. Working with Birgit Meyer's idea of "sensational forms" and Melani McAlister's concept of "enchanted internationalism," I argue that large-scale pageants and smaller dramatic skits produced a cosmopolitan aesthetics that invited White women to luxuriate in a spiritually enchanting diversity while also working through the challenges it presented.[38] These chapters introduce Christian imperial feminism and its related practices in the context of the White women's missionary movement.

The next four chapters focus on the 1920s and 1930s as White women formed new ecumenical and often interracial churchwomen's councils that took up much of the practices and combined the programs of the older home and foreign missionary societies. Chapter 3 offers an institutional history of White-led churchwomen's organizations at the local and national levels. Examining the different invocations of "cooperation" in the practice of committee meetings, I argue that Protestants' developing ecumenical movement can be interpreted as an imperial form. This chapter explores the means by which White Protestants strategized how to maintain and increase their influence amid concerns about religious and racial diversity in northern cities, and how White Protestant women preserved the missionary movement's Christian imperial feminism as they justified the value of their separate women's organizations and redefined "missions" to a much larger program of "Christianizing" social, racial, and world relations. Chapter 3 also introduces the Council of Church Women in Rochester, New York, one of the earliest and best organized local ecumenical women's councils. Rochester's Council provides a case study for how national leaders' plans played out in a local setting.

Chapter 4, "Christian Americanization and the Tri-Faith Movement," examines how White home and foreign missionary women turned their attention to assimilating immigrants in the 1920s. Christian imperial feminism structured Protestant women's Christian Americanization programs as churchwomen participated in mission study classes examining the different "racial groups" coming to American shores. White women studied different definitions of "race," and in their pageants and Americanization outreach efforts, they emphasized a racially inclusive Christianity to downplay their often evangelistic intentions. I examine the sentimental politics of White women's "friendly visits" and Protestant settlement houses, and I show how the local practices focused on European "races" were meant to display a racially tolerant and cosmopolitan Christianity but could also be used to exclude Black Protestants. This chapter also examines the tri-faith movement as itself an Americanization program of sorts. When White ecumenical Protestants joined forces with some White Catholics and Jews, they produced a narrow conception of religious freedom that resonated with the "religious liberty" defined in their earlier Protestant Americanization texts. In addition, I discuss how many White Protestant women interpreted their interreligious cooperation to distinguish their brand of Protestantism (and themselves) as thoroughly aligned with American democracy and their proscriptive vision of the nation.

Chapter 5, "The Spiritual Feelings and Religious Politics of Interracial Cooperation," turns to the complexities of interracial cooperation in the late 1920s and 1930s. In this chapter, I build on the scholarship of Judith Weisenfeld, Nancy Marie Robertson, Betty Livingston Adams, and Bettye Collier-Thomas, who have written about Protestant interracialism in the North largely from the perspective of Black Protestant women. My approach differs in my focus on how White women approached interracial cooperation through the lens of Christian imperial feminism. This chapter begins with a discussion of how "interracialism" was defined as a Christian project and a solution to racism by Black sociologist and churchman George Haynes in *The Trend of the Races*, a mission study book for 1924. I then examine the Church Woman's Committee on Race Relations' interracial conferences and committee meetings as practices of interracial cooperation. I also compare how churchwomen's councils in Oakland, California, and Rochester, New York, implemented, ignored, or went beyond the recommendations of the Church Woman's Committee. Not unlike their approach to Christian Americanization, White women viewed interracial gatherings as an enchanting opportunity for self-reflection and spiritual growth, while Black women more often saw them as a strategic opportunity to win White women's support for their ongoing political projects advanced through their other organizational commitments. Black women achieved a measure of success as they shaped the agenda of the United Council of Church Women's Social Relations Department. Black and White churchwomen pointed to this "progress" toward racial liberalism as they presented the postwar United States as a model democracy for the world to follow.

Chapter 6, "Christian Citizens, World Citizens," analyzes the evolving discourse of Christian citizenship and world citizenship, two terms that became staples of churchwomen's vocabulary in the 1930s and 1940s and that transitioned Christian imperial feminism and their aspirations to manage the "empire of Christ" into a vision of a postwar Christian world order. This chapter focuses on how churchwomen interpreted political activism as Christian citizenship, both a responsibility and formative religious practice. They also brought politics into their juxtapolitical practices of prayer services and pageants like the World Day of Prayer and World Community Day. In the aftermath of World War II, White and Black churchwomen strengthened their efforts to campaign for a Christian world order through many political action items including promoting the United Nations and advocating for refugees.

By ending the book with the formation of the UCCW, I depart from the UCCW's own histories as well as outsider accounts that more often make the 1920s and 1930s the prologue. By centering on those transitional years, I show how Christian imperial feminism born in the foreign missionary movement was reinterpreted and preserved in these post-missionary liberal initiatives. This allows for a greater focus on the continuities evident in churchwomen's repetitions of cosmopolitan practices and ongoing appeal to cosmopolitan feelings. These familiar practices and emotional responses were, I think, comforting and stabilizing to Protestant women living amid social upheavals that included two world wars. These continuities are also important to consider because so many histories of twentieth-century US Protestantism privilege change over time, in some cases replicating the same progress narratives that White and Black Protestant women told of their own history. This book does not attempt to explain the decline of mainline Protestantism, but rather seeks to show how organized Protestant churchwomen's beliefs, practices, feelings, and aesthetics continue to resonate in Protestant, interfaith, and secular contexts.

A Note on Terms and Naming Conventions

Because I am examining the creation of a White liberal Protestant identity as well as how those White Americans involved in the missionary societies conceptualized and defined racial categories for others, I capitalize "White" and "Black" to denote that these are socially constructed identities.[39] Additionally, married women in the book were typically identified by their husband's name in meeting minutes and publications. Upon first introduction, I put their husband's name in parentheses after their given names. Unmarried women are introduced by their given name alone. This approach also serves to alert readers to individual women's marital and related social status as most unmarried women were paid employees of Protestant institutions, while most but not all married women held voluntary positions.

1

Christian Imperial Feminism and Mission Study

In 1902 Caroline Atwater Mason published *Lux Christi: An Outline Study of India, a Twilight Land*, the second textbook in White Protestant women's United Mission Study (UMS) program. Mason set out to document the errors of Hinduism, the religious tradition's negative implications for Indian social mores and family life, and especially its production of "women's wrongs" as opposed to the women's rights attributed to the expansion of Protestant missions in India. *Lux Christi* also contained a brief section addressing what Mason viewed to be a growing and perplexing problem in the United States. White Protestant American "Apologists for Hinduism" had gained ground in recent years because missionary supporters had perhaps shied away from discussing the "darker features of Hindu worship." Consequently, some White Americans were inclined to romanticize the "exotic East" and elevate Asian religious traditions more generally "for the admiration of the Christian world." Mason warned that this phenomenon had become a "crisis in the history of missionary endeavor."[1]

Mason dramatized the "crisis" in her novel *The Little Green God*, also published in 1902. In the didactic novel, Mason's missionary protagonist, Titus Fletcher, has recently returned to the United States after twenty years in India. While staying with an old seminary classmate in Cleveland, he realizes that his friend's wife and daughters regularly attend meditation and yoga classes with a "swami" named Mrs. Sylvester who had been invited to give "Lenten lectures" at their church. While Fletcher has spent his adult life spreading the gospel among Indian villagers, he now intends to show these American "Apologists for Hinduism" the error of their ways. Fletcher displays the jade Krishna statute (the titular "little green god") he plans to use as an object lesson for his upcoming fundraising lectures. Instead of recoiling in horror, his American hosts are delighted and ask to display the statue in the parlor. When Fletcher explains that the object is meant to illustrate the demeaning treatment of women within Hinduism and particularly the forced sexual servitude of "temple girls," his hosts scoff at what they see as his narrow-mindedness. "With a cold little smile," one of the daughters tells him that the "temple girls" and other "heathenish" rituals Fletcher condemns are not actually part of Hinduism at all. As Mrs. Sylvester taught them, "beneath all these symbolic forms and the popular parables which the ignorant accept, perhaps literally, there is the purest and most elevated monotheism."[2]

If Fletcher's shabby clothes and earnest piety mark him as desperately old-fashioned to his sophisticated Cleveland friends, the missionary is later revealed to be an expert scholar of Sanskrit who had given up his academic career to serve India's poor. This plot twist is revealed at a dinner party thrown in honor of an esteemed English novelist. To Fletcher's hosts' chagrin, the novelist recognizes Fletcher as none other than his childhood tutor and proceeds to spend the rest of the evening in conversation with the missionary. Fletcher's glory is fleeting. His cosmopolitan credentials do little to improve his communication skills, and his missionary tour is a failure. At the end, he decides to return to India, where he has experienced real Christian community in contrast to the supposedly Christian civilization of the United States.

If *The Little Green God* articulated a problem that concerned White Protestant missionary leaders, Mason's other 1902 book, *Lux Christi*, and the larger United Mission Study program, was their solution. Launched in 1901 and overseen by the Central Committee on the United Study of Foreign Missions, the UMS series and related pedagogical exercises were meant to educate existing missionary supporters and recruit new women to the cause.[3] Comprised of White women from the largest women's foreign missions boards, the Central Committee promoted the UMS textbooks as distinct from existing literature by virtue of their "scientific" approach to studying foreign people and places. Central Committee members presented the UMS series as a new stage of the missionary movement and White Protestant women's authority to weigh in on Americans' perceptions of the world. The UMS textbooks taught missionary supporters about the histories of different "races" and the benefits and failures of western imperialism and encouraged them to evaluate how "ethnic" religions hindered the modern advance of women's rights. The UMS program emphasized the importance of factual knowledge to missionary women's humanitarian concern and evangelistic zeal. Through portraits of the "New Women of the Orient," the UMS program also encouraged White American women to see themselves as members of a "worldwide woman's movement" made possible through their Protestant missionary program.[4]

In this sense, missionary leaders created a *Christian* cosmopolitan sensibility that provided a morally sound mode of engagement with "the world." Mission study textbooks and classes enabled White Protestant women to delight in the thrill of cosmopolitanism while avoiding both the consumerist materialism of acquiring foreign goods and the religiously tolerant spiritual cosmopolitans who idealized the spiritual superiority of Eastern religious traditions.[5] As they promoted mission study, White Protestant women did not reject the nineteenth-century gender ideology that White women's innate piety and feminine sympathy fueled their moral reform activism, but they increasingly stressed the merits of a more Progressive-era notion of knowledge-based expertise.

Missionary leaders urged White Protestant women to understand themselves as Christian imperial feminists. To be sure, the term "feminism" had only just entered the popular discourse in the 1910s and its meaning would be debated by missionary women and others, although the "woman's movement" had existed since the 1840s.[6] Scholars have used "imperial feminism" to describe White suffragists who tied their own power to the expansion of US empire and who prioritized White women's political rights over those of Black, Indigenous, and colonized men and women.[7] The architects of Christian imperial feminism in the early 1900s similarly tied White Protestant women's power to an evangelical Protestant imperial project that overlapped and reached beyond the formal bounds of US empire. White Protestant women had reaped the benefits of a Christian civilization, missionary leaders argued, and their privileges as well as their faith should spur them to acquire the "missionary intelligence" that equipped them to act. Even if relatively few mission study participants would go abroad and become missionaries themselves, they could still play a role at home. Mission study taught White Protestant women to channel their moral sense in particular ways through educating them in their responsibility toward the conduct of US empire and to interpret racialized people, their "ethnic" religions, and the too-frequent "women's wrongs" to a wider American public. Further, the UMS series' textbooks on comparative religions became an incubator for White Protestant women to make a biblical argument about women's equality.[8]

Finally, Christian imperial feminism charged White missionary women to manage their own communities as religious liberalism would certainly result in gendered and racial disorder. Mason's *The Little Green God* showed what happened when White women became swamis and when minister's wives looked fondly on Hindu statues. Mason's tale also suggested that well-meaning missionary men like Titus Fletcher lacked the social skills and sophistication to communicate their genuine *Christian* cosmopolitanism to these should-be Protestant White women. Mason's novel made a silent appeal to its women readers that the task of managing religion, race, and gender fell to them, a point that the UMS textbooks and mission study classes would make explicit. More than just keeping a Christian home and praying (and donating) to the missionary cause, missionary women had a more public role to play. The women who created the UMS program claimed that they would teach White women the "truth" of Hinduism and other "ethnic" religions. As Christian cosmopolitans, mission study participants accepted their duty to educate the public about the proper arrangements of religion, race, and gender gleaned from their mission study lessons, and that knowledge fueled their Christian imperial feminism.

The United Mission Study Program

In the 1880s and 1890s, the editors of missionary magazines promoted "mission study" as a corollary to bible study, and as a form of programming that would improve the average monthly missionary society meeting.[9] Missionary magazines had begun to print model meeting agendas along with suggested Bible readings, hymns, and topical articles, while some denominational boards like the Methodists developed their own study programs.[10] One writer extolling the benefits of well-ordered study programs noted that poorly conducted meetings fostered "chaos" and "confusion." As a remedy, leaders should approach the work systematically. Take "one field at a time," she advised, and present it in "an *interesting* manner." Leaders should also make sure that only "the brightest and the best" were asked to do readings and presentations.[11]

Missionary leaders saw mission study as an instrument for improved organization and fundraising and as an indication that the missionary movement itself was a vehicle for women's improvement and progress.

In addition to missionary leaders' enthusiasm for mission study, they also pointed to the growth of the movement itself as evidence of the centrality of Christianity to the American women's rights movement. This was evident in several speeches given at the 1893 Woman's Missionary Congress at the World's Columbian Exposition in Chicago. Some speakers seemed quite aware that the women's foreign missionary movement received relatively little attention from those women active in the suffrage movement. Perhaps they had read the recently published first volume of the *History of Woman Suffrage* by White suffrage leaders Susan B. Anthony, Elizabeth Cady Stanton, and Matilda Jocelyn Gage. Missionary readers would have been disappointed (although perhaps not surprised) to see that Protestant Christianity more often came into play as a source of women's oppression rather than women's emancipation. As one passage early in the book explained, there was little difference from the oppression women experienced in Muslim lands or in the United States. "The same principle that degrades her in Turkey, insults her in this republic. Custom forbids a woman there to enter a mosque, or call the hour of prayers; here it forbids her a voice in Church Councils or State Legislatures. The same taint of her primitive state of slavery affects both latitudes."[12] The speakers at the Woman's Missionary Congress told a different story of Christianity and the foreign missionary cause as the basis for women's rights, a narrative of White women's progress focused on Christianity's gendered contrasts with decidedly un-feminist "ethnic religions."

Most of the women's foreign missionary societies had been established in the 1870s and early 1880s, and in just a few decades, they had gained thousands of dues-paying members spread out over hundreds of American cities and towns. In her address, Ellen C. Parsons, a future member of the UMS's Central Committee and the editor of the Presbyterian magazine, *Woman's Work*, praised the organizational prowess of Protestant missionary women. "The history [of foreign missionary societies] is a record of women called forth from the conservatism in which they were entrenched," she said. "Through *participating* in the direction of missionary work multitudes of women have acquired the sense of responsibility, and give their money with the feeling of a shareholder."[13] Parsons described the emotional, spiritual, and financial investment in foreign missions as an integral part of White Protestant women's identity, and she emphasized how they used their skill set to transform the lives of women through the missionary work they funded. Their seemingly small donations connected them to a global project of enormous magnitude.[14] Another speech by Emily White Smith (Mrs. Moses Smith), a Presbyterian missionary leader, addressed "Women Under Ethnic Religions." Smith used comparative religions methodology to illustrate the Christian roots of the women's rights movement and to contrast a universal Christianity with "ethnic religions." She noted that the World's Parliament of Religions had taken place just a few weeks earlier, and that the "philosophies of religion" discussed at the Parliament might seem "to some minds fascinating in their grace and mysticism." But if those men had also considered the "practical workings of these religions" as it pertained to women's status, they would be forced to see how they perpetuated "women's wrongs."[15]

The United Mission Study program had its origins in the nexus of mission study, organizational cooperation, and an interest in centering White Protestant missions in narratives of women's progress. The series also exemplified how White Protestant women's Christian imperial feminism took shape in the context of the late 1800s. In her 1893 speech, Parsons rejected a secular feminism that viewed all religion as antithetical to women's emancipation, while Smith made the case against those religious liberals who romanticized non-Christian religions. Instead, Christian imperial feminists would trace Christian feminism to the Bible and through Protestant women's organizations, and the UMS program elaborating on these themes offered White Protestant women a cosmopolitan knowledge of other cultures, but without idealizing the religious traditions deemed degrading to women.

These goals were evident when Congregationalist Abbie Child laid out the plan for the UMS program at the Ecumenical Conference on Foreign Missions in New York City in 1900. As the editor of *Light and Life for Women*, Child had a good deal of experience on the subject of missionary literature. She had been instrumental in coordinating earlier meetings among women's mission board leaders as well, and she viewed her proposed textbook series as furthering ecumenical cooperation.

She proposed a "systematic study of missions: a uniform scheme for all women's organizations."¹⁶ Child explained that a shared study program represented a new phase in the women's missionary movement that would demonstrate White women's progressivism as they prioritized big-picture objectives rather than quibbling over doctrinal differences. When they engaged in the same readings and mission study practices, "there would be a great inspiration in knowing that others are studying in just the same way that we are," Child declared, suggesting that the mission study program would forge bonds of common purpose and shared identity as White Protestant women. A Christian imperial feminism born out of the "scientific" study of world history, racial science, and comparative religions would invite missionary women to see themselves as part of a bigger millennialist project than just the particular work of their own missionary society.

The audience of missionary leaders agreed enthusiastically with Child's plan. A number of attendees noted that it would enable them to compete with the more intellectual bent of women's clubs. Ellen Parsons spoke about how an organized mission study program could improve the quality of the monthly missionary society meeting and attract new members. She noted that "a very active, intellectual woman of our church told me that she belongs to a club which meets every Monday afternoon" that had been studying one American city for the past three years. Parsons added that "the ordinary time-honored method of leaflets and little cuttings from our papers, placed upon cards" served to alienate the "young woman accustomed to study."¹⁷ Methodist Annie Ryder Gracey (Mrs. J. T. Gracey), who would also serve on the Central Committee, focused on the need to combat misinformation at home. She complained of a growing "live and let live attitude" among American women and reported that a woman she had recently encountered in New York attested "that the women of India are having a delightful time, that they are not in bondage at all, and that we could take some lessons from the delightful way in which they live." As Gracey concluded, "we want to be thoroughly informed ourselves, to contradict such things as these."¹⁸

After a summer of planning, the women who headed the denominational mission boards formed the Central Committee for the United Study of Missions in September 1900, and the first series of seven textbooks was underway to be published with Macmillan. Initially the Congregational, Episcopal, and northern Presbyterian, Methodist, and Baptist women's mission boards appointed delegates to the Central Committee. Child served as the chairwoman until her death in 1902, when the Baptist Lucy Waterbury Peabody (Mrs. Henry W. Peabody) took over the position and headed the Central Committee for nearly three decades.[19] Wellesley professor and editor of the Methodist *Woman's Missionary Friend*, Louise Manning Hodgkins, agreed to write the first book, *Via Christi*, a history of Christian missions from the early church to the nineteenth century. Caroline Atwater Mason, author of *The Little Green God*, wrote the second book, *Lux Christi*, on India. A Congregationalist missionary named Arthur Smith wrote the third book on China, and the next three focused on Japan (*Dux Christus* by William Elliot Griffis), Africa (*Christus Liberator* by Ellen Parsons), and the Pacific Islands (*Christus Redemptor* by Helen Barrett Montgomery). The series was supposed to conclude with the seventh book, Anna Brown Lindsay's *Gloria Christi*, on missions and social progress, but the Central Committee decided to extend the program and to abandon the abstruse Latin titles going forward. Through the 1920s, sales of the old textbooks and new volumes provided the primary income for White missionary women's expanding interdenominational work that became the Federation of Woman's Boards for Foreign Missions in the 1910s. The final UMS textbook published in 1938 was comprised of chapters by several Asian Christian women, including Madame Chiang Kai-Shek.

As material objects, the UMS textbooks proved popular among the thousands of Protestant women who participated in missionary societies and mission study classes. Missionary magazines touted mission study as extending beyond the books' sales, and in June 1903, Central Committee members claimed that as many as 1.5 million people took part in the study classes on Mason's *Lux Christi*, even though only 32,000 copies were reportedly sold.[20] Sales did increase over time as older volumes continued to find an audience. By 1906 and the publication of the sixth textbook, the foreword from the Central Committee reported that 250,000 copies of earlier books had been sold in addition to the sales of the new volume.[21] The editors of missionary magazines constantly promoted the books to their audiences, describing the object itself as an outward sign of the owners' piety and intelligence. "A copy should be in every Christian home," declared one missionary magazine that praised the series' first volume, Louise Manning Hodgkins's *Via Christi* as "a marvel of condensed historical information."[22] New "library" editions of the first ten books with blue and gold bindings and gilt-edged pages marked them as serious literary fare rather than more cheaply made missionary magazines or pamphlets.[23] Missionary leaders often differentiated the books from other kinds of missionary literature by emphasizing their modern and fact-based approach in contrast to the literature they saw as sentimental. The UMS books' physical appearance and the inclusion of lengthy bibliographies for further reading gave the books more of a textbook character that lent credibility to the contents within.

While the sales of the textbooks fluctuated depending on the topic and the author, missionary leaders viewed the series as a way to bring more women into the movement, and they touted their informational value and potential appeal to those who shunned missions. The books might cross over to a secular audience (or so the Central Committee members hoped) and then entice those readers to join a missionary society. The Central Committee described the textbooks as a "recruiting agency" and encouraged missionary women to purchase extra copies to donate to the library, hospitals, and the "old ladies' home," or to give as Christmas presents. They might also "get up a study class in the woman's club."[24] A librarian from Dayton, Ohio, wrote to the Presbyterian *Woman's Work for Woman* with the suggestion that missionary supporters request that their local libraries purchase the books. "The average city library is a publicly supported institution, and must respond in its book purchases to any considerable and representative call for books, along the lines of reading demanded in the community, such as the study in women's clubs," she explained. With the UMS textbooks, the same now applied to missionary literature. "For the first time in its history, mission study has now been placed on a footing with club study, being systematic, undenominational and interdenominational, and of general religious and educational interest." Not only would this help missionary women access the textbook, but it would also ensure that "missionary literature is placed on public library shelves, and finds its way, afterwards, into general circulation."[25]

While missionary women recognized the value of the physical books, they were equally enthusiastic about how the textbooks set the stage for creating innovative mission study programs that could rival secular women's clubs. The editors of women's missionary magazines (many of whom served on the Central Committee) frequently published suggestions for how to incorporate the books into missionary society meetings. Of course, not all missionary women liked mission study and the changes it had wrought on their missionary meetings. At least a few women wrote to the Central Committee with complaints that mission study distracted from the true purpose of a missionary society, which was prayer and Bible study. In her report on the status of the UMS program in early 1904, Central Committee chairwoman Lucy Peabody answered these complaints. One "dear old sister" thought that mission study was "a mistake" that relied on "sensational methods" and took attention away from Bible study. Another critic feared that mission study would replace "the tenderness and prayer which should characterize our meetings." Peabody responded that mission study offered women a "new mount of vision" from which they could "watch the wonderful working of the God of nations," and, she asked, "shall we not gain an added faith in prayer, and a more earnest desire to understand all our Master's teaching, and to obey all His leading?"[26] Missionary leaders also saw the textbooks as an opportunity for White women to organize joint mission study classes across denominations. At the Federation of Woman's Boards for Foreign Missions' triennial meeting in 1912, attendees reported that there were "Union Classes," or mission study classes made up of women from different denominations, in dozens of cities.[27]

The White northern Baptist Helen Barrett Montgomery (Mrs. William A. Montgomery) played an important role in the UMS program as an author of six UMS books and as the contributing editor of the *How to Use* handbooks prepared for mission study teachers. For Montgomery, the practice of mission study presented an opportunity to develop White Protestant women's confidence and feelings of expertise and confidence through their cosmopolitan and colonial knowledge about the world. Born in 1861 in New Jersey, Montgomery came of age just as the women's foreign missionary movement was coming into existence. She graduated from Wellesley and became a teacher in Rochester, New York, where she was also active in the women's suffrage movement and Progressive reforms. She served as the president of New York State Federation of Woman's Clubs in 1896 and 1897, and had been a cofounder with

Susan B. Anthony of Rochester's Women's Industrial and Educational Union. In the 1920s, Montgomery became the first woman president of the Northern Baptist Convention.[28]

Montgomery's experiences in an array of women's organizations shaped her broad vision for what the foreign missionary movement could become. At the Ecumenical Conference in 1900 Montgomery admitted that she had long been frustrated by the "smallness" of many women's missionary societies and urged her audience to see the potential power vested in the many thousands of local missionary societies around the country. "We have done very little original work," she stated, and "we have made very few demands upon the brains of the women in our missionary circles." Montgomery insisted that there was "no reason why the State Federation of Women's Clubs should have a higher average of intellectual caliber" than the women's missionary society. While many White Protestant women had already begun to engage in politics through temperance work with the WCTU or various Progressive-era reform projects, Montgomery believed that they could do still more and that foreign missions had prepared them to take on the world. For Montgomery, missionary work had no bounds "when we come to realize that in this cause of foreign missions are included statecraft, and civilization, and geography, and history, and biography, and philosophy, and poetry, and art, and the living history of the living kingdom of the living God."[29]

Although Montgomery was not an official member of the Central Committee until much later, she had an inordinate amount of influence on shaping the books' reception because she prepared the accompanying *How to Use* handbook for each volume. Beginning in 1906, the Central Committee offered Montgomery's *How to Use* handbooks for sale along with other related materials like maps. In these supplemental handbooks (that grew longer and more detailed each year), Montgomery provided outlines of the textbooks' chapters along with suggestions as to how to present and discuss the information within. The handbooks drew material from the annual summer workshops Montgomery and other women led at interdenominational women's "summer schools" held across the country. While little evidence can be found of local leaders explaining how they used Montgomery's handbooks, it is easy to imagine a local missionary leader turning to their concise chapter summaries, discussion questions, and ideas for classroom activities as well as the included templates for maps, charts, and other visual aids. Montgomery also used the books to weigh in on what factors constituted an effective missionary meeting.[30]

Montgomery's discussion of the ideal missionary meeting provides insights into how she and other missionary leaders understood it as a formative practice. She considered the tensions between traditionalism and "modern" approaches to the missionary movement, and she also gave thought to the proper role of heart and mind, emotions and knowledge. Like many of her colleagues, Montgomery focused on the importance of systematization for both learning facts and sincere prayer. Missionary society meetings had once been mostly "devotional services," she wrote, but "what these pioneer societies lacked in the way of interesting program and organization was more than made up in the spirit of prayer and consecration." She admitted that without an "atmosphere of devotion" mission study would "prove powerless," while a meeting that became only devotional prayer would also be lacking. Without the specific details learned from mission study, prayers could become "dull and lifeless," and they would "degenerate into formality" and "may even become superstitions." To remedy this, Montgomery advised that one woman be put in charge of choosing Bible readings and hymns and writing prayers that were aligned with the mission study lesson. "Let us not mock God by prayers that drizzle along," she added. "Scripture, prayer, song, and program should all combine to deepen the one impression, to drive home the one lesson of the day."[31] Montgomery's description of bad prayers ("superstitious," "formality") relied on language White Protestants commonly applied to Catholicism and the "heathenism" described in missionary literature. By describing missionary society meetings in these terms, Montgomery aligned mission study and its imperial knowledge with Protestant progress as she hoped to convince her readers to modernize their practices.

The informational portion of the meeting also required the same attention to protocols as did prayer. Montgomery explained, "in these days missions is becoming increasingly a science. We no longer speak of the unnumbered millions who wait in darkness, with a conception of the task as vague as the terminology. It is the day of scientific study of our problems and statesmanlike effort to grapple with and conquer them."[32]

All attendees should come prepared with the appropriate objects, a "notebook and a textbook," and the students should assemble around a large table set up with the relevant maps.[33] Noting that "we have far too little real discussion and interplay of ideas in our meetings," Montgomery also offered advice for how to conduct an effective discussion. She reminded leaders that "the danger of making a discussion a sham is real. Don't be afraid to disagree. Give a chance for opinion. Hold to time. Be courteous. Don't allow the society to wander from the question."[34] For Montgomery and her colleagues, "scientific study" did not mean they had abandoned the spiritual purpose of missionary meetings. In this way, mission study reflected what Kathryn Lofton has described as a Protestant modernist methodology that emphasized "*how* Christians ought to pose theological questions," as well as "*how* they should pursue the answers to these questions, and, ultimately, how Christian men and women will reenact the tactics of Jesus Christ through this discursive process."[35] The UMS program and especially Montgomery's handbooks show how foreign missionary society meetings became sites for White Protestant women to engage in these modernist practices with respect to subjects that included missions, geopolitics, comparative religion, and women's rights.

Montgomery's handbooks were filled with activities meant to help missionary women learn the material in the textbooks. These activities turned the often dismal stories of women's degradation and the dire social effects of "superstitions" into entertainment. For example, at a "Progressive Question Party," different teams competed to answer the most questions correctly. In the "Missionary Spelling Down," participants were lined up into two teams. If a woman did not know the answer to a question about the assigned chapter, she had to sit down and the question went to the other team.[36] A less competitive activity was the "Progressive Conversation Party." Organized like a dance, half the participants tied handkerchiefs on their arms to indicate that they were "gentlemen" who then mixed with the other half of the group who were equipped with a topic on a notecard. "Soft music played" during the conversations, changing when it was time to switch partners. In the spirit of the activity, Montgomery recommended that the leaders "see that no woman remains as a 'wall flower'" and that "strangers" were welcomed and introduced. She also added that the topics should be circulated in advance so that "each woman may prepare herself by diligently practicing her mental steps."[37] In her 1906 *How to Use*, Montgomery reminded leaders that mission study was meant to be entertaining as well as informative, and she encouraged leaders to use different methods for each class or meeting that would make learning pleasurable rather than a chore. "Variety is not only the spice of life, but of missionary meetings as well," she wrote.[38]

These pedagogical activities were not necessarily focused on cultivating sympathy for distant others but were instead meant to build White women's confidence as knowledgeable Christian cosmopolitans. Mission study lessons also integrated colonial knowledge with participants' spiritual practices. Maud Mary Raymond elaborated on the relationship between knowledge, emotions, and Christian formation in her 1913 UMS textbook that articulated missionary women's idealized Christian cosmopolitan sensibility. "We need the tonic of real study to overcome apathy and indifference, and to furnish a great objective for purposeless lives; we need the hand-to-hand conflict with actual conditions and problems, to guard against a conception of missions, remote, superficial, or sentimental." Mission study practices acted "to incite permanent habits of study and thinking along missionary lines," Raymond wrote. Writing little about evangelism or missionary work abroad, Raymond instead focused on how mission study gave White Protestant women's lives purpose by converting them, that is, transforming how they viewed the world through the habitual practices of imagining a Christian cosmopolitanism. Mission study classes could "build Christian character in its highest sense and thus help to bring God's kingdom in all the world." In other words, mission study empowered White Protestant women to "be receptive to large visions," a necessary condition if they were to contribute time and money to the sufficiently "large" program of converting the entire world to Protestant Christianity. Yet Raymond and the UMS series also tasked White Protestant women with the related work of winning over those closer to home, or as she put it, they must "develop the world-consciousness in others."[39]

Mission Study and American Empire

Helen Barrett Montgomery would have been the first to endorse Raymond's call for American women to develop "the world-consciousness" in other White Americans, and this was a frequent topic in the six UMS textbooks she wrote as well as in her other writings. Her first contribution to the UMS series, *Christus Redemptor*, a survey of the history of missions in the "islands of the Pacific," made the case that a "world-consciousness" might begin with stoking an interest and a responsibility toward US colonial possessions. This was the only UMS book that directly addressed the obligations of White Protestant women to US empire, as Protestant missions in American colonies were classified as "home" rather than "foreign" missions. In *Christus Redemptor*, Montgomery presented Hawaii, the Philippines, and other islands seen as potential US territories as vital to the larger work of missions in Asia. For Montgomery, the reputation of Protestant Christianity and American Protestant missions hung in the balance as the world watched the United States' imperial policies. She argued that missions-supporting women had a responsibility to ensure the moral conduct of US empire, and this required study.

Before *Christus Redemptor* came out in 1906, missionary leaders had already noted the value of mission study to educating White women about US imperialism and more precisely, about the territories occupied by the United States after the Spanish-American War. In 1898, the United States' war to liberate Cuba and the Philippines from Catholic Spanish despotism resulted in both an anti-imperialist movement and strong support for the creation of a transoceanic American empire. For White missionary women, the questions that arose in mission study books did not dispute this colonial project but rather hoped to salvage it by ensuring the moral conduct of American imperialism. At the planning meeting at the Ecumenical Conference, P. J. Walden, who published the Methodists' *Missionary Friend*, made a direct comparison between missionary intelligence and imperial geography, evangelization, and colonial rule. American women had to *know* about the people and land that the United States now possessed. Walden suggested missionary meetings use the "map roll," an activity that required members to learn the geographical details of the world, and especially American territories. It was a "lamentable fact" that too many "women of our churches" are ignorant of existing and needed missionary activities in areas now under US governance. "In the Spanish-American War, when Admiral Dewey entered the harbor of Manila and gained such a wonderful victory, many of us had no new atlases in which to find just the location of the Philippines. We had an intense interest in these islands, and our secular papers, always a way to the thing that will bring money and interest, issued maps, that they might tell us exactly the location, size, and all that would interest us in regard to these islands."[40] American imperialism also offered an opportunity to generate interest in Protestant missions from the wider public *and* an opening for missionary women to play a more public role as both sympathetic and knowledgeable experts.

As implied by the title *Christus Redemptor*, Montgomery presented the new era of US Protestant missions and American imperial ventures into the Pacific as redemptive, not only in terms of spreading the right kind of (Protestant) Christianity, but also in terms of redeeming "Christian civilization" itself from the un-Christian behavior she attributed to craven White Americans and Europeans who had exploited peaceable islanders and had stolen their natural resources. In a sentence that implicitly connected Whiteness to a colonial Christianity, she wrote, "the deeds of the white man, untouched by faith and love, make so black a story in the islands of the Pacific, that the least we can do, in very shame, is to give all that we can in money and men, in schools and hospitals and churches, to remedy the wrongs our race has wrought."[41] Montgomery alluded to the Black Legend long used by Protestants against Spanish Catholic colonialism, but throughout the textbook, she also chided White Protestants. She implied that these men were not Christians, not only because they were "untouched by faith" but also because they had no capacity to "love." These men might have been White and the products of predominantly Christian countries, but without "faith and love," they were certainly not Christians by Montgomery's definition. *Christus Redemptor* parsed good and bad imperialism and separated out true White Christians from those other "white men." The latter served as the foils for the righteous Christian imperial feminism Montgomery attributed to her White Protestant women readers.

To be sure, Montgomery generally praised the United States as a benevolent empire while also insisting that its moral character depended on the ongoing interest and activism of White Protestant women. In the *How to Use* handbook for *Christus Redemptor*, Montgomery elaborated on the particular importance of this topic to missionary women. "It is part of our business in furthering the coming of the Kingdom of God on earth, that we be intelligently aware of present-day conditions in these island possessions." She advised the women leading mission study classes on the textbook to transform the distant and obscure territorial possessions into familiar and knowable places. The stakes could not be higher, she explained, and instructors should pay particular attention to the American territories of the Samoan Islands, the Philippines, and Hawaii. "Our churches are on trial before the bar of history," and "if we fail to so energize the moral convictions of the people as to secure the administration of the islands in the interests of fair play and civilization we shall be found wanting when history takes account of the world battle fields of today." Montgomery went so far as to describe missionaries in the Philippines as "unselfish trained observers," who would "know and report injustice if it occurs." Montgomery acknowledged the debate about the US occupation of the archipelago among Americans, but argued that this debate had little relevance to the reality on the ground. "Whether we wish it or not Americans are to be responsible for the conditions of the Philippines for the next generation, possibly for a much longer period," and this was a "solemn responsibility."[42]

What did this responsibility entail? A missionary society member did not need to become a missionary to the Philippines or elsewhere to become knowledgeable about its history, peoples, cultures. Montgomery advised mission study teachers to consult the textbook's included pronunciation guide and glossary of Hawaiian and Tagalog names and words in addition to memorizing the details of the islands' geography, racial groups, and religions. In contrast to other *How to Use* handbooks, in which she often suggested that leaders skip over the specifics of geography and history, no such shortcuts were recommended with regard to current or future American colonies. "Drill on geography and names until they are familiar," Montgomery instructed in the *How to Use*. Montgomery looked to women to do "all that is necessary for the Christian sentiment of the nation to control the situation is a close and intimate acquaintance with the facts, and a vital interest in the outcome."[43] She tasked White missionary women with fostering a national

"Christian sentiment" through sharing their UMS-gleaned knowledge with their friends and neighbors.

In *Christus Redemptor*, Montgomery walked her readers through debates about race science and the challenges it raised for Christian missions. Montgomery recapitulated scientific theories of racial groups in a matter-of-fact style while also grounding her Christian critique of some of these theories in empirical evidence. For example, she outlined the origins and characteristics of different "Polynesian racial groups" and attended to "the result of mediaeval civilization superimposed on the Malayan social structure" in the Philippines, as well as the different religio-racial categories of urban Catholics, Muslim "Moros," and rural "pagan" Filipinos that informed how the United States governed the islands.[44] Yet she also set out to debunk what she considered to be dangerous and inaccurate ideas about race held by many White Americans. To this end, Montgomery dismissed the notion that exposure to "civilization" and conversion to Christianity had weakened Pacific islanders' physical health and reproductive capacity. If there had been illness or a lower birth rate, it was due to the introduction of vices from White people such as alcohol and, she implied, sexually transmitted disease. To correct such misconceptions about the biological capacity of Pacific islanders to become Christians, Montgomery suggested that local leaders focus on Tonga, where the Gospel had arrived "unhindered" by other detrimental European and American influences, people were "increasing in wealth and members as well as in spirituality." This was evidence to "refute the common impression that these races fade away before Christianity," Montgomery explained.[45]

In this and other UMS textbooks, writers celebrated and often described a diverse and racially heterogenous Christianity that functioned as a protest against competing ideas that attached true Christianity to Whiteness. Yet if Montgomery and many other White Protestants were adamant that all people could become Christians, they mobilized this case for Christian universalism to denigrate what they called "ethnic religions" and, more notably, they defined "Christian universalism" based on their own quite particular values and circumstances. Of course, Montgomery's conception of a universalist Protestant Christianity was also an "ethnic religion," that is, the religious vision of middle-class White Americans.

The particular middle-class Whiteness of Montgomery's universal Christianity was evident throughout *Christus Redemptor*. As noted above, she highlighted Tongans' industriousness as a sign of their Christian character. Physical appearance also mattered. She encouraged mission study leaders to find ways to get their students to see Pacific islanders as physically attractive to show their compatibility with Christianity and their worthiness as potential converts. Such passages also reflected how a more popular cosmopolitan fascination with exoticism and "noble savages" could be incorporated into mission study programs dedicated to "civilizing" those same people. For example, in *How to Use*, she advised mission study leaders to draw attention to "the beautiful side of primitive life." The Samoans' "evils, errors, and weaknesses . . . should not be ignored, but there is so much that is noble and attractive that it would seem wise to avowedly confine attention to the attempt to bring our societies in sympathetic contact with these primitive folk." In other words, Montgomery found little use in depicting Samoans as unredeemable "savages" and instead sought to paint them as likely converts. What made them appealing to White Americans? In a skit, perhaps, mission study leaders should highlight "their chieftans, stately etiquette, pride, love of music and flowers, their simple and genuine acceptance of Christianity."[46]

In contrast to such cheerful depictions of Samoans, the Muslim Moros, who had been villainized in the American imperial imagination as the enemies of freedom, democracy, and Christianity, were barely even candidates for conversion in *Christus Redemptor*. Instead, Montgomery encouraged mission study teachers to consult and use recent newspaper articles about the 1904 World's Fair in St. Louis, where the organizers had put Filipino Moros on display as representative "primitives" and a justification for American imperial rule.[47] The European Catholic friars who had missionized the islands and maintained Catholic institutions after the US invasion received similar scrutiny. In her chapter on the Philippines, Montgomery gave her readers an overview of "the friar question," or how Americans should think about the Spanish Catholic missionaries who had wielded enormous power over the lives of Filipinos for centuries. As Katherine Moran notes, some Americans had come to see the friars' methods as necessary for managing a "backwards" population, while others were more likely to associate the friars with the Black Legend, the centuries-old Anglo-Protestant polemic contrasting the cruelty of Catholic Spain's imperial ventures with a supposedly benign English imperialism. True to form, Montgomery recommended that mission study participants stage a debate. "It will be good discipline for our Missionary Societies to have a companion and contrasting picture presented along with the very severe arraignment of the Friars, which truth compels us to make." Instead of only criticizing the friars' "hoary institutions that have outlived their usefulness," Montgomery recommended that one woman should "represent the Friars" and explain "the services performed for the Filipino people by her order."[48] Such roleplaying practices created the appearance of a cosmopolitan and liberal tolerance to different points of view, and the willingness to engage in the activity itself became an illustration of White Protestants' qualifications to manage a diverse society.

In contrast with some Protestant missionaries in the Philippines, Montgomery expressed open admiration for what she termed the "independent Catholic movement under Aglipay." Gregorio Aglipay, a Catholic priest, broke with Rome to form the Iglesia Filipina Independiente in 1903, and he argued for Filipinos' religious and political liberty, which appealed to a Baptist like Montgomery who saw religious freedom as her denomination's heritage. Montgomery did not seem to struggle with the idea that politics should be kept out of religion, a combination that many White Protestant Americans found objectionable when the religion in question was anything other than a White middle-class Protestantism. Instead, Montgomery suggested that mission study leaders present Aglipay's "partly political, partly religious" movement by comparing it to the English Reformation during King Henry VIII's reign.[49] By mapping the Filipino present onto Anglo-American Protestant history, Montgomery downplayed the racist assumptions that Filipinos were not yet equipped to organize a Christian church without the guidance of White missionaries. Her comparison of a modern Filipino church to the nearly 500-year-old English Reformation also implied that Filipinos were delayed in their inevitable progress toward a future that would necessarily resemble the Protestantism of the United States. Montgomery presumed a racialized hierarchy in her sense of time even when she avoided explicit statements on Filipino's "backwardness" or tendencies toward superstition.

Montgomery was a leader in the woman suffrage movement and, as her remarks at the Ecumenical Conference showed, thought that missionary societies could be mobilized for political action on matters of empire. Montgomery recommended that women's missionary societies form committees focused on advocacy for Hawaiians and Filipinos as US colonial subjects. "Such committees would report to their societies whenever questions came up that seemed to demand the creation or expression of public opinion; and if vigilant and well organized might powerfully affect congressional action in regard to these far away possessions." Montgomery pointed to recent "disgrace which befell the entire country" when the Senate failed to pass a tariff bill that would have restrained "selfish private interests."[50] The reputation of the United States as well as Protestant Christianity was on trial in the eyes of the world, and missionary women had a duty to both state and church. To this end, Montgomery encouraged auxiliaries to prepare petitions and send letters and telegrams to call upon their senators to "pass the tariff reduction bill, which elementary notions of justice and considerations of national honor alike require." Montgomery, well-versed in women's political activism through her suffrage and woman's club work, called on local missionary societies to flood the offices of the Senate with "petitions from societies, county and state organizations, individual letters and telegrams. . . . How much influence can the United Women's Missionary Societies of the United States exert?"[51]

This was not only a matter of national reputation but essential to the future of Protestant missions in Asia. Montgomery believed that Hawaii provided a "unique opportunity" for Protestant missionaries to reach out to East Asia since "this youngest of our territories" brought many people "in close touch with American life and thought, under friendly circumstances." This was also providential. "The hand of God has shaken together this garden of the Pacific seed corn from many nations," she wrote, as "the stream of life ebbs and flows between China, Korea, Japan, and Hawaii."[52] Women missionaries were not only "beneficent imperialists," in historian Carol Chin's term, in their evangelistic, humanitarian, and women's rights projects, but the missionary women who supported them from the United States also were the beneficiaries of imperialism.[53] Mission study in the age of American imperialism put missionary supporters at the center of world events and tasked them with the role of populating these "many nations" with missionaries and influencing those around them to see their Christian cosmopolitan sensibility as the right attitude, as the correct "Christian sentiment for the nation."[54]

As her 1906 textbook showed, Montgomery was deeply invested in mobilizing the women's foreign missionary movement when it came to US empire, and on matters of American foreign policy. She also argued that White American women's potential political power and social influence was a product of Protestant Christianity, and a cosmopolitan Protestant Christianity held the answer to stabilizing a racially and culturally diverse US empire. In Montgomery's second textbook, *Western Women in Eastern Lands*, she would develop these ideas further by encouraging White American women to assume an even bigger role that extended beyond US imperial possessions.

Comparative Religion and Christian Imperial Feminism

Beginning in the fall of 1910, Montgomery and Lucy Peabody and a host of current and former missionaries toured the United States as part of a jubilee celebration honoring the fiftieth anniversary of the first independent women's foreign missionary society. Montgomery, Peabody, and their colleagues attended hundreds of prayer services, luncheons, and other events put on by interdenominational committees of local women. As local newspapers covered the events, the jubilee tour also generated publicity for the women's missionary movement and Montgomery's Christian and imperial framing of women's rights. Materially, the jubilee events raised more than $3 million that missionary leaders set aside for new ecumenical programs, such as a fund for Protestant women's colleges in Asia and a new committee that would translate Christian literature for women and children abroad.[55] The tour also sparked even greater interest in interdenominational mission study as women from different missionary societies had gotten to know one another while planning for the scheduled visit from Montgomery, Peabody, and the team of speakers. Importantly, Montgomery's Christian imperial feminism explicated in the textbook, *Western Women in Eastern Lands*, and in her speeches, created a common identity and a set of objectives for White Protestant women embarking on a new era of ecumenical organizing.

Montgomery began *Western Women in Eastern Lands* with a chapter narrating the recent progress of mostly White women across what Montgomery called the "woman's century," and showing how the women's missionary movement had grown from meager gatherings collecting mere pennies to national organizations with budgets of hundreds of thousands of dollars. In contrast to the triumphs of American (Christian) women, Montgomery presented the unfortunate conditions facing women in other countries in the second chapter, entitled "Ladies Last." Organized around sections on the "ethnic faiths" of China, Japan, Korea, and India, and then a section on Islam and a much shorter section on "pagan and savage tribes," she listed the tropes that had become associated with each of these places and traditions, but focused more minutely on what Orientalists had deemed to be the sacred texts of these religious traditions. In a nod to fairness, Montgomery explained that she would exclude "exceptional cases of horror," noting that one could write a damning indictment of Christianity were one to focus exclusively on the rampant vice in American cities. Instead, Montgomery set out "the disabilities and wrongs of heathen women" through what she presented as a fair analysis: "so far as possible Oriental authorities will be quoted."[56] Her comparative religions method consisted of pointing to quotations from writings of Confucius, the Qur'an, and the Hindu *Laws of Manu* to reveal the intractable customs and practices that harmed women, or, as the subtitle of this section succinctly stated: "the wrongs against womanhood in non-Christian lands shown to rest on the direct teachings of the ethnic religions."[57]

This distinction between exaggerating harms and her supposedly fact-based presentation was in part a measure to deflect criticisms that terrible things befell women in the Christian United States as well. Montgomery also elaborated on this point in the *How to Use* handbook, noting that "a pitiful tale of suffering" can easily be dismissed if someone remarks, "'O well, we have plenty of cases as bad in our own land.'" She instructed local leaders to be sure that they emphasized the point that "the aim is not to show that women are abused in heathen lands, but to show that this abuse arises naturally out of the religious teachings and ideals of the people." As an example, she suggested that a group could compare prostitution in the United States and "temple prostitution in India" and they would find that while prostitution was illegal in the United States, "reprobated in custom, forbidden by law, condemned by religion, practised by the lawless and criminal," it was, by contrast, "considered almost respectable" in India where "no wedding is solemnized without the presence of the temple girl. These girls are a part of worship, are consecrated to religion." In making this point here and in the textbook, Montgomery underscored a key tenet of Christian imperial feminism that presented the "women's wrongs" in so-called Christian civilization as an aberration while diagnosing the women's wrongs in other places as endemic and unchangeable results of other religions.[58]

As she went about analyzing the different texts associated with each tradition, Montgomery painted a claustrophobic picture of narrowly defined "religions" in which modern-day people were held captive to ancient texts and unreformable rituals. She then contrasted this with a liberatory Christianity, playing on the evocative binaries of bondage and freedom and hierarchies of dominance and submission. For example, her section on China discussed both Confucianism and Buddhism, explaining how both had exerted an influence on "Chinese ideals." Confucius did not value women even as he had sought to "remedy" other social ills. In the Buddhism practiced in China and elsewhere, woman's "hopeless inferiority is assumed and her impurity taught." As she analyzed passages from the Qur'an and the Laws of Manu, Montgomery repeated the process, drawing a tight connection between the core religious texts, centuries of traditional teachings, cultural attitudes, and women's suffering.[59] She quoted the fourth surah of the Qur'an, "Men shall have preeminence over women because of the advantages in which God has caused the one to excel the other," and then observed, "It is easy to see how teachings like these would work out into practice among a people who regard every word of the Koran as inspired, and who follow faithfully all the duties laid down by their religion." She made a similar point in relation to the "Code of Manu" in Hinduism, isolating this "sacred code of Hinduism" as the basis for "the deepest degradation of womanhood" that "inheres in the very religious standards of the people."[60]

Anticipating her critics who might ask about the patriarchal teachings found in the Bible, Montgomery explained what made the Bible and Christianity different from these other traditions. As she did so, she laid the groundwork for her case for Christian feminism. First, unlike other traditions' sacred texts, the Bible contained many women characters. She listed Eve, Rebecca, Rachel, and Miriam, as well as the New Testament's several Marys, Martha, and those noted in Paul's epistles. These "godly women that adorn the pages of the Bible" had stories which "cannot be surpassed for tenderness and beauty." Montgomery also argued that the Bible had a "tone of moral purity" throughout, as exemplified by its writers' condemnation of adultery and "punishment of Sodom." To be sure, it had a "frank plainness of speech in regard to facts and vices which belongs to a primitive time and people," yet it was lacking in "evil suggestion" and "obscenity" or in "immoral beautifying of ugly sin under fine names." This stood in stark contrast to the way "the facts of sex" had appeared in the texts of "ethnic faiths" or in Greek or Egyptian stories. Compared to what had been "recorded in carving and temple and hieroglyph, the White glory of the Book shines out."[61]

To contrast the Bible with other sacred texts, Montgomery relied on a progressive and supercessionist interpretation that had much in common with earlier abolitionists' efforts to use the Bible as a weapon against slavery. Montgomery applied the parable of the seed growing secretly from the Gospel of Mark to the whole of the Bible when she argued that the truths set down in the text took millennia for humans to realize. The Bible "enunciated the principles which will finally lead to the complete emancipation of women," she explained. The Old Testament was put in its place by the "democracy of the New Testament" in which Jesus "took up the old teaching of the prophets, obscured by the prejudice of centuries, brushed aside the dishonoring conventions which the rabbis had built up, and associated with women in the plane of a beautiful, free, human relationship." Montgomery noted that "his disciples could not rise at once to the height of his example and teaching," and pointed to the norms of the time as the reason. Montgomery discussed Paul's infamous instruction in Corinthians that women should be silent in the church. This was, Montgomery acknowledged, "a stumbling-block to so many," and she attributed it to Paul's own opinion, made "in light of conditions then existing in Greek society" rather than divine inspiration.[62]

Even if she believed the Bible to be a morally pure and ultimately (if secretly) feminist text, Montgomery still grappled with the problem of what she called "delayed recognition," or, why Christians had been so slow to realize and apply the Bible's feminist principles. In the paragraphs that followed, she folded together her comparative religions analysis with a justification for Christian supremacy premised on what she saw as the biblical basis for "democracy" and "women's rights." She wrote, "the Bible doctrines in regard to women are the last word in democracy," and, "women do come to their rights in exact proportion as Christian ideals become dominant in a nation." As she elaborated, "step by step democracy must fight its way against the self-interest, the pride, the passion, and the prejudices of mankind."[63] As Montgomery confidently stated in a 1911 speech given during one of the jubilee events, "once the Eastern nations become thoroughly Christianized, they will no longer lag behind the modern nations.... They are steadily becoming more progressive as they adopt Christianity."[64] A worldwide empire of Christ stood opposed to provincialism, selfishness, and "prejudices," all qualities she associated with "ethnic" religions and, as she would next suggest, conservative opponents of women's rights within White Protestant institutions.

There was, for Montgomery, no question as to White women's qualifications for sharing power with White men. Montgomery addressed the perennial question of whether the women's boards were siphoning donations from the male-led general boards and wastefully duplicating their work. She put this common complaint into a rhetorical question: Had the women's boards' income "been collected at the expense of the general missionary funds, so that Peter has been robbed to pay Paulina?" Montgomery contended that the women who had created organizations that brought in large sums had a right to manage that money as an "opportunity for self-expression." She declared that "the modern educated woman has ideas not only on the way to collect money but on the way to spend it, and the purpose for which it should be spent." She also argued that any mergers would result in women being pushed to the margins because of men's reluctance to see women as competent equals. "Are men ready for it?" she asked. Drawing on the same language she would apply to her analysis of womanhood in other countries, she wrote, "are they emancipated from the caste of sex so that they can work easily with women, unless they be head and women clearly subordinate? Certain facts seem to indicate that in spite of the rapid strides undoubtedly made in this direction we still have a long stretch of unexplored country to be traversed before the perfect democracy of Jesus is reached." After all, if the result of a supposedly equal merger was to "have two or three women on a Board who are assigned to unimportant committees [that] would hardly be satisfactory to the women."[65]

While Montgomery's textbook reached missionary women, her message of a progressive Christian feminism combined with her "scientific" assessment of "women's wrongs" in other religions found a much broader audience during her speeches and the press coverage of the jubilee tour. She and her colleagues' arguments that Christian evangelism would save and liberate the world's women rebuffed the critique of conservative Protestants found in the women's suffrage campaign, while it also equipped skeptical church women with a biblically and missionary-oriented Christian feminism. Writing about her first stop in Oakland, California, the *San Francisco Chronicle* reported on Montgomery's speech under the headline, "Would Free Women of the Oriental Countries." The article summarized Montgomery's address, including her argument that "it is in Christendom only that women eat at the same table and the same time with the men," and her discussions of what she presented as the views of women according to Confucius, Buddha, and Mohammed.[66] One of several articles on the jubilee meetings in Louisville, Kentucky, also tied White women's power and expertise to missionary work. The *Courier-Journal*'s headline read, "Five Reasons Why Women Should Help Christianize the World," and long excerpts from Montgomery's speech to a thousand people at the Broadway Baptist Church followed.[67]

While Montgomery and the Central Committee worked to envision a "worldwide woman's movement" with White women at the lead and in charge of managing exactly how and what "feminism" became, they were almost entirely silent when it came to any kind of alliance with Black women or other women of color within the United States. In a chapter on the "New Woman of the Orient" in *Western Women in Eastern Lands*, Montgomery began with an anecdote about Harriet Tubman, who "with autocratic authority, absolute fearlessness, and a genius for avoiding detection" led "trembling fugitives" to freedom. Rather than connecting Tubman to a long history of Black women's activism or even to contemporary Black churchwomen, Montgomery instead used Tubman as a metaphorical bridge that enabled her to connect the rhetoric of spiritual liberty associated with the abolitionist movement to the now international Christian feminist results produced by White women missionaries. Black women did not appear in the pages that followed even as Montgomery cited the accomplishments of Pandita Ramabai, who led Mukti, a community of Indian widows; Lilavati Singh, who had been a teacher at Isabella Thoburn College and who had addressed the Ecumenical Conference in 1900; and Hü King Eng, a Chinese surgeon. The discussion questions that concluded the chapter were also revealing as Montgomery invited readers to compare the different types of "piety" between Indian and Chinese Christians, or to ask "what worldwide organizations are already binding women of all races together?"[68]

Montgomery and other missionary leaders also argued that feminism without Christianity could be destructive to women in a different way. In the early 1910s, they expressed concerns that western feminism had infiltrated Asia, and that secular and socialist feminist movements that had shunned Protestantism might "emancipate" women in the wrong way. China was a primary site of concern as many Chinese women had joined the 1911 revolution to overthrow the Qing Dynasty. At the 1915 meeting of the Federation of Woman's Boards for Foreign Missions, participants heard about the need for more Christian literature addressing women's rights alongside a cautionary tale. Chinese women "with hair cut short" had "joined the army as Amazons" in part because "they had fed on literature—socialist, feministic, anti-Christian; not translations but perversions of Ellen Key, Olive Schreiner, Charlotte Perkins, and others."[69] Notably, missionary women did not directly criticize Key, Schreiner, and Perkins, but rather feared that Chinese women were not yet capable of interpreting their feminist writings accurately, that is, in a way that did not lead them to turn against *all* religion. This would be a central theme in Montgomery's third UMS textbook, *The King's Highway*, that contrasted a godless "crude" feminism with a Christian feminism. Women were "in danger of swinging over to undisciplined individualism," she wrote, "from believing, as she has always been taught, in her own inferiority and subordination, she is going to an extreme of self-assertiveness which frightens and amazes her uncomprehending husband. The swaggering, mannish, suffragette type is all too common among younger 'advanced' women in the cities." These women offered a lesson to American women about the importance of the examples they set for the women of the world, Montgomery argued, since Chinese women who might read western feminist writers or see images of them were now making a "poor copy of the luxurious vices of the West."⁷⁰

White missionary women also viewed Black American women as in need of guidance and supervision rather than as potential partners. While Montgomery and others reveled in a diverse Christian cosmopolitanism in the abstract, women's Protestant organizations closer to home remained segregated. Black churchwomen's organizations, including Nannie Helen Burroughs's Woman's Convention of the National Baptist Church and the Woman's Parent Mite Missionary Society of the AME Church, were listed on the 1909 and 1912 annual reports of the Federation of Woman's Boards for Foreign Missions, yet no women representing these organizations attended the conference in 1909, and it seems that only one Black woman, Burroughs, attended the 1912 meeting in Philadelphia. In contrast, there was much more representation from White southern Methodist, Presbyterian, and Baptist women.⁷¹ Further, even though Montgomery and Peabody addressed Black audiences during the jubilee tour, White missionary women had yet to incorporate interracial cooperation among women in the United States within their global Christian cosmopolitan vision, as they would do in the 1920s. When the jubilee arrived in Washington, DC, in February 1911, Nannie Burroughs presided over one meeting where Peabody spoke along with several other missionaries.⁷² In Charleston, South Carolina, the White Episcopal bishop William A. Guerry and Black Congregationalist minister Abraham Lincoln DeMond introduced Peabody and two White missionary women to a "large audience." Guerry, who in 1914 would propose the appointment of a Black suffragan bishop for his diocese, compared missions in China to evangelical outreach to African Americans in the South, reportedly saying that "as the Chinese were being Christianized by Chinese, so negroes [sic] must be evangelized by negroes."⁷³ In the eyes of White Protestants engaged in foreign missions and home missions, most Black Americans were perceived as the object of missions rather than fellow missionaries.

White women involved in the Federation and the Central Committee prioritized regional reconciliation over racial justice. Both organizations were created and run by northern women who belonged to northern denominations, but several White southern women also began to join in these ecumenical bodies. The work of White southern women's missionary societies had become legible to Peabody and Montgomery during the jubilee tour. At several points during the 1912 meeting of the Federation that followed the jubilee events, participants commented on how missionary women might bridge the divisions between northern and southern churches.[74] Lucy Peabody reported that even though "conservatism and prejudice against anything like public effort by women" prevailed in the South, she was impressed with those who had organized for the jubilee events. The topic also came up in Mrs. H. S. Prentiss Nichols's address on "efficiency." A "separated church" was a less effective organization at a time when the spirit of ecumenical unity was on the rise. Nichols had been moved by recent scenes of regional reconciliation and pinned her hopes on White missionary women to heal the wounds of the Civil War. "There, where men who bore the blue and gray were assembled to dedicate a monument to peace was the sad spectacle of the northern church and a southern church. I believe that one great fruit of the Jubilee is going to be a closer bond between the women of the church, and that as time goes on and knowledge increases differences will disappear."[75] In this 1912 meeting, none of the speakers commented on the numbers of Black women who had attended jubilee events, or what role Black women might play in uniting Protestant churches.

For White Christian imperial feminists who located themselves in a history that included the abolitionist movement and who continually proclaimed God's desire for women's emancipation, Black women remained mere symbols (like Harriet Tubman) or needy objects of missionary aid. In mission study textbooks celebrating the "New Woman of the Orient" and urging White Americans to interrogate their own "intolerance," Christian imperial feminists projected their vision of a diverse and universal world Christianity outward and elsewhere. While White women could see some Asian Christian women as worthy partners, if still in need of some ongoing tutelage, Black American women remained apart. Not only did White missionary women in the North and South not encourage racial integration in their own organization in these years, they ignored the Christian activism of Black women who confronted lynching as a moral crisis in their own supposedly Christian nation.

* * *

When White missionary women agreed to create the UMS program in 1900, they saw it primarily as a way to improve the quality of the local missionary meeting and to foster cooperation across denominational lines. They also hoped that providing "missionary intelligence" about other religions would stave off what they feared to be the growing popularity of "American Hinduism" in the United States, and that the books' quality would win over college-educated and more sophisticated women who tended to view missionary societies as old-fashioned and sentimental. By the 1910s, the ambitious plans of Lucy Peabody, Helen Barrett Montgomery, Ellen Parsons, and others on the Central Committee had turned the modest seven-book series run into a permanent program that integrated the textbooks' "missionary ethnology" into the devotional practices of White Protestant women's missionary meetings.

Helen Barrett Montgomery's popular contributions to the series most clearly articulated her vision for how White Protestant women involved in foreign missions could become more active in secular politics and in their churches. Her *How to Use* handbooks and her own textbooks proffered a Progressive and Christian cosmopolitan vision of diverse women from around the world cooperating together for the betterment of society. She identified White American women as the leaders of this movement. She also used the textbooks to hone her progressive Christian feminism, a position that emerged directly out of a racist and imperialist method of comparative religions. Working from a progress narrative that separated a "universal" (White) Protestant Christianity from all "ethnic" (racialized) religions, Montgomery made the case that the Bible itself endorsed women's equality, and that only Christian feminism—and not secular feminism—would lead to the full emancipation of women.

The UMS textbooks' Christian cosmopolitanism did not seek to erase racial hierarchies, but to manage them. The UMS textbooks and mission study reinforced White Protestant women's moral authority and command over a normative secularism by locating them in this racially diverse empire and world. As the next chapter will show, the missionary pageants and dramatic skits performed in mission study classes gave life to the cosmopolitan aesthetics of Christian imperial feminism and drew White women's power not only from their "scientific" knowledge of other people and places, but also from the enchanting spiritual experiences drawn from diversity.

2

Performing Christian Imperial Feminism in Missionary Pageants

On a Monday afternoon in July, two hundred women attending the 1910 Interdenominational Woman's Foreign Missions Conference in Northfield, Massachusetts, put on a pageant. White women donned costumes and processed across the lawn of the Northfield Inn in a rousing opening scene, and then proceeded to act out scenes set in India, China, Japan, Turkey, and Africa that showed the slow progress of the women's missionary movement. Based on Helen Barrett Montgomery's United Mission Study (UMS) textbook, *Western Women in Eastern Lands*, the pageant depicted tropes of "women's wrongs" and then illustrated how Protestant missionaries' educational and medical work had produced the emancipation of women's bodies and souls.[1] Montgomery's *Pageant of Missions* garnered praise in the Protestant and missionary press. One review of the Northfield premiere described the performance as "a new and excellent kind of missionary sermon."[2] Another observer found the experience of watching scenes set in "non-Christian lands" to be educational in large part due to the evocative experience of the pageant's materiality. Performers in particular "were helped to realize conditions there simply by wearing the costumes."[3]

Like many Americans in the early twentieth century, Protestant missionary women adopted pageantry as an entertaining and aesthetically pleasing performance medium to rally the faithful and broadcast their good news to a wider audience.[4] Historian David Glassberg's study of historical pageants traces the phenomenon to the English Arts and Crafts movement's revolt against industrialism. Unlike the English pageants that sought to revive rural traditions, however, American pageants had more varied forms. Civic and heritage organizations staged pageants for centennial anniversaries and for the Fourth of July. These typically mythologized the American past and present, softening settler colonial violence into stories of White pioneers' perseverance and Native Americans' voluntary withdrawal. Progressive educators and settlement workers also wrote pageants that reified the "folk cultures" of newer immigrants, and presented their distinctive ethnic cultural gifts as what made the United States exceptional.[5] Although some White Protestants may have been skeptical of religious pageantry's seeming similarity to Catholic rituals, their interest in the famous passion play at Oberammergau had grown in the late nineteenth century.[6] Yet unlike nativity scenes, passion plays, or children's plays of Noah's ark, the missionary pageant more closely resembled popular history pageants. Rather than illustrating a diverse and democratic United States born out of the sacrifices of White settlers, they instead embodied a world Christianity that grew out of the labors of generations of Protestant missionaries.

Missionary leaders embraced pageantry in the 1910s as an expressive and narrative form that straddled tradition and modernity and that was viewed by many commentators as a spiritual (if not religious) enterprise in terms of how pageants embodied community. Missionary pageants can be interpreted as a "sensational form," what anthropologist Birgit Meyer defines as "authorized modes of invoking and organizing access to the transcendental, thereby creating and sustaining links between religious practitioners in the context of particular religious organizations."[7] This analysis of religion with respect to its mediation through aesthetics and the senses calls attention to the conditions and objects that produce religious experiences and how those embodied experiences strengthen communal bonds as well as a person's relationship with the divine.[8] Missionary leaders promoted pageants as religious pedagogies that illustrated the lessons of mission study textbooks and transformed those "facts" into an embodied and sensous experience meant to arouse the religious emotions of both performers and spectators. The performers who dressed in costumes, the people behind the scenes who sewed costumes, painted sets, and publicized the event, and the audience all became part of the sweeping narrative of missionary progress and the unfolding millennial vision of the Kingdom of God that they embodied on the stage. While individuals involved in the pageant undoubtedly had their own specific experiences, missionary leaders' commentary on what made effective missionary pageants illustrates how they were meant to "tune the senses" of participants on a collective level.[9] Women's missionary pageants integrated Christian imperial feminist knowledge with shared religious feelings of sympathy, triumph, and the thrill of belonging to a cosmopolitan Christian community. The globe-hopping panoramic pageant and the smaller-scale dramatic skit made the world's Christian conversion synonymous with women's emancipation, and pageants' cosmopolitan aesthetics created a visual shorthand for White Protestant missionary supporters' Christian imperial feminism.

Missionary pageants offer a rich text for thinking about how the information in missionary literature was translated into embodied performances. Hillary Kaell has described pageants and other humanitarian practices as "participatory techniques" meant to cultivate "engaged empathy" in American Christians.[10] In this sense, pageants promised to collapse the spatial distance that protected the sympathetic missionary woman from the object of her sympathy.[11] White performers inhabited this ambiguous space between medium and intermediary as they both became and sought to represent women of color who might be potential converts or already were Christians. When performers stepped in and out of the roles that were, of course, written by White Protestants in the first place, pageants also secured and reinforced the leadership of White women at the top of the racial, imperial, and religious hierarchies of the missionary movement, as they remained the "pageant masters" in control of the story. To imagine and play another person could create a powerful experience of border-crossing communion and membership in the vast body of Christ while also illustrating the White performer's Christian cosmopolitan credentials that reinforced her sense of power. To a wider audience, pageants presented the foreign missionary cause as a cosmopolitan, liberal, and modern Protestantism by measuring it against racialized "ethnic religions" that were stuck in the past and against conservative and ethno-nationalist White Protestants in the United States as well.[12]

It is also important to consider missionary pageants in context with White people performing in blackface or "playing Indian." Although those involved in pageants worked hard to differentiate what they considered to be art from crass entertainment, pageants also reflected White performers' and audiences' "racial aversion and racial desire."[13] Pageants also followed similar rules about who could dress up as whom. In pageants performed in the United States, White people could portray people of color, but people of color never played White characters. This custom illustrates how White Protestants' rules of embodiment differentiated them in terms of both race and religion.[14] In a missionary pageant, White performers' capacity to switch religions and races underscored their sense of being the universalist norm rather than members of an "ethnic religion," while people of color could play Christian converts, new inductees into the universal empire of Christ, but they could not similarly escape their racial identity.[15]

In this chapter, we will first examine the popularity of pageants in the 1910s and how some theorists at the time celebrated pageantry as a communal and spiritually productive antidote to an atomized and secular society. We will then examine two categories of missionary pageants: large-scale panoramic pageants and more informal dramatic skits or "impersonations" used in mission study classes. Panoramic pageants like Montgomery's *Pageant of Missions* tended to be performed for wider audiences on special occasions and as fundraisers. Women's missionary societies publicized them in local newspapers along with short summaries of the pageant, including the expected number of performers. These pageants featured (mostly) White women in costumes meant to represent missions in many locales, and they usually included at least one ensemble scene that illustrated the Protestant missionary movement's imagined world Christian community. In contrast to panoramic pageants aimed at outsiders, dramatic skits and "impersonations" were regular features of mission study classes. They often but not always involved costumes, and they involved more dialog as the characters debated topics from UMS textbooks. Still the playacting involved in dramatic skits referenced the more occasional panoramic pageant and as a repetitive ritual they conveyed a sense of "stability" in participants even if the topics under discussion could raise potentially unsettling questions.[16] In both panoramic pageants and dramatic skits, White missionary women performed their well-ordered vision of an aesthetically diverse kingdom of God. On stage and off, White women played out conflicts and resolved them, demonstrating to themselves and others White Protestant women's liberal ability to secure modern women's rights for all and their expertise in managing religious, racial, and national diversity.

The Pageantry Craze

In 1913, the *New York Times Magazine* ran a full-page article on pageants with the headline that the United States had, like England, become "pageant mad."[17] The article's author, William Chauncey Langdon, was hardly a disinterested observer as he served as the president of the newly organized American Pageant Association and was a pageant writer himself. Langdon explained how the largely Greek and medieval-themed pageants of the English Arts and Crafts Movement had taken on new life on American soil. Praised for their educational benefits and wholesomeness, pageant boosters argued that the amateur performance art was distinct from vaudeville or traveling shows that merely entertained. Pageants were a "communal pastime," wrote one enthusiast, who declared that the art form created a "visible manifestation of the community soul" and was no mere "sensational exhibition."[18] Many pageant writers and directors were women who were marginalized in other artistic forms. Women were seen as well-suited to pageants' community focus, affective qualities, and homespun charm. The fact that a pageant relied on amateur "local talent" instead of "professional showmen" meant that the performers and producers as well as the audience shared in the "emotions and feelings—pleasures and profits of the entertainment."[19]

For a brief period of time before they were eclipsed by movies, pageants could be found in all corners of the United States. Historical pageants became common fare for centennial anniversaries and at Fourth of July festivities. Favored by the White middle-class Progressives of the "City Beautiful" movement, pageantry, like parks and monuments, was thought to combat social ills and social disintegration through pleasing aesthetics and wholesome recreation. Pageants told a selective version of the past, reviving interest in local history in a way meant to foster a spirit of cohesion. They encouraged civic pride and patriotism through an optimistic vision of the city's prosperous future as part of an imperial nation.[20] As David Glassberg notes, the 1914 *Pageant and Masque of St. Louis* featured a cast of thousands acting out the distant and recent history of the city, and the performances represented "the ecstatic communion of all St. Louis." Some pageants reframed the religious history of the United States in their reconsideration of the positive contributions of Catholic missionaries as a model for American imperial ambitions and

Protestant missions alike. The stories of Spanish and French missions had become a popular subject for pageants set in the West and Midwest in the early 1900s, and Katherine Moran argues that the histories of earlier Catholic missionaries not only softened divisions between Catholics and Protestants in the present and stoked the tourism industry to these historical sites, but also rendered this Catholic colonial past as an example for ongoing Protestant colonial projects.[21]

Pageants were also adopted for different ends by Progressive educators and reformers, clubwomen, and by more radical activists. At northeastern women's colleges, White students donned togas to perform classical scenes or medieval costumes to act out Arthurian legends. These pageants situated young White Americans within the triumphant narrative of western civilization that also structured their curriculum.[22] In contrast, African American students used pageants to tell a different narrative centered on Black progress, and in the 1920s, Black students at Atlanta University wrote a pageant celebrating its fiftieth year called "The Open Door." Its scenes moved from "wild men" in Africa" to the oppression of slavery and the joy of emancipation, to scenes of promising Black scholars learning and expressing "Truth, Beauty, and Love" through knowledge. Atlanta's students performed the pageant in the North as a fundraiser for the college.[23] In urban settlement houses and in public schools, schoolchildren put on pageants wearing someone's idea of ethnic folk costumes, usually either to act out a story of assimilation or to isolate and celebrate "cultural gifts" attributed to each "race" of immigrants. Protestant home missionary societies produced pageant scripts for immigrants' assimilation as well, either to be performed by native-born White missions supporters in costumes or to be used as a form of outreach to local immigrants who would be recruited to play themselves.[24] Clubwomen regularly organized costume parties with Orientalist themes like Japanese teas or bazaars as fundraisers for various charitable causes.[25] Even radical socialists appreciated pageantry's democratic ethos, and in 1913, striking silk workers from Patterson, New Jersey, and Greenwich Village bohemians staged a pageant sponsored by the International Workers of the World at Madison Square Garden. That same year, W.E.B. Du Bois premiered "The Star of Ethiopia" in New York City, and White women dressed in a variety of costumes for the Suffrage Parade in Washington, DC, and in smaller-scale pageants around the country.[26]

Perhaps because of pageantry's varied messages, the White pageant supporters affiliated with William Langdon's American Pageantry Association appointed themselves gatekeepers as they sought to "establish a uniform standard."[27] They distinguished pageantry as White Protestants' wholesome drama and spiritual qualities from other kinds of performances branded lowbrow, immoral, and even "savage." For example, in his handbook for pageantry, the White New Englander Ralph Davol insisted that pageants be performed outdoors and in the daylight. This differentiated them from vaudeville and minstrel shows and the largely Jewish theater scene found in New York, Chicago, and other cities.[28] Even when a Protestant pageant took place in a church, organizers were careful to explain how it was different from "pagan" feast day celebrations of Italian Catholics or what they saw as sexually promiscuous Native American dances, even if it shared certain "universal" affinities with those other performances.[29] Pageant theorists worked from a Weberian secularization narrative as they expressed a sense that they had lost some kind of religious or spiritual community, and they presented pageants as the restorative solution that maintained White middle-class Americans' "civilized" status and respectability.[30]

This was evident in a 1916 treatise on pageantry by Barnard College dance professor Mary Beegle and Yale English professor Jack Crawford. Pageants reintegrated religion and drama four hundred years after the Protestant Reformation had severed the two, but it did not demand a return to medieval belief. In a narrative beginning in Ancient Greece and moving through medieval Europe, the two academics described how the connection between drama and religion had produced a democratic religion and performance art, one that existed outside of institutions and professionalization. They romanticized the unification of religion and art in the past, writing that "as long as these peoples lived their religion they kept drama in their own hands." Pageantry revived what had been lost, but in a religiously diverse United States, the question of what kind of religion should be dramatized created a problem. There was simply no way to restore "the religious significance to drama," as "we should have to have a different drama for each sect." Yet pageants could operate on a spiritual level seen as transcendent of particular religious traditions. Like other modernists who aspired to create a pluralist spirituality through art, pageants generated religious experiences outside of religious institutions and sectarian identity. Unlike museums or the theater, it was also a "cooperative art." A well-managed pageant moved participants (the "pageant worker") and audience alike, allowing ordinary folk to "take part in art's mysteries," and it could "add color to modern life as well as play its part in community cooperation."[31]

As a sensational form, the pageant's spiritual spark stemmed from the community spirit of those who produced it and the communities it depicted on stage. In his handbook for pageants, Davol explained that "pageantry must pull toward the centre against forces constantly tending to pull apart."[32] For Davol, the "centre" was the White Protestant middle-class home and all that it represented. "There is no theme that comes nearer to the heart of men and women than that of the home," wrote William Langdon in his *New York Times* article celebrating pageants, and he defined "the home" as either "the private family or the community home of the town."[33] It was not a coincidence that more than half of the people listed in the American Pageantry Association's Who's Who were White women considered to be experts on the home, whether private, civic, or national.[34] Historical pageants domesticated the violent process of American homemaking that was settler colonialism. When foreign missionary supporters adopted pageantry for their own purposes, they expanded the borders of the "home" to include the whole world and the imperial project of White Protestant missionary work.

While progressive White missionary leaders immediately recognized the usefulness of pageantry for publicizing missionary work, they still had to justify the moral value of a pageant to those who saw such performances as sensationalist distractions. Writing for the Presbyterian magazine *Women's Work* in 1914, Gabrielle Elliot, a recent Vassar graduate and editorial assistant for *Woman's Home Companion*, wrote that a "well-knit pageant" focused on an idea rather than on a hero, and that "the evangelization of the world offers fascinating opportunities for contrast and effect." Elliot suggested a pageant comprised of scenes set in "Africa, Japan, China, Turkey, Alaska, Mexico, and the New York slums," noting that such a performance had "the advantage of novelty" for fundraising. Just as the UMS textbooks had been pitched as a recruitment tool, pageants also provided a modern method for promoting the missionary movement to wider audiences of White women. Like all pageant enthusiasts, Elliot also touted the benefits of cooperation for those who participated in the pageant, writing, "nothing promotes friendship more than working together."[35] In a 1916 article for the Congregationalist *Mission Studies*, Milwaukee librarian Margaret Reynolds made a similar argument, asking, "is it not natural that churches should use this means to stimulate interest in their work? Is there any reason why churches should not use this picturesque, elastic and genuinely instructive form of entertainment?"[36]

Religious pageants quickly found support among White Protestants as an acceptable activity for adults, teenagers, and children. In the 1910s, the Federal Council of Churches formed a Committee on Religious Drama to coordinate and publicize these efforts. By the early 1920s, the ecumenical Missionary Education Movement had published dozens of pageants, both scripts as well as detailed suggestions for tableaux, or living pictures, that could be adapted by local Sunday school teachers and missionary societies. In 1921, the YWCA's Board of Pageantry and the Drama published a bibliography of hundreds of "pageants, masques, ceremonies, and pantomimes" written for adult and child performers, and a number focused on missionary topics. Prompts and fully developed scripts for pageants and dramatic skits formed a significant part of the pedagogies in the *How to Use* handbooks Helen Barrett Montgomery wrote to accompany the annual UMS textbooks.[37]

Madeline Miller's 1924 book on *Church Pageantry* opened with the dramatic claim that "God teaches through pageants." She explained that pageants enabled performers and audiences to "visualize world situations," and the ability to represent vast swaths of time gave spectators a God's-eye view on the world. Performers and audiences alike were made to see their own positionality as White American Protestants as the objective observers of those mired in the provincialism of the so-called ethnic religions. Yet pageants also imbued this secular positionality with warm religious feelings as performers prided themselves on their heightened sympathy and loving concern for the suffering stranger. Miller explained that the "heightened emotions" during a pageant made the contents and message "vivid" when compared to merely listening to a sermon or reading a book. To prove her point, Miller described a pageant about India performed in McMinnville, Oregon, that had resulted in three attendees declaring their intention to become foreign missionaries. Missionary pageants were a rehearsal for future missionary volunteers, and she speculated that many current missionaries had likely "first *imagined* themselves in these situations in some 'life-play'."[38] This resonated with a line from Langdon's article more than a decade earlier as he noted that participants in a history pageant "were re-living rather than acting" the parts.[39]

Panoramic Pageants: Christian Progress and Ethnographic Tableaux

Panoramic pageants narrated the progress of Christian missions through an arrangement of discrete scenes rich in missionary tropes. Depending on the pageant, some scenes were tableaux, a "living picture" that captured a moment in time, while other scenes had more of a narrative arc, a short story contained within the scene. Panoramic pageants began or ended with the cast assembled to show the unity of the Christians depicted in the different times and places. The pageant reflected unity and diversity in the Christian cosmopolitan aesthetics of (mostly White) people wearing colorful costumes, all singing in unison as the momentary embodiment of the elusive kingdom of God. Pageants provided a way for missionary supporters to take part in a respected art form and to indulge in the exotic thrill of cosmopolitan make-believe, all within the moral structures of White middle-class Protestantism.

Two of the more widely performed panoramic pageants included *The Pageant of Darkness and Light* by the English Congregationalist John Oxenham and Helen Barrett Montgomery's *Pageant of Missions*, which was likely inspired by Oxenham's work.[40] Oxenham's pageant premiered in London in 1908, and it became a huge draw for several missionary expositions in the United States beginning with The World in Boston. The success of Boston's exposition and pageant prompted other Protestants in Chicago, Cincinnati, Baltimore, and elsewhere to organize their own missionary expositions in 1912 and 1913 that also made Oxenham's pageant the centerpiece of museum-like displays of maps and curios.[41] Indeed, the organizers in Baltimore continued the money-making pageant for a few weeks after the exposition closed in order to repay the debts incurred from the exposition.[42] Montgomery's *Pageant of Missions*, first performed at the Northfield interdenominational conference in 1910, had been written to be used throughout the women's missionary jubilee year, and it would be performed in part and in full at jubilee events throughout 1910–1911. Montgomery's *Pageant of Missions* played for smaller audiences and most performances had a much smaller cast than the *Pageant of Darkness and Light*'s five thousand singers and performers.

Oxenham's *Pageant of Darkness and Light* depicted the perilous lives of missionaries and their converts across four scenes set in the North (among "Eskimos"), South (Central Africa), East (India), and West (Hawaii). The threat of death and martyrdom hung over all four scenes, but unlike other missionary narratives that focused on persecuted Christian martyrs, Oxenham's story instead portrayed Christian missionaries as lifesaving and soul-saving as well as the mediators equipped to resolve conflicts. In the fifth and final scene, a "processional" of the characters from the previous four scenes joined in a "final tableau." The narrator repeated the refrain, "They come! They come!" and recited the many "perils" that were overcome as these people were "climbing through darkness up to God." Each scene's cast delivered a short speech in verse. Each speech ended with the same lines imploring the audience to take action: "To-their-night," and "Take-the-light." Then, together, the full assembly sang a hymn that would become a regular feature of churchwomen's prayer services and meetings and mainline Protestantism more generally, Oxenham's "In Christ There Is No East or West."[43]

Performed twice daily in April and May 1911 at The World in Boston, the *Pageant of Darkness and Light* was the key attraction to what one journalist called the "World's Fair for the Gospel."[44] A chorus numbering five thousand flanked both sides of the stage, with the men in green robes and the women in white, as the "prolocutor," a role typically played by local clergymen, narrated each scene. The American debut of the pageant received glowing reviews, and its mixture of religion and drama fascinated audiences. One reviewer wrote that this final flourish "took the pageant out of the realm of theatrical shows and placed it upon the level of religious observances." To illustrate the point, the reviewer reported overhearing someone ask, "Is this Presbyterian theatricals?" to which the friend replied, "This is the American Oberammergau."[45] When the pageant was staged once again at The World in Baltimore in 1912, another reviewer praised it as "spectacular, gripping, with pleasing music and a wide variety of scenes" that tell audiences about the "strange customs of the world's darkened nooks."[46]

Perhaps inspired by Oxenham's pageant when it premiered in Boston, Montgomery wrote the *Pageant of Missions* to illustrate the progress of the White women's missionary movement. The pageant began with a prologue entitled Pilgrims of the Night in which the entire cast in diverse "oriental" costumes assembled on stage with their eyes downcast. This could number as many as two hundred women at some performances. When a bugle sounds, the "heralds of the dawn," women dressed in white flowing angelic robes, streamed through the ensemble while singing a hymn. They led the newly awoken "oriental" women off the stage. The pageant's progress history then began. The first scene was set in a cozy New England parlor. A few women costumed in "old-fashioned garb" gathered around a table decide to start collecting money to support a future mission in Japan. This scene referenced the first chapter of Montgomery's UMS textbook, *Western Women in Eastern Lands*, and Montgomery's argument that missionary societies had been integral to American women's progress over the course of the nineteenth century. As they donned Victorian dresses, the scene also provided a visceral reminder of performers' own modern-ness while also enacting a gesture of gratitude to their forebears.[47]

The rest of the pageant's scenes were set in foreign mission fields. The pageant's structure rendered it a living missionary map displaying "hierarchies of heathenism" that focused on the status of women.[48] Scenes in rural India and China relied on stereotypes that were shorthand for "heathenism" and "primitiveness" and depicted the early setbacks missionaries faced. In the Indian village scene, a missionary prayed with a group of Indian "Bible women," early converts who played a significant role in forming Christian communities in India. Other characters ignored them even as the Bible women begin to sing a "native hymn." The Chinese scene took place in a missionary clinic. A missionary physician treated her patients, but as patients left the clinic, they unwrapped their bandages, and one comedically swallowed a whole jar of pills. Western medicine was useless where "superstition and ignorance" prevail, annotated the pageant script. The following scenes took place at a Japanese kindergarten and at a girl's school in Turkey. Both showed Christianity's importance to educational advancements and women's rights. Decades of missionary literature had primed spectators and performers to see these two countries as more modern and therefore more receptive to Christianity. The Turkish scene featuring Muslim converts most easily conveyed women's emancipation and conversion through the removal of the veil. It began with veiled women in a harem, and then contrasted those performers with another group dressed in academic regalia. As the program notes specified, the latter pantomimed a graduation scene at the American College for Girls in Constantinople. Finally, the pageant concluded with the most recent mission field for American Protestants, "darkest Africa." This scene also focused on education, but unlike the kindergarteners or college graduates, the performers playing African villagers mimed "sewing and various kinds of industrial work," the industrial education skills deemed most suited for African-descended and rural people. Still, the scene marked this as a liberating departure from patriarchy as their fathers, "savage chiefs," stand in the background and "peer through the palms" at their children.[49]

While it lacked the life and death scenarios found in the *Pageant of Darkness and Light*, for missionary women, the story of Christianity as a vehicle for women's emancipation—both their own and others—brought them into an intensified spiritual experience. If they had thought about their missionary society work as just another social obligation, the pageant reminded them of its world-changing importance, and it did so by provoking emotions of women's physical and mental suffering and the subsequent relief of Christian conversion. In addition to the performers' actions on stage, those performers wearing "oriental" costumes could also enact another escape from what they saw as degradation when they returned to their regular clothes and posture. Viewers also commented on the pathos on display that drove home the missionary message. A review in the Congregationalists' *Life and Light for Women* described the emotions on display at the Northfield premiere of the pageant. "Even the picturesqueness of their strange garb and the brightness of Oriental color did not relieve the unutterable sadness of the scene," read the description of the opening prologue, and "tears filled many eyes" as the pilgrims of the night stood on the stage in silence for several long moments. The contrast between the "Turkish" women's "depressing black robes" and those acting out the graduating ceremony was "striking," and the diploma became "a symbol of emancipated womanhood."[50]

The Northfield performance's final processional also included four little boys dressed in costumes "of a Chinese, an American Indian, a Negro, and an Esquimau" who carried a large frame that made them into a living tableau version of a cartoon found in Lucy Peabody's children's magazine, *Everyland*.[51] Like the "Pilgrims of the Night" prologue, this kind of Christian cosmopolitan aesthetic was a common feature of panoramic pageants. When Montgomery, Peabody, and their colleagues visited American cities for the 1910–1911 jubilee tour, versions of the *Pageant of Missions* were often part of the program, and over the next few years, other local missionary societies adapted and improvised on the pageant's themes and materials. For example, a missionary pageant put on by women of First Presbyterian Church in Wilmington, Delaware, included two scenes that both referenced the prologue of the *Pageant of Missions*. In the first part, costumed White women representing "various heathen tribes such as Koreans, Burmees [sic], Africans, Chinese, Japanese, Moslems, and Hindus" assembled on a platform after a procession led by "angels attired in white flowing robes." A reader then said a few things about each country. In the second scene, the "pilgrims" reappeared dressed in black robes and veils. The "heralds" fanned out among the "pilgrims" and gave many but not all of them the gift of a Bible and a lit candle in order to symbolize the need for more missionary workers.[52]

Ethnographic tableaux could be found in less formal performances as well. Take, for example, a 1904 fundraiser organized by the Disciples of Christ's Young People's Missionary Society in Lincoln, Nebraska. Children dressed as "Oriental pilgrims," a category that also included Africans, as they enacted scenes they had learned about at their missionary meetings. As their guests (most likely parents and perhaps other children) visited the four homes designated as China, India, Japan, and Africa, the costumed children played the part of hosts. Visitors to the Chinese house viewed curios while the children playing the part of "grave Chinese matrons served rice, mince, nuts, watermelon seeds, and chopsticks." At the Japanese house, children wearing kimonos staged a tea ceremony alongside a "genuine Japanese gentleman" about whom no more details were given. In the Indian house, they donned turbans to become "stately Hindus" who served "ices and sweet cakes" to their visitors. These scenes played on stereotypes, to be sure, but they were respectful when compared to what happened in the "Africa" house, where

"The Oriental Pilgrims," *Missionary Tidings*, July 1904, 81.

children in blackface performed the role of "hospitable African cannibals" and served guests "blood (red lemonade) and flesh (lady fingers) from a huge cauldron."[53]

In some panoramic pageants, organizers found ways to cast women of color in some of the parts, and such efforts at authenticity made the experience of Christian cosmopolitanism even more meaningful to White viewers and participants. At the Northfield premiere of the pageant, the Japanese kindergarten scene's teacher was played by Tsuru Arai, a graduate student who would shortly become the first Japanese woman to earn a doctorate from Columbia University. This scene and one in which an unnamed "Karen girl" playing the "Bible Woman" sang a hymn in the Indian scene received special note.[54] When women in Portland, Oregon, staged the "Pilgrims of the Night" prologue, the organizers reported to one missionary magazine that "many nationalities were presented in the procession of heathen women," including a "converted high-caste Hindu woman and a Christian Nez Perces [sic]."[55] At the final event of the 1910–1911 women's missionary jubilee celebration in New York City in March 1911, Black children from the Howard Colored Orphan Asylum played the role of the African youths in the staging of the *Pageant of Missions*.[56] Only White performers had the power to cross racial and religious lines and to move in and out of other people's clothes and perspectives. In contrast, Japanese, Indian, Native, and African American performers were only permitted to play the "diverse" parts rather than getting to play the part of the White missionary. In an "original missionary pageant" produced by the Women's Society of Chambers Memorial Church in Rutledge, Pennsylvania, several White children played "wild Indians" alongside "one genuine Oneida and one Chippewa," who said the Lord's Prayer "in Indian dialect." The pageant also featured two "Syrian immigrants" who were "'living epistles' of [missionary] Dr. Jessup's work" who "sang a Christian hymn in Arabic." This pageant also included a Black man who played "an unevangelized African in scant clothing, bone necklace and armlets." In his scene, he stood next to a Black girl, which was meant to represent how far African Americans had come in contrast to their "heathen" past.[57]

By drawing attention to diverse casting in descriptions of pageants in missionary literature and secular newspapers, White Protestants scripted these performers into a narrative about their own appreciation for Protestant missions. These "real" examples of Christian cosmopolitanism in a pageant also reinforced White Protestant women's idea that Christianity held the solution to racial, religious, and national conflicts. The limited inclusion of people of color in pageants also relates to a point Ralph Davol had made in his 1914 *Handbook of American Pageantry*. Writing about his preference to include Black people as pageant performers, he argued that a pageant could transform "racial elements into an ethnic *ensemble*." Drawing a hard line between pageantry and minstrelsy, Davol complained that a pageant he had seen in New England had "a white girl wearing a black mask" instead of casting "a colored boy" in the role. He proposed that interracial pageants could contribute to "harmonizing the black and white races" if they brought Black and White performers together on the stage.[58]

White missionary women's enthusiasm for these "authentic" characters also anticipated how they would interpret Christian Americanization programs and interracial cooperation in the 1920s and 1930s. A racially diverse Christianity offered proof of its universal appeal and capacity to be both diverse and unified. Pageants reinforced White Protestant women's confidence in their ability to manage this heterogeneous yet orderly kingdom of God. It is worth considering the parallels between these early twentieth-century missionary women and more contemporary efforts to visualize multiculturalism. Writing about twenty-first-century "diversity work," Sara Ahmed comments on how liberal institutions like universities use photographs of racially diverse groups in marketing materials, but that "the very idea that diversity is about those who 'look different' shows us how it can keep whiteness in place."[59] The missionary pageant's Christian cosmopolitan aesthetic functioned similarly. White Protestants' representations of a racially diverse Christianity existed as a visual spectacle rather than an interrogation of White settler Christian theologies or the financial arrangements and decision-making structures in White-led missionary societies. Though people of color might get to perform on a stage, their presence reflected back onto White Protestants' cosmopolitan sensibilities and the successes of their missionary movement.

In some instances, the quest for "authenticity" in pageants could unintentionally expose the limits of White women's racial liberalism. This was the case when Helen Barrett Montgomery wrote the handbook for the 1928 UMS textbook, *An African Trail*, about West Africa. Given that the dramatic skits or impersonations would mean that her White readers would be playing Black people, Montgomery opted to advise against blackface and caricature, one of the only times that such concerns arise in one of her *How to Use* books. As discussed further in a later chapter, White churchwomen had only just begun embarking on serious interracial cooperation efforts with Black churchwomen in the mid-1920s, and these interracial collaborations developed very slowly. White Protestant women's foreign and home organizations had not issued strong support for Black Protestant women's moral arguments and activism against lynching, segregation, and anti-Black violence in the late 1800s and early 1900s. White home missionary societies still classified Black Protestants under "Colored" or "Negro" work as well.

In the handbook, Montgomery warned readers against "blacking up," and instead suggested powders that could slightly darken the skin. She explained that blackface "vulgarizes and caricatures the African and does not make vivid the scene."[60] Presumably, Montgomery wanted to distinguish the genteel and morally rigorous missionary dramatization from a commercialized and crude minstrel show. At several points in the handbook to *An African Trail*, Montgomery instead recommended that local groups invite African Americans to play the part of Africans. Since the second chapter of the textbook focused on "the African people,"[61]

Montgomery suggested that local leaders might ask "African friends to take the parts."⁶² She meant, it seems, Black Americans rather than visiting university students from Africa. This was evident in the instructions for another dramatization entitled "The Annunciation" that involved a young African evangelist bringing the Gospel to a group of Africans sitting around a campfire. Montgomery wrote, "If it could be given by a group of colored students the effect would be even better. The audience will forgive absence of accuracy; they cannot be serious in the face of the grotesque."⁶³ Montgomery believed that an effective pageant must not descend into minstrelsy, but in this example, she also noted that Black Americans were not an "accurate" equivalent for Africans. Montgomery's discomfort with blackface did not lessen her commitment to pageants as a meaningful pedagogical tool. By the late 1920s, however, new interpretations of pageantry had begun to develop in White Protestant women's interracial prayer services for the World Day of Prayer and Race Relations Sunday. In these renditions of a racially diverse yet hierarchical world Christianity, Black Americans would play Black characters from the past and present, often signing spirituals, alongside performances of European ethnicities and sometimes Asian women as well.

Long after the popularity of the panoramic pageant faded, its aesthetics and its Christian imperial feminist message continued to inform White Protestant women's practices and material religion. In the early 1940s, the Rochester, New York, Council of Church Women held an "International Bazaar and Food Fair" that was intended "to develop fellowship and understanding among women of different races and nationalities through emphasis on the common ground of preparation of meals, wearing apparel, and the adornment of the home." The Council reported that a hundred women had taken part in the "colorful events." These included a Food Fair, arts and crafts displays from European immigrants, and a "Costumes of the World on Parade" in which White women who had lived abroad wore the costumes of "war-stricken nations" to show the "common ground of suffering throughout the world today" and the "supreme value of Christian brotherhood."⁶⁴ While the Rochester women's event was not a pageant, it referenced the sensational forms of the missionary pageant, the aesthetics, material, and sensory practices as much as the Protestant-secular forms of a world's fair exposition. White churchwomen invested in the ongoing relevance of foreign missions blurred the distinction between their explicitly evangelical Protestant missionary past and a secular liberal cosmopolitanism. Even without scenes of costumed women's conversion, the International Bazaar and Food Fair played out the familiar Christian imperial feminist script of the missionary pageant.

Managing World Religions in Dramatic Skits

While a panoramic pageant required dozens of performers, Helen Barrett Montgomery developed a variety of pageant-inspired dramatic skits as more everyday mission study practices. In the *How to Use* handbooks she wrote for the UMS textbooks, Montgomery pointed readers to the usefulness of dramatizations and "impersonations" as a pedagogical technique. These pageant-inspired techniques were so familiar to local leaders that in many cases, Montgomery provided just a couple of sentences of instruction with the assumption that her readers could fill in the details. This was the case in a brief sketch she proposed in her first *How to Use* handbook for her 1906 book, *Christus Redemptor*. In this skit, one character played "Expansion," that is, potential American colonies in the Pacific, and another would play "Columbia," the United States as the potential bride. Montgomery's directions were simple. "Expansion . . . tells of his home, family, resources, and prospects, and Uncle Sam promises as the bride's dowry, commerce, education, and missionary effort, and the marriage is consummated." The mission study class could then debate whether the promises had been kept.[65] This particular example shows how skits could introduce gendered power dynamics explicitly to discussions of empire. Many dramatic skits similarly sought to embody abstract ideas.

Montgomery addressed some of the finer points of putting on dramatic skits in her 1915 *How to Use* handbook. She noted that "a few costumes add very much to the effectiveness of any program," and local leaders could find sewing patterns for particular "oriental costumes" that had been published by the different women's missions boards.[66] Yet costumes should not become a distraction from the substance of the activity. As she wrote in another *How to Use*, "no costume is at all necessary to make a most effective meeting," and "it is not advisable to have costumes so often that the society grows to demand some sort of dressing up." Montgomery recommended moderation, perhaps one costumed performance per UMS course.[67] Still, the sheer number of ideas for pageants and other performances found in Montgomery's handbooks suggests the popularity of pageant-inspired skits among White Protestant women. It seems likely that these more informally produced dramatic skits produced a glimmer of the powerful feelings and majestic Christian cosmopolitan aesthetics of the panoramic pageant.

Montgomery wrote dramatic skits for virtually every mission study topic, and she found them a particularly useful format for the study of comparative religions. Christian apologetics took center stage in the mission study skits prepared for two textbooks: Montgomery's *Western Women in Eastern Lands* from 1910 and Robert E. Speer's *The Light of the World* from 1911.[68] Montgomery's *Pageant of Missions* took on the broad themes of her textbook, but the mission study skits she recommended for her second chapter, "Ladies Last," provided a more detailed assessment that compared Christianity and Christian feminism to the "ethnic" religions' unreformable patriarchy. Montgomery's skits for Speer's book amplified "women's wrongs." Yet both textbooks and Montgomery's *How to Use* handbooks focused on moderating the responses of White Protestant women to these other religious traditions. This reflected Speer's and Montgomery's accurate concern about the reputation of those involved in foreign missions. As Speer wrote in his preface, he did not set out to attack other religions as this had not served the missionary cause particularly well.[69] Speer instead encouraged readers to "bathe the whole investigation in the atmosphere of missionary sympathy and of a Christian faith, at once open-minded and perfectly fearless and assured."[70]

In the *How to Use* for Speer's book, Montgomery felt the need to explain precisely why a churchgoing woman needed to bother herself about comparative religions in the first place. In one skit, the reason concerned college-aged children who would be exposed to other religions in their classes. In this skit, entitled "What Our Minister Told Dorothy," the main character was "a recent college graduate, troubled over her study of comparative religions." The "minister" answered not only with evidence from the Bible, but with statistics about the material, social, and political benefits of Christianity, particularly for women.[71] Another skit pointed to the ways travelers visiting other countries could get the wrong idea about missions. In this skit, "a party of tourists just home from a trip around the world," one of them named Mrs. Rich, insists that missions were a waste of time and money. The rest of the characters defended the good works of missions, each focusing on a benefit to women's lives (education, medicine, and so forth). These didactic skits did not achieve the soaring emotions participants attributed to panoramic pageants, but rather offered an opportunity for White Protestant women to practice their missionary apologetics. Participants learned to downplay discussions of evangelism or detailed descriptions of "heathenism" that would mark them as old-fashioned, and they instead learned to rehearse the string of Christian feminist progress found in UMS textbooks.[72]

Another kind of Christian apologetic skit was the impersonation, and these more closely resembled panoramic pageants. These skits staged debates between White missionary women representing other religious traditions and those who got to play the part of Christians. In one impersonation, someone played the "Inquirer" who questioned five women playing Hindu, Muslim, Chinese, Korean, and Japanese characters, and another five women playing Christians. The object of the exercise was "to test the great religions by their teaching on the woman question." While there are no archival records reporting mission study participants' reactions to dramatic skits like this one, Montgomery's commentary on how these skits should be performed offers some insights into how she intended the performances to go. She stressed that the dramatic presentations "should be fair and sympathetic, but should not gloss or conceal evils or imperfections." In Montgomery's instructions for one in which missionary women spoke about the "founders" of different religions from the perspective of "an ethnic believer," Montgomery advised that "an enthusiastic *hero* presentation would be good, if skillfully done *from the viewpoint* of *an ethnic believer*. The unconscious revelations of defects would be all the more striking." In other words, the performer must inhabit the version of the Muslim, Hindu, or Buddhist found in the UMS textbook. As she further explained, the Muslim "does not seek to justify the slaying of the infidels but glories in it," and this "unconscious" attitude would be revealed as "he enumerates the number of women who were honored by being selected by the prophet as his wives, etc." The performers who played their parts as Montgomery intended became passionate defenders of the very customs and beliefs that they had been taught to find abhorrent. By making such performances as sincere and unbiased representations of those other religious traditions, impersonations could make the "facts" in the textbook seem all the more authentic. Montgomery insisted that impersonations performed in this fashion had impressive results. "If this can be well done it is more effective than the critique, but it takes more skill and imagination."[73]

Other comparative religion skits relied on the imperial and Protestant comparative religions premise that "religion" was a universal phenomenon and that all religions could be defined by the same (Protestant) features: places of worship, founders and leaders, sacred texts, moral teachings, and styles of prayer.[74] This idea structured many of the mission study lessons for *The Light of the World*. One class might deal with "the world's bibles," for example, or have mission study students each describe "their temples."[75] One skit from 1915, titled "The Appeal of the Nations," pursued a similar tactic to compare how prayer worked in different religions. Ten "Oriental women" each performed a prayer that ended with a plea that God save them from the dire circumstances they faced as a woman in their religious tradition.

In another type of comparative religion skit, an Asian Christian woman played the protagonist. While these performances sometimes had White missionaries as minor characters, they offered White Protestant women the opportunity to play the part of what Montgomery called the "New Woman of the Orient." Unlike White missionary characters, these Asian Christian women often addressed what they saw as the sins of the Christian West and spoke favorably of an indigenous rather than a missionary-imposed Christianity. In one such skit, Luksmi, a Hindu who had recently graduated from the Protestant Isabella Thoburn College, asks a Theosophist, two reformist Hindus, and a Christian about their religious traditions. Luksmi had "become disgusted with popular Hinduism" and, in a very Protestant way, was looking for a new religion. In addition to elaborating on their traditions, the Theosophist and Hindus also dissuade Luksmi from Christianity. The (White American woman playing the) Theosophist asks, "Is England free from caste? Would all English children attend the same school? Does an American eat with a Chinaman or an African negro?" To no one's surprise, Luksmi chooses Christianity despite those questions as its benefits for womanhood convince her.[76]

White American performers of this dramatization had an opportunity to display their knowledge of Theosophy and different Hindu reform movements, and they reiterated the textbooks' analysis that ranked them in terms of how closely they approximated a White western and modernist Protestantism. Alongside this expected rehearsal of colonial knowledge and imperial hierarchies, however, these characters also raised pointed questions about the social outcomes of White Protestantism as manifested in the United States and in England. The concluding lines of the skit also insisted on the need for Indians to create their own kind of Christianity. The Christian representative does not disagree with those critiques. She rejects the authority of western missionaries, telling Luksmi that it is the "responsibility" of Indian women to bring "this religion, which we have made our own, to our own people, in our own way."[77] If the performers followed Montgomery's script to this point, they were then invited to discuss the importance of devolution, or turning over control of missionary institutions to local Christian communities. Although this had been a topic of discussion among Protestant missionary leaders since the movement began in the early 1800s, the devolution idea had gained even more currency among missionary leaders during World War I. In the Christian Indian character, Montgomery provided the mission study class participants with a useable historical narrative, a progress history that enabled them to relegate such "bad" social practices to the past along with a coercive missionary policy of assimilation. Further, the pageant created the illusion of cooperation as it was a New Christian Indian Woman (named "Ramabai") who appealed for their assistance rather than the abject figure of a child widow or other missionary trope. If White missionary women followed this fictionalized version of Pandita Ramabai, a White fantasy of the Indian convert, they could see themselves as a modern cosmopolitan Christian vanguard with none of the uncomfortable guilt of imposing their White Protestantism onto unwilling Indians. Christian imperial feminism underwent critique in this pageant when the performers pointed out the hypocrisies of so-called Christian nations, but it emerged undefeated and strengthened as White women imagined their work to be endorsed by Indian Christian women.

Intergenerational drama was the subject of another play with an older and younger Chinese woman. This scene took place in a Chinese home complete with a "shrine for ancestor worship" set up behind the characters. An American missionary and a friend visiting from the United States come to the home of a "Chinese bride," a young woman who had attended the American's missionary school, and who had just married and moved into her husband's home. Her mother-in-law, Mrs. Ming, plays hostess, and as the women sit down, a concubine to Mrs. Ming's husband serves the group tea. During the first half of the scene, Mrs. Ming debates the Americans about the value of women's education and Christian ideas of family life. "I confess that I am not one who believes in these new fangled notions," says Mrs. Ming, wondering why her new daughter-in-law had wanted to attend school in the first place. The missionary asks, "without giving offence, Mrs. Ming, may I ask you to explain to my friend the Chinese theory of concubinage?" Following the textbook's information, the performer playing Mrs. Ming relates it to "ancestor worship," saying, "if a wife does not bear a son, all the spirits of the ancestors are denied their accustomed worship, and wander disgraced in the spirit land." The dialog briefly pauses so that the participants can pantomime ancestor worship with the makeshift shrine. For accuracy, one supposes, Montgomery pointed readers to a different textbook that explained what this looked like.[78] The skit concluded with a speech from the daughter-in-law, who "timidly" explains her observations of Christianity that emphasized "the position of women." After she finishes, Mrs. Ming "reproves her for boldness" but also admits that she likes some aspects of Christianity, such as the "absence of idols" and the "happiness of Christian neighbors of hers." But she is not fully convinced, and she voices some criticisms that might just as easily come from American conservatives. Mrs. Ming questioned that "such young men are put forward as ministers" and she "thinks Christianity has a tendency to make women imagine themselves as good as men."[79]

Like the Christian apologetic dialogs, in this skit, Montgomery used the Chinese setting to weigh in on debates taking place among American Protestant women concerning Christian feminism. In her skit, she put the conservative views she found disagreeable into the mouth of a traditionalist and "backward" Chinese mother-in-law rather than attributing them to a White minister or an older White woman. Although the emotions in play for these didactic skits were quite different from the panoramic pageant, the skit still tapped into the bigger pageants' sweeping progress narratives and channeled participants' feelings of millennial urgency that included women's rights. Further, the skit forged bonds between the White American performers and the imagined young Chinese woman, placing them on the same side against what they conflated into an anti-feminist, "backward," and conservative position. If a panoramic pageant like the *Pageant of Missions* sought to stage a diverse and feminine world Christianity through the spectacle of hundreds of costumed performers, the skit about Mrs. Ming aimed to create more intimate (but also imagined) connections between White American women and Montgomery's New Women of the Orient.

By the late 1910s, the UMS textbooks' content and the Christian cosmopolitan aesthetics of mission study began to emphasize the agency of Christian women of color. This theme was evident in the 1918 UMS textbook by Margaret E. Burton called *Women Workers of the Orient*. Focused on the ways women in different Asian countries grappled with rapid social transformations of industrialization, urbanization, and, in the case of China, the 1911 republican revolution, Burton focused on missionary institutions like women's colleges and groups like the YWCA as vital resources for these young women. As noted earlier, Burton stressed the importance of Christianity—and Christian institutions—on Asian women. She also emphasized the leading role Asian women would play in their countries' future as mothers, workers, teachers, and social activists, suggesting that the need for western missionaries had run its course. Almost twenty-five years younger than Montgomery, Margaret Burton had graduated from the University of Chicago (where her father had taught and briefly served as president). Burton had traveled the world as a YWCA secretary rather than as a missionary. In her textbook and in the illustrations that Montgomery used in the *How to Use* for Burton's book, the benighted "pilgrims of the night" were eclipsed by a forward-looking and progressive history of racially and religiously diverse Christian feminist activists.[80]

One visual aid in the *How to Use* offered an updated version of the panoramic pageant's ethnographic tableaux. The women wear "ethnic" dresses, like the costumes used in pageants, but instead of standing with heads bowed as "pilgrims of the night," they are presented as feminists, perhaps marching in a parade, as they carry a banner. The caption for the image reads: "More significant than anything . . . men are doing" a

How to Use Handbook for Women Workers in the Orient, 1918.

quotation from the textbook's fifth chapter, "Women Working Together." Below were the additional lines: "For the cause of education and progress among women of the Orient, is the way in which women different in race, creed, caste, and color unite in service to country and public good." Above the women's heads appeared four different religious identities: "Parsee, Moslem, Christian, Hindu," further emphasizing that this was an interreligious group of women. Following Burton's argument in the textbook, the poster's message was that not all women involved in social work and modernization had to be Christian, because Protestant missionary institutions exerted enough power to change the culture of those who did not convert.[81]

Yet in the skit Montgomery prepared for the same chapter of Burton's textbook, she made clear that White American women had been responsible for producing these revolutionary changes abroad. In the skit, a character playing "America" sat on a "raised platform" as White women wearing costumes from Persia, Turkey, India, Japan, and China approach with their scripted lines about women's progress in each country. Each explains how the First World War has challenged religious, political, and sexual conservatism in their countries. In each country's speech, Montgomery ties together a vision of Christian internationalism and the breaking down of borders with women's progress and liberation from religious custom. In this pageant, modernization is represented not by conversion to Christianity but to an embrace of a secular religious tolerance. To this end, the Persian and Turkish characters speak of escaping from "the harem" while the Indian notes that "Hindu, Mohamedan, Parsee, and Christian women are meeting together to sew for the Red Cross, women who never had any intercourse with those of any faith before." Yet Montgomery's nod to religious diversity here and in the poster were contained within a Protestant frame. Later in the pageant, the characters playing Japan, China, and India all attribute their advancements to the YWCA, and "America" concludes with the following lines: "In the name of all these Christian women here assembled I thank you for the cheer which your reports have brought us, and I ask you to join with us in the great hymn in which all women everywhere can unite to bring in the Kingdom of Love and Light." The mission study class would then proceed to sing "We've a Story to Tell to the Nations."[82] Rather than seeing such presentations of religious diversity as a problem, Christian cosmopolitan churchwomen would instead come to see a degree of religious tolerance itself as an expression of the imperial capaciousness of their Christianity and its ability to accommodate and consume those differences, that is, as long as those *other* religious women adhered to White Protestant women's Christian feminist values.

* * *

In the 1910s, White Protestant missionary women embraced the sensational form of pageantry to manifest and embody a world Christianity. In the panoramic pageants of Montgomery's *Pageant of Missions* or in Oxenham's *Pageant of Darkness and Light*, triumphant stories of the Protestant and Christian imperial past were woven together in ways that mirrored other historical pageants of the day that softened violent

White settler colonialism into a celebratory patriotic story of pioneers and progress. They also became a site for White women to demonstrate their authority through embodying the colonial knowledge obtained in mission study textbooks. More than just presenting the "facts," however, the act of performing different races and religions demonstrated how White Protestant women felt themselves to be unmoored from racial and religious boundaries as their race and religion granted them universal access to embody others. In contrast, when people of color played parts in pageants, their race remained a permanent fixture marking them as "native" or, in later missionary parlance, "national" Christians who remained distinct from the White Protestant missionary.

Panoramic missionary pageants forged a visual and affective Christian cosmopolitan aesthetic that also found expression in less formal improvisational performances and skits used in mission study classes and missionary meetings. Created more for educational purposes than for fundraising, these skits staged debates about modernity, feminism, race, and empire that gave White Protestant women a venue by which to discuss changing gender norms and missionary policies, often through the lens of foreign women. Like Helen Barrett Montgomery's Christian feminism that took shape in the context of comparative religions, the Christian imperial feminist sensibility informed how American women approached their own status and conception of Protestant womanhood. Pageants offered opportunities for White Protestant women to construct historical narratives for themselves as well as for those who were the objects of their missions abroad. They could narrate the decades-old Protestant missionary movement as one of evangelical success in terms of conversions won but also as a process of their own growing cosmopolitan sophistication and racial liberalism. While the White women's foreign missionary movement remained largely silent on Jim Crow segregation and lynchings of Black men in the United States, pageants presented White missionary women as humanitarians and liberators abroad.

The debates about the meaning of foreign missions and changing mission policy intensified in the post–World War I era as the Anglo-American leaders of Protestant missionary operations worried about an inevitable postcolonial future. Would Protestantism survive if anticolonial nationalists associated it with Western imperialism? How could policies like devolution and an expansive vision of "world Christianity" replace the more obvious structures of imperial Christianity? The leaders of the women's missionary boards would also face more immediate questions about the purpose and necessity of their separate organizations. Was it "modern" to segregate men and women, or should their organizations combine? As White Protestants grappled with these questions in the 1920s and 1930s, they invoked the ideal and practice of "cooperation" almost constantly. Cooperation was in many ways the object of a missionary pageant, not only in terms of the words and movements on the stage but in terms of the effort required to stage the pageant in the first place. This same cosmopolitan ethos of cooperation would also be developed as a cosmopolitan practice in the less glamorous rituals of committees, councils, and federations as White Protestant women reorganized in the interwar era.

3

Learning to Cooperate by Cooperating

"Coming from the simplicity of the Congo, I was completely confused by all the committees."[1] The White Disciples of Christ missionary Myrta Ross (Mrs. Emory Ross) was not a stranger to Protestant bureaucracy, yet even she was stymied by the many ecumenical committees, federations, and councils in New York City in the early 1930s. The executive secretary of a local churchwomen's group had a similar experience. In 1935 she reported attending more than 250 meetings, a feat that she joked "might put her in the class of the tired official who stipulated that on his tombstone should appear the legend, 'Committed to death.'"[2] Many White Protestant women had once channeled their time and money into denominational missionary societies, but most of those organizations had become obsolete in the 1930s as they merged with their male-led counterparts. Meanwhile, the women's mission boards' executive secretaries and officers participated in the Federation of Woman's Boards of Foreign Missions (FWBFM) and the Council of Women for Home Missions (CWHM) and, in many cases, sat on committees within the Federal Council of Churches. Each of these interdenominational groups consisted of departments and committees with representatives from the different participating denominations.

In his 1959 address to the American Society of Church History, the prolific historian Robert Handy described the period 1925–1935 as a "religious depression" in which spiritual life and church memberships sank along with the economy.[3] If official church membership lagged and donations dried up, White Protestants' organizational apparatus expanded and so too did their definition of missionary work. White Protestant women presented the practice of cooperating among themselves as training for their part in creating a cooperative vision of a cosmopolitan Christianity. Or, as one churchwoman put it in 1941, "People learn to cooperate by cooperating."[4]

In this process of reorganization and interrogation of what constituted "missions," White women confronted two related dilemmas. Did separate Protestant women's foreign and home missionary societies have a value and purpose, and how could missions best continue to develop the kingdom of God? The answers to both questions would be found through their Christian practice of cooperation. As denominational mission boards struggled, White Protestant women practiced "cooperation" with each other on their many committees, councils, and federations that would eventually replace the women's missionary society. They also called for cooperation between foreign and home missionary organizations, a process that contributed to a new and expanded program of "missions" as Protestants dedicated themselves to "Christianizing" all social, racial, and world relations. The bureaucratic practice of cooperation was connected to this reinterpretation of missions. In their many committees, churchwomen experienced "a collective new Pentecost" that enabled them "to meet present-day human needs." Foreign and home missions and community service combined, and "recognizing the desperate need of the world for the leadership of Jesus the Christ in all areas of life, we hereby declare that it is imperative that the Christian womanhood of America become a united force for bringing in the Kingdom of God."[5]

Before the ecumenical movement existed as such, White Protestants hailed "cooperation" as the solution to the sinful greed of robber barons charged with exploiting workers. By pitching cooperation as Christian, social gospel Protestants encouraged the faithful factory owner to share his wealth with his workers and cultivated what amounted to a moderate Christian alternative to the more radical demands of other labor activists.[6] Cooperation took on new meaning as White Protestants formed ecumenical organizations in the early 1900s like the women's Central Committee for the United Study of Foreign Missions, the FWBFM, and the CWHM. At this time, some Protestant mission boards combined their efforts abroad as well. When northern Methodists, Baptists, and Presbyterians joined with Episcopalians and the Disciples of Christ to create the Federal Council of Churches in 1908, they committed to cooperating across denominations and theological differences to better consolidate their moral authority and to coordinate their social service and missionary programs. In theological terms, cooperation also reflected their ecumenical missionary vision of creating one universal church for the whole world, a united world Christianity. By the early 1920s, ecumenical Protestants celebrated cooperation in reference to their own expansive bureaucracy and as a spiritual practice that manifested God's kingdom in the world.

This did not mean that the imperial underpinnings of the missionary movement underwent substantive critique. The ecumenical movement reflected its White Protestant organizers' desire to be seen as a unified religious (and racial) group as American Catholics and Jews had formed their own organizations. Further, White Protestants would align cooperation with White Protestant and American democratic values. Cooperation for non-Protestants often required submission to a normative secularism defined in White Protestant terms. Like other White liberals who constructed a "consensus culture" in the 1930s, White ecumenical Protestants used the discourse of cooperation to include and to exclude those seen as "uncooperative." Cooperation, then, grew out of the universalizing Christian cosmopolitanism of the White Protestant missionary movement that encouraged diversity so long as those differences did not threaten Christian unity.[7]

Examining how "cooperation" functioned as a practical strategy and a religious practice for White Protestant women as they began a new era of institution building and as they redefined "missions" illuminates the relationship between ecumenicalism among White Protestants and their expansionary Christian imperialism at home and abroad. On one level, we will explore two institutional histories of post-missionary organizations: the negotiations that led to the United Council of Church Women in 1941, and the local Council of Church Women in Rochester, New York. Through these institutional histories, we will track the way in which cooperation factored into how White Protestant women came to see themselves as "churchwomen" instead of "missionary women." By imagining these sometimes contentious meetings at a granular level, we gain a better understanding of when and how local and national leaders invoked "cooperation" both for practical ends and to reimagine missionary work as a much broader campaign to manage heterogeneous communities, the nation, and the world. These were sometimes painful meetings as participants had attachments to their old missionary organizations. By examining moments of conflict in what are fairly sparse meeting minutes, we will see how churchwomen formed committee meetings and cooperation into a practice that they considered to have a direct connection to their spiritual development.

Pittsburgh, 1924

In the early 1920s, the leaders of missionary organizations debated whether "missions" should be distinct from other kinds of Protestant reform efforts and activism. They also debated the role of separate women's organizations in this new phase of ecumenical Protestantism. The Central Committee for the United Study of Foreign Missions, along with the FWBFM and CWHM, had organized the leaders of the different women's foreign and home missionary societies in the early 1900s. In the 1920s, however, these White-led women's organizations faced a host of setbacks. First, the leaders of the women's boards noted a generational divide. At the 1924 meeting of the FWBFM, one woman presented mission study and "discussion groups" as a way to "get away from the 'mental hangers-on'" at missionary society meetings. Discussions were the answer as "mothers, aunts, and grandmothers must keep step with the young people by having independent thinking and freedom of discussion among themselves."[8] Even so, missionary leaders recognized that the younger generation of White churchgoing women were often critical of the assumptions of Christian imperial feminism. The 1927 Annual Meeting of the FWBFM included an assessment of the recent Christian Conference of American and Oriental Students held at Princeton University. The student participants were "remarkably free from a national or provincial point of view," and "they expressed their conviction that the responsibility for extending Christ's Kingdom throughout the world is a task for East and West together rather than the task of the West alone."[9]

Besides criticisms of missions, the women's missionary societies and interdenominational organizations faced financial deficits that would grow worse during the Great Depression. In the face of depleted budgets, the heads of the male-led general boards voiced concerns about efficiency: Was it necessary to have separate women's boards that duplicated the general boards' work? This combined with a sense that single-sex organizations were old-fashioned and out of sync with modernization led missionary leaders to move to merge the women's organizations into those of their male-led counterparts.[10]

Unsurprisingly, many White Protestant women remained deeply invested in continuing women's organizations in the 1920s as they feared women would become subordinates in male-led ecumenical organizations.[11] Helen Barrett Montgomery had addressed this in her 1910 book, *Western Women in Eastern Lands*, noting that while women's organizations contradicted the principles of sex equality she found in the gospel, they were a practical necessity as long as men shunted their female colleagues to the margins. Yet not all women agreed, and the different sides of this debate are evident in a discussion that took place at an FWBFM meeting in 1922. Montgomery's longtime friend and fellow Baptist Lucy Peabody proposed that the FWBFM support her proposal for a new global women's organization, the Federation of Christian Women of the World. She argued that Protestant women around the world must unite to bring about a Christian world order. Peabody also believed in women's distinctive contributions. Peace and internationalism could not be achieved "through political means and [male] political leaders," and she asked, "should not the women unitedly pray and study and learn better ways of working for the great ends of the Kingdom of God?"[12] A lone voice of opposition came from a British guest at the meeting named Muriel Underhill. The Oxford alumna had been a missionary in India and now worked for the London-based *International Review of Missions*.[13] Underhill thought women's organizations were old fashioned, arguing that "there should be no definite lines between men and women on politics, religion or social questions and that women's organizations did not appeal to her."[14] Even if many women at the FWBFM meeting agreed with Underhill's rejection of gendered differences in principle, their experiences taught them that in practice, men tended to ignore women when they sat together at the decision-making table. When women were "on joint boards there was always courtesy and good fellowship" but it still came down to "the men make the plans and hand them over for the women to endorse."[15]

Both the issue of defining missions and the question of separate women's organizations were at the heart of a meeting of executive secretaries that took place in Pittsburgh over two snowy December days in 1924. The meeting had been called by Roy B. Guild of the Federal Council of Churches, who had spent the past five years encouraging the formation of local councils of churches around the United States and the related women's councils. He invited representatives from some of these new women's councils to the meeting to connect with representatives from the FWBFM and CHWM for a discussion of a list of questions that had come up at the Federal Council's quadrennial meeting the previous week in Atlanta. Could local ecumenical church federations replace home missionary societies? Was there still a need for separate women's organizations or could women just join their local federation as equals to men?[16] As was clear in the meeting's organization, Guild and others at the Federal Council had already answered these questions. They saw the new ecumenical women's councils as the natural replacement for the older women's missions boards, and they viewed the former as a first step in integrating "women's work" with that of the male-led local federation. Yet few of the meeting's women participants would end up agreeing with Guild, and those who were on the fence left Pittsburgh even more convinced of the need for women's organizations. While Guild and the White women in attendance agreed on the necessity of cooperation if White native-born Protestants were to remain influential in a demographically changing United States, they had quite different ideas about how this should be done.

Upon arriving in Pittsburgh, Florence Quinlan, the executive secretary of the Council of Women for Home Missions, was aware that many of the women in attendance had little interest in supporting missionary organizations that they viewed as out of touch. She expected to hear criticism from "women more or less distant to the missionary groups," but she was taken aback when "Miss Sampson of the Methodist Board" stood up and "said that missionary organizations went around patting themselves on the back instead of looking to see what could be done to actually better conditions."[17] Quinlan described this and other thoughts and reactions to the meeting in a frank letter to her colleague, Carrie Kerschner. Kerschner, the executive secretary of the Reformed Church's Woman's Missionary Society, was a member of both the CWHM and the FWBFM.

In spite of her frustrations, Quinlan admittedly had an easier time of it than her counterpart, Ella MacLaurin, the newly appointed executive secretary of the FWBFM. MacLaurin left Pittsburgh feeling "disappointed" that the subject of foreign missions had barely come up at all except at the end of the meeting when some in attendance pushed for a resolution recognizing their role in educating Americans about the "pressing issues" of the "abolition of war and the establishment of a

Christian world order."[18] Quinlan chose not to discuss foreign missions in her own remarks given the conference's planners' clear enthusiasm for women's work on behalf of "community interests" and her status as a "missionary woman." She felt there was a need "to be careful or there would be a real explosion and we would make no headway."[19] She also kept her remarks "extremely brief." When it was time to form a Findings Committee to write the meeting's conclusions, she initially refused to be nominated, arguing that the committee should be comprised of women from the local councils since this was an FCC meeting. Although Quinlan nevertheless became a member, she insisted that she not serve as the chairwoman. She admitted to Kerschner that one of other participants "quietly said to me, 'You are the best politician in the room.'" This woman "had been watching some of the moves and could read through them what others in the room did not see."[20]

While Quinlan's remarks at the Pittsburgh meeting might have helped win over some reluctant churchwomen in the audience, the more significant unifying factor would be their shared annoyance with the FCC men and a growing sense that women excelled at cooperation in ways men did not recognize. The congeniality she found in her office was in short supply at this meeting. "Had there been women on the committee which planned the conference," Quinlan wrote, "it would undoubtedly have attacked the problem from a somewhat different angle." As the men on the first panel addressed the question about the need for separate women's organizations, they described women's missionary societies as useless when it came to addressing the social problems of the day. One panelist declared that the denominational women's missionary societies "centered around two things—money raising and educational work," and, according to Quinlan's account, "he implied very strongly that the latter was purely in the theoretical realm." At this, she reported, the "women in the room rustled considerably." The next speaker "informed us that the women practically did nothing along international or inter-racial lines; that all moral and political issues were dealt with by non-church organizations and civic affairs by groups outside the church" and that church groups "practically ignored the human problems." Quinlan confided to Kerschner that "the room nearly exploded at this point."[21]

Quinlan responded in her own brief remarks on a later panel. She emphasized that women's missionary societies had long considered both "moral and political issues." She explained that the foreign and home mission study textbooks were not, in fact, "theoretical" but practical guides related to "the project line." The CWHM's recent publications encouraged local women's activism on "racial and interracial matters, in housing conditions, conditions among the foreign-born, etc., etc." Quinlan also pointed to the CWHM's adoption of *The Trend of the Races*, by African American sociologist and head of the FCC's Commission on the Church and Race Relations George Haynes. In noting how Haynes's book was a mission study textbook, Quinlan made the point that organized Protestant women did not define "missions" narrowly or in sentimental or abstract terms as women's missionary societies might once have done.[22] For this reason, Quinlan and her fellow attendees were frustrated and angry that while the men had a "real ignorance of the women's denominational programs" as they currently existed, they still "did not hesitate at all to indicate the lines of procedure that they thought the women should take." When the Findings Committee met to summarize the conference's conclusions at the end of the second day, Roy Guild initially sat down with the group of women even though he was not technically on the committee. Quinlan wrote: "in a jocular way, I then asked whether Dr. Guild was to be present or whether he vanished from that point on, and he said that he vanished and he was not with us again. I feel pretty certain that I did not hurt his feelings in any way, but I was determined personally that we as women would not be run by any of the men!"[23] The Pittsburgh meeting was a learning experience for Protestant women leading the CWHM, the FWBFM, and the local councils, and in the coming years, representatives from each would begin to meet among themselves rather than under the aegis of the Federal Council.

"Protestantism Is Disorganization": Ecumenicalism in the Churchwoman's Council

In the years before that Pittsburgh conference, Roy Guild had traveled the country to encourage local groups of White Protestants to form interdenominational church federations. Guild came to this work with a background as a Congregationalist minister who had excelled at coordinating Protestant churches as social service agencies in Topeka,

Kansas. He also served as the co-chairman of the national Men and Religion Forward Movement in 1911.[24] When he was hired as an associate executive secretary at the Federal Council in 1915, Guild sought to make community-based churchwork appealing to businessmen and civic leaders, and he advocated for clergy and laymen to form local federations of churches. Such ecumenical organizations fulfilled White Protestants' theological ideal of creating a universal Church and strengthening White Protestants' social and political power. This was evident in Guild's 1919 book for the YMCA, *Practicing Christian Unity*, in which he analyzed what he called the "Christian reconstruction" of the United States (and the world) taking place in the aftermath of World War I.[25] He encouraged Protestant clergymen and churchgoers to take charge of mapping and managing their communities on issues of temperance, religious education, eradicating vice, political corruption, and other matters. He also emphasized that they should not "police the city" but rather influence "public opinion" through the pulpit and the press. "The biggest, most irresistible policeman in America is public opinion," he wrote, and "the churches can create this public opinion."[26]

Guild aimed to draw Protestant men into this work, and he did so by describing Protestant power in business and military terms that flattered the men in his audience and suggested how their talents were suited to this work. In a speech to Topeka's ministers, for instance, Guild predicted that rural communities would be unable to support multiple churches and would be better served if the churches "fused into one big organization with the denominational executive bodies guiding all of them." Churches must avoid "entering into the keenest competition" and instead "co-operate in winning souls to Christ, in a systematic manner never before tried."[27] Military metaphors and international diplomacy infused Guild's presentation of church federation to laymen and clergy when he visited Rochester, New York, in December 1918, just weeks after the November armistice.[28] He described the meeting to plan the city's church federation as a "Versailles conference" and the federation's future executive secretary would be "a General Foch to direct the Protestant battle against evil in Rochester" coordinating his "Christian force." Whomever they chose to be the executive secretary must be a "master religious strategist who will throw the regiments of Baptists, Presbyterians, Methodists and other denominations into line for the battle for right and justice." He would be tasked with running "evangelistic campaigns" that would publicize church events, promote their social services, and generally launch a "new era of religious education through the pulpit and the press."[29]

As it turned out, the laymen and clergy who established the Federation of Churches of Rochester and Monroe County found themselves too busy to be either the generals or foot soldiers, and they instead invited women to organize an auxiliary group that would take up this work. In January 1922, Orlo Price, the executive secretary of the Federation of Churches of Rochester and Monroe County, and its president, Samuel Tyler, invited a small group of women representing different Rochester churches to a meeting in which they were asked to form a woman's council. It would "fill a long felt need," they explained, as "matters were constantly coming to the Federation which could be better handled by a woman's organization."[30] In 1926, Rochester's Woman's Council hired Alice T. Walker (Mrs. Irving Walker) as a part-time executive secretary, and the position would become a full-time salaried job in 1938. Unlike Guild and the clergy who ran the city's Federation of Churches, Walker belonged to the dense network of women's and other civic associations in the city and the state. In 1936, Walker reported her meetings for "the Allied Temperance Forces, the Executive Committee of the [Rochester] Federation of Churches together with membership on a number of its departments of work, the Rochester World Peace Committee, the Emergency Peace Conference, the Executive Committee of the State Council of Churches and Religious Education and numbers of temporary committees on all sorts of subjects."[31]

Married to a psychologist who had retired early from his work at the state asylum in Rochester due to illness, Walker became a vital node in a network of Protestant and other organizations.[32] Notably, Walker was a Universalist, a more theologically liberal tradition than most of the Protestant traditions represented on the Woman's Council. She would even serve as an officer and president of the Universalists' Women's National Missionary Association in the 1930s. Walker earned accolades for her organizational skills, and the women working to organize a national Protestant women's group praised both Rochester's Council of Church Women and Walker's "interdenominational consciousness." Walker, they added, "combines the efficiency of a professional woman with the graciousness of a charming hostess."[33]

Established in 1922, the Council of Church Women in Rochester, New York, was one of the earliest councils of churchwomen that would eventually be the local affiliates of the UCCW, and its structure would be presented as a model for other councils around the United States. Early on, it joined other such local groups in modeling its bylaws and structure after the recommendations of the CWHM and FWBFM.[34] The Council's strong missionary orientation was not a surprise given that its membership included Helen Barrett Montgomery, who had helped found the FWBFM. In a speech to Rochester's Council at one meeting, Montgomery was full of optimism for the future of the new Women's Council. She made a direct connection between the cooperative work of women at the local level and the larger objectives of Christian women to bring about a better world. The Council reflected "the beginning of interdenominational conscience" and she believed that "denominations must co-operate before nations will co-operate."[35]

Cooperation meant improved organization to White Protestant women, and an opportunity to expand their moral influence as Protestants beyond their churches. At the fourth meeting of the Rochester Woman's Council in April 1922, churchwomen heard a "most excellent inspirational talk on 'The Power of an Organized Idea'" by Cornelius Savage, a Baptist minister from nearby Oswego. Savage compared Protestant groups to organizations like the Red Cross and the Roman Catholic Church, noting that while anyone might "have their dreams and ideas and ideals, these ideas must be organized in order to become efficient and effective." Pointing to the historical evidence, Savage complained that "Protestantism is disorganization, a breaking up of the church into several bodies." Yet Protestants had turned a corner with the new local ecumenical organizations. Rochester's churchwomen believed that their new council would stand as a successful example of "re-organization for more effective service" as they practiced an "applied Christianity" through their missionary outreach and community services. Savage concluded with a stirring appeal on this point that invited the churchwomen to bring their missionary vision to Rochester. "The slums of Rochester need our help," he implored, "and we must get the feeling that Jesus loves the unwashed soul in the street just as much as he loves us."[36] Over the next year of meetings, planning, and projects, the Woman's Council made itself a known presence among Rochester's Protestants and in the larger community. Donald B. McQueen, the pastor of Rochester's First Baptist Church, praised the group as an exemplary model of ecumenicalism. "We need a more complete understanding with one another in the religious world," he said, and the Woman's Council's willingness "to bring good will" as well as to "co-operate" meant that it was "leading the churches to be that which is better and that which is to be."[37]

Who belonged to the Rochester Woman's Council? A 1923 list of members shows that mostly White Presbyterian and Baptist women (with sixteen and fourteen representatives respectively) were the early majority, with ten Methodist women coming in a close third. The city's Congregationalist, Disciples of Christ, Presbyterian, Episcopal, Reformed, Lutheran, and Unitarian churches also had representatives on the Council. Most of these women were White, married, and middle class, although some unmarried women (often affiliated with the University of Rochester) held leadership positions in the Council. Most representatives were leaders of women's missionary societies or other organizations in their own churches rather than minister's wives. One of Rochester's wealthiest citizens, Episcopalian Georgiana Sibley (Mrs. Harper Sibley), was also active in the Council, serving as its president in the mid-1930s. A decade later, Sibley would also be the United Council of Church Women's president. While the Council's officers and committee chairwomen were all White women in the first two decades, at least three Black women from Mt. Olivet Baptist Church, Trinity Presbyterian, and Memorial AME Zion were also listed as church representatives. Mt. Olivet's representative, Carrie Dukes Rose (Mrs. James E. Rose), was a Spelman graduate who had worked alongside Lugenia Burns Hope (Mrs. John Hope) in Atlanta's Neighborhood Union. She moved to Rochester after marrying Mt. Olivet's pastor, who was himself active in the local Federation of Churches and NAACP chapter. In addition to her duties as a minister's wife, she was the superintendent of the Dorsey Home for Dependent Colored Children.[38]

Rose and other Black Rochesterians shared some common interests with the White women on the Council of Church Women, but the Council's agenda very clearly reflected White Progressive women's moral reform activism and their relative affluence and means. They monitored the enforcement of Prohibition, they learned about local government reforms, and launched a volunteer Motor Service Corps to drive those in need to doctor's appointments and the like. They also signed several petitions protesting the "demoralizing" effects of "bathing beauty contests" for the "false ideas" it created for men and girls, and they investigated the display of "improper literature" on newsstands.[39] Their meeting minutes show how they took up issues from the missionary-oriented FWBFM and the CWHM, but were also in conversation with many other groups that represented the city's and state's White Protestant establishment.

The Woman's Council grew quickly in its first decade, and its regular monthly meetings, open to all members, often had several hundred women in attendance.[40] Seeking to expand their programming and needing to increase the budget, in 1926 the officers launched a new membership campaign focused on individuals in addition to the dues paid by member churches, and they had the ambitious goal of securing 1,500 sustaining members paying $1 dues per year. By the end of 1927, they neared their goal with 1,338 members.[41] Spurred on by their success, in late 1927, Rochester churchwomen renamed their organization the Council of Church Women of Rochester and Monroe County. Instead of being "affiliated with" the Federation of Churches, they now "cooperated with" it.[42] With an income of almost $3,000 for 1927, that included an existing balance plus new dues paid by churches and from individual sustaining memberships totaling more than $1,400, Rochester's churchwomen joined the many other women's clubs in their midsize city whose luncheons, fundraisers, and social service projects were regularly reported in the city's newspaper.[43] Yet social activities and social services were always framed as an expression of Christianity. In 1932, the tenth anniversary of the Council, its president Ida Post (Mrs. Walter Post), described the Council as "the body of Christ" performing God's work in the world. While "in the early Christian century He depended on His disciples. Today He depends on us, the members of the Council of Church Women."[44]

Where did missions fit into the Council's varied activities? Foreign missionary women were well represented on the Council. Grace Hondelink (Mrs. Garrett Hondelink), the chairwoman of the Rochester Woman's Council's Missions Department, had been a Reformed Church missionary in Japan before marrying and moving to Rochester, where her husband worked as a pastor, in 1913. Hondelink quickly became active in ecumenical missionary organizations, serving as the president of Rochester's Women's Missionary Union, an interdenominational organization focused on the United Mission Study textbooks.[45] She also represented Rochester's Woman's Council at the Pittsburgh meeting in December 1924. Even if she might have identified as a "missionary woman," and a foreign missionary at that, the discussions about cooperation as a necessity to asserting Protestants' authority in their local communities at the Pittsburgh meeting would have been familiar territory. She left the meeting feeling a sense of pride in what Rochester's churchwomen had accomplished since their formation in 1922. She reported that "Rochester was almost if not quite the best organized and in the best working condition of any of the women's organizations."[46]

The Missionary Institute illustrated how Rochester churchwomen engaged in more traditional missionary society programs while also expanding "missions" more broadly. The inspiration for the Institute was a one-day event in 1922 focused primarily on workshops for the upcoming UMS and home mission study textbooks. Hondelink led a session on "How to Conduct the Class Meetings" on pedagogy, and James Rose spoke on the year's home mission study textbook, FCC secretary George Haynes's *The Trend of the Races*. This provided at least one example of Florence Quinlan's contention that Protestant women had studied this text and topic as Roy Guild had wanted. In addition to the workshop on the UMS book for 1923, foreign missionary interests were represented by the luncheon's speaker, Dr. Mathilda Hunt, a Christian Indian physician visiting the United States to raise money and awareness about her work with children on the subcontinent.[47]

The annual Missionary Institute shows an example of how the Rochester Council and Hondelink were already reinterpreting "missions." The event connected (mostly White) Protestant women's missionary expertise to matters of local politics and social relations. It asserted organized Protestant women's ability to address big questions and manage the challenges of a diverse community while also coordinating the whole proceedings in a pleasing manner. Alongside mission study workshops, Protestant women heard speeches from keynote speakers like the Christian internationalist and former missionary Sidney Gulick of the Federal Council of Churches, Rochester's Jewish Congressman Meyer Jacobstein, and the Universalist minister and columnist William Wallace Rose. Council member, suffragist, and politician Helen Probst Abbott was a frequent speaker as well.[48] These discussions of cooperation, tolerance, and Protestant women's responsibilities to Christianize their communities also included entertainment that echoed missionary pageants. The closing banquet at the 1924 Missionary Institute featured a "chorus of Ukrainian young people dressed in native costumes."[49]

The Missionary Institute's range of topics illustrated how White-led Protestant women's groups had expanded beyond the narrow concerns of temperance and evangelical missionary work. Yet this broadening agenda was not without its challenges. One small but revealing incident shows how the Council of Church Women's members had to make a choice about whether to support an upcoming lecture by Maude Royden. The English "woman preacher" and Christian internationalist had arrived in New York City in late 1927, where she planned to begin a lecture tour on her new book, *I Believe in God*. The Anglican Royden was best known for establishing the Guildhouse Fellowship, an ecumenical chapel and community center in London.[50] While her previous US visits had raised little notice in the press, this time, Hearst newspapers across the country published stories disparaging Royden as the "smoking evangelist," who not only smoked cigarettes and drank, but who also supported socialism, "companionate marriage," and free love.[51] The Archbishop of Canterbury defended Royden in a letter to the press, but even so, White Methodist women canceled Royden's scheduled appearances before their missionary society meetings in Boston, Philadelphia, and Chicago.[52]

In Rochester, New York, several members of the Council of Church Women had concerns about Royden's January visit, and at a meeting held a couple of weeks before her visit to their city, the Council's Executive Committee revoked their initial sponsorship of her lecture.[53] Would White Protestant women's traditional support for temperance and moral purity take precedence over their shared support for Royden's social Christianity and internationalism? Over the course of the next week, local ministers took up the subject of Royden in their sermons, and the liberal editor of Rochester's newspaper defended Royden and railed against what he saw as religious persecution. Boundary lines were being drawn, and it seemed that Rochester's status as a modern and cosmopolitan city was on the line. One local Episcopal priest attacked the "intolerance" and "provincialism" of Royden's opponents, while another clergyman invoked the recent Scopes Trial when he commented that the uproar "seems like Dayton, Tennessee, not Rochester."[54] Council member Georgiana Sibley would be hosting Royden in her home, and she called a special meeting of the Council to try to change her colleagues' minds. At the special meeting, Sibley "spoke of the great work done by Maude Royden and pointed out how customs have varied in the different ages." In other words, Sibley contended that there was no single standard of Christian morality with respect to cigarettes and alcohol, and the Council's support for Royden need not imply that its members condoned drinking or women's smoking. Perhaps because of her social power and influence, and perhaps because she successfully appealed to the modernist and cosmopolitan aspirations of the Council women, Sibley's resolution to reinstate funding passed easily with a vote of 36–7.[55] Reading between the lines, it is also possible that the Sunday sermons and editorials penned by Rochester's clergy helped change some of the Council members' minds as well. The Council's endorsement of Royden, along with the newspapers' coverage of Rochester's leading Protestant ministers, shows how ecumenical White Protestants sought to influence public opinion. The Council's decision to side with Sibley also provided an example of how the absolutist moral purity that had once defined Protestant womanhood was replaced in this instance with Sibley's cosmopolitan appeal for cooperation and a view that Royden's Christian internationalist politics mattered more than purity on the temperance question.

Georgiana Sibley's own understanding of the purpose of Protestant missions also marked a significant departure from the old guard leaders of the earlier foreign missionary movement and her more evangelical-leaning contemporaries. For example, in the 1930s, Lucy Peabody, the Baptist who had long chaired the Central Committee overseeing the UMS series, and Helen Barrett Montgomery were both critical of the Laymen's Inquiry Report, a major study surveying Protestant missions in Asia. The findings had been published in 1932 and called for greater emphasis on providing social services than evangelism, and suggested that in some places, Protestant missionaries might cooperate with non-Christian local groups and governments.[56] Not long after, Peabody resigned from her post on the Central Committee and left the Northern Baptist Convention. Along with her daughter and son-in-law, both missionaries in the Philippines, Peabody helped establish a Fundamentalist Baptist missionary society that emphasized "Bible-trained evangelists." Peabody chafed at her new Fundamentalist colleagues' pre-millennialism and conservative attitudes toward women. Her decision proved all the more remarkable given the fact that her longtime collaborator, Helen Barret Montgomery, had in the early 1920s fended off a Fundamentalist advance when she served as the first woman president of the Northern Baptist Convention.[57] Montgomery had died in 1934, shortly before Peabody made her move. It is likely that some other women also abandoned what they saw as overly liberal ecumenical women's organizations in the 1930s, but the ballooning of local churchwomen's councils in the 1940s and 1950s suggests that many more stayed or would be recruited.

The Maude Royden incident in Rochecster is instructive because it foreshadows how Georgiana Sibley, who served not only as Rochester's Council president in the mid-1930s but also as the president of the UCCW in the late 1940s, navigated these kinds of conservative-liberal divides. Sibley was, notably, one of the few women on the Laymen's Inquiry Commission, along with her husband, Harper. They also had a close friendship with Ernest Hocking, the author of the Laymen's Report. In 1958, the Sibleys gifted Hocking with a new biography of Rufus Jones, the Quaker philosopher who had also been with them on the Laymen's Inquiry. Hocking's thank-you note in Georgiana Sibley's papers reminisced fondly of when he and Jones were chastised for spending too much time in conversation with Buddhists and Shintoists during their time in Japan.[58]

In a different folder, Sibley preserved a handwritten statement of her own views of foreign missions. While it is unclear if she wrote this as part of a speech or article, it illustrates how her modernist view of Christianity was not incompatible with the missionary movement's Christian imperial feminism. Sibley believed missionaries should preach "love one another, the brotherhood of man" and should tell "of the fulfillment of divine spirituality in a man, Jesus." But for her, missionaries also worked "to defeat superstition, ignorance, and the terrible shackles of disease, hunger, and poverty." On this point, she and Peabody would have been in full agreement. Yet, Sibley also offered a statement of her own beliefs as she continued her thoughts, and here she firmly rejected virtually all of the "Fundamentals" that conservative Protestants defended. Sibley wrote,

If the missionary goes out to teach the supernatural appearance in the world by virgin birth of a deliverer, who used mysterious otherworld magic rather than the highest use of natural law, who rose physically from actual death and walked abroad, who continues in human form beside the personality of God in human form—if an after life is to be a reward and prize for present goodness. If these things are a necessary belief for a missionary of the Christian Church—for a member of the Christian Church, then I do not and can never fully qualify.[59]

When Sibley led the UCCW in the 1940s, she did not foreground those aspects of her liberal theology that would certainly have scandalized some UCCW members, but instead would build on the shared desire to eradicate superstition, ignorance, and, of course, women's oppression. She also relied on the flexible language around cooperation that developed in the 1920s and 1930s as foreign and home missionary women united with other churchwomen to lay the groundwork for the UCCW. In contrast to the sharp institutional schisms taking place in other corners of White Protestantism amid the Fundamentalist-Modernist debate, Protestant women's organizations would be looking for ways to unite their organizations.

From Missionary Women to Churchwomen: National Reorganization

In a series of meetings taking place in the late 1920s and 1930s, mostly White Protestant women representing the FWBFM, the CWHM, and local organizations like Rochester's Council of Church Women moved haltingly toward creating a single organization. To this end, these three entities began to form joint committees that represented a new stage of cooperation. In her 1926 presidential address to the FWBFM, Katherine Silverthorn (Mrs. E. H. Silverthorn) made "cooperation" her theme. She highlighted that the "cooperative activities" among different Protestant and even secular agencies had expanded "the outreach of Foreign Missions, showing the interrelation of the missionary enterprise with many things which not very many years ago we thought bore no relation to missions. We are gradually learning that Christian principles need to be applied to all of life and its relationships everywhere." Silverthorn's parting remarks further defined missions in terms of "abundant life," a phrase gaining currency among liberal Protestants in the 1920s. "We are finding it increasingly difficult in this age of complex relationships to narrow our missionary activities and interests to what we used to designate as 'Missions per se.'" She instead suggested that "if 'Missions' implies sharing the Gospel Message, 'Good News,' the abundant life Christ came to give to all, then our message touches all of life, and its relationships, Godward and Manward."[60] That same year, at a meeting of the leaders of the FWBFM and CWHM in Cleveland, one woman declared, "We have been home missionary or foreign missionary women, now the inclusive term—church women."[61]

With this process underway, the leaders of the FWBFM and CWHM sent out a survey to their members asking about the relationship between missionary societies and new women's councils. The anxiety of the missionary groups was clear as the letter explained that there was a "growing feeling among groups of church women that the missionary program is not sufficiently inclusive to hold or interest the majority of church women." The letter was also protective of missionary women's organizations. It noted that newer churchwomen's councils dealt with "international questions, peace, law enforcement, interracial relationships, and Christian Social Service," but that these issues had long been of interest to women's groups as part of "the technically-termed missionary enterprise." The survey also asked readers to weigh in on how the "missionary program" could be made more "flexible" in order to address local community concerns of interest to churchwomen's councils "without spreading the missionary interest so thin that our missionary interest will be lost."[62] At the meeting in St. Louis, the FWBFM and CWHM agreed to redefine missions "to include all the activities of church women," and they set a course for the future. They created a "Guiding Group," later renamed the National Commission of Protestant Church Women. Practically, this meant that local churchwomen's councils should send reports about their activities to the Council's Florence Quinlan, who would then ensure that the national program responded to local interests. Quinlan would work in consultation with her counterparts at the Federation as well. In the Findings Committee report written after the 1927 conference (and chaired by Rochester's Alice Walker), the delegates at St. Louis reported their optimistic hope that a shared program would "provide a bond of unity and a medium of cooperation for all activities for which church women should be responsible."[63]

The changing view of missions was also evident when a joint committee renamed the CWHM and FWBFM's annual Day of Prayer for Missions to the World Day of Prayer in 1926. Since the nineteenth century, missionary societies had set special "days of prayer" that included prayer services and collecting offerings for foreign missions. In their own histories of the event, churchwomen traced the event to 1887 and a Presbyterian day of prayer for missions. In 1920, Helen Barrett Montgomery and the Central Committee's chairwoman Lucy Peabody had formalized the ritual Day of Prayer for Missions, and over the next several years, the proceeds for this event would be distributed to two foreign and two home missionary causes: Protestant women's colleges in Asia, the Committee on Christian Literature for Women and Children, migrant ministries, and religious workers at Native American boarding schools.[64] The World Day of Prayer committee encouraged local women to form interdenominational *and* interracial committees to plan the event. "In order to realize the full purpose of the day," the World Day of Prayer committee's chairwoman Mary Hough recommended in 1927, local committees "should be international in character and include all Christian women and girls of the community, regardless of race."[65] In many cities and towns, these World Day of Prayer committees had laid the groundwork for local churchwomen's councils.

In addition to the broadening missionary objectives in the World Day of Prayer services, the FWBFM also began to think about missions more expansively as Christian world relations. At the 1927 annual meeting, speakers emphasized the importance of "international, interracial, and industrial relationships," including individual friendships and cooperation in organizations and in communities. As had been the case in mission study programs, they also called for more fact-finding studies to "familiarize ourselves with conditions and movements in foreign countries and the relation of our own countries thereto, not relying alone on the public press, but using every known means to ascertain the facts." Local leaders were encouraged to "create a right public opinion" and to "write to our representatives in the legislative bodies . . . on bills dealing with international relations, urging passage of those which represent justice and tend to create goodwill among the nations, and disapproving those which foster suspicion, jealousy or race hatred."[66]

In 1929, the Findings Committee of the FWBFM meeting issued a similar statement. "The responsibility of Christians is not alone to take the message of salvation to individuals, but to Christianize all human relations. Peace is an adventure of faith. We must demobilize the mind of the world for war—and as definitely mobilize it for peace."[67] While critical of older expressions of White women's Christian imperial feminism, the new calls to "Christianize all human relations" represented a new iteration rather than a rejection of US churchwomen's sense of moral authority to manage a heterogeneous world. Instead of focusing solely on the conversion of individuals to Christianity, organized Protestant women saw the purpose of their own cooperative efforts as empowering them to transform larger structures by shaping public opinion and mobilize politically on behalf of policies they believed to be in accordance with their Christian vision.

As churchwomen advocated for Christian cooperation on a global scale, they continued to navigate the challenges of cooperating within their own organizations. The National Commission of Protestant Church Women they had created at the St. Louis conference in 1927 had not worked out as planned. Churchwomen would later describe it as an "experiment, a high adventure in fellowship in service." In reality, it generated confusion and some local leaders took issue with its attempts to collect dues for what they saw as a pointless bureaucracy.[68] It was made even less relevant when, in early 1930, the local churchwomen's councils agreed to establish their own organization, the (confusingly similarly named) National Council of Federated Church Women.[69] That same year, representatives from the FWBFM, CWHM, and this new organization met for a two-day conference in New York to determine how they would work together.

While many attendees likely arrived at this meeting with the political savvy Florence Quinlan displayed at Pittsburgh, this meeting's presiding officer, M. Katharine Bennett (Mrs. Fred S. Bennett), sought to set a different tone. She opened the meeting with a passage from theologian Henry Nelson Wieman's 1928 book, *Methods of Private Religious Living*. Wieman's book was a spiritual advice manual of sorts, and it exemplified Protestant modernism in its emphasis on methods of spiritual and intellectual self-examination.[70] His aim was to equip readers with the practices that would "produce definite observable results in improvement of human living."[71] Bennett read from the fifth chapter of Wieman's book entitled "Meeting a Crisis." "A crisis is dangerous," she began, "like a wave we must ride it to victory or be whelmed beneath its flood." The "wrong ways" of meeting the crisis included failing to see it, fearing it, or being "so custom bound and habit ridden that we cannot change our ways and meet the new strange demands that are made upon us." Wieman told his readers and Bennett instructed her audience, "To meet a crisis and ride it to victory we must be alert, fearless and plastic. We must face the issue squarely, and unafraid."[72] Wieman concludes his chapter with a discussion of disintegration: "A crisis shatters the little dome of daily life," and forced people to change their habits. This period of creativity was "the call of God to join with Him in the making of a better world."[73] If one of the principles of Christian imperial feminism concerned creating unity out of diversity globally through Christianity, and if it also called upon people to meet different viewpoints with openness rather than defensiveness, then Bennett's opening prayer exercise can be seen as a subtle call to White women's shared missionary past as they navigated those same issues among themselves.

During this meeting, the delegates returned to the debate about how to define "missions" and what this might mean for women's church work in the future. In an illuminating discussion, representatives from the Federation, Council, and new National Council of Federated Church Women each described what they saw as their organization's purpose. Speaking on behalf of the Federation, Halla Johnson (Mrs. F. I. Johnson) described its purpose as "to promote greater efficiency in the work of the Women's Boards of Foreign Missions" and to "stimulate united prayer and study," and, finally, "to secure a fuller development of resources and a truer conception of the scope and purpose of women's work for missions." In contrast, the speakers for the Council and the National Council of Federated Church Women offered much broader program goals that had a great deal of overlap. The National Council's Frances Ferguson was the most capacious as she declared her organization's purpose to be "the unification of the efforts of church women in the task of establishing a Christian social order in which all areas of life shall be brought into harmony with the life and teachings of Jesus Christ."[74]

Cooperation, however, was not easy, and this was evident in the minutes even if no behind-the-scenes letter was preserved in the archives. Florence Tyler, the Federation's executive secretary, took the minutes. She noted that some in attendance still sought "to guard rather than merge their interests." Some of the attendees sharply criticized women's missionary societies. Even if "national agencies think of missions with the larger implication," local missionary leaders still thought the purpose of a missionary society was to raise money alone. The missionary women in attendance contested this point and defended local missionary women. "The women at the center of this great movement are the missionary women," said one attendee. "These missionary women are the ones who have carried the great weight of responsibility in the years past," and it was also noted that the "inclusive program" described by churchwomen had "been practiced in the mission stations at home and abroad, as public health programs, Christian citizenship ventures, religious education movements, etc." Further, and perhaps most important, missionary women had "carried the responsibility for the raising of millions of dollars—ten million dollars this past year." Although she was hardly unbiased on the question, Tyler wrote in the minutes that the consensus in the room was that local missionary women "will be the backbone of the local federation."[75] Over the next few years, Tyler and her FWBFM colleagues confronted declining contributions from denominational mission boards and a worsening budget crisis amid the Great Depression that would eventually result in their merger into the (male-led) Foreign Missions Conference of North America in 1934. The White woman's missionary movement's Christian imperial feminism would persist in the local churchwomen's council through the continued use of the last few UMS textbooks and an increasing focus on the international relations and peace issues that the FWBFM had begun to endorse in the late 1920s.

Like the earlier joint meeting in St. Louis, those in attendance at the 1930 New York meeting agreed on the task at hand but felt keenly the need to defend their sources of income and institutional history. At the same time, they all came to recognize that having multiple national organizations meant that "the local woman is confused."[76] Invoking a business-minded approach that "the ultimate consumer is the woman in the local church," the delegates were driven to cooperate in part out of fear that they would lose their supporters entirely if they remained in competition with each other.[77] The National Council's wide-ranging objective of creating a Christian social order seemed to encompass the work of home missions and, in its international relations concerns, it drew in foreign missions as well. Florence Tyler reported that there was general agreement that "missions is no longer an exclusive term" but could be interpreted as including a wider variety of humanitarian, political, and social reform programs. "Church Women must think unitedly, see unitedly, act unitedly."[78] The meeting ended with the shared singing of a verse from the hymn, "Blessed Be the Tie that Binds." The new Relationships Committee created at this meeting and made up of representatives from the three organizations along with a growing number of joint committees became the sites for practicing cooperation.[79]

* * *

In the 1930s, White Protestant women affiliated with denominational and interdenominational missionary organizations had begun to reimagine themselves as Protestant churchwomen with a vastly expanded missionary field. They drew a connection between the "cooperation" they practiced in their bureaucratic meetings amid organizational restructuring and their capacity to influence public opinion and advance their vision of a Christian social order. While some Protestant men viewed women's missionary organizations as irrelevant to the modern concerns of the day, the leaders of those organizations emphasized how programs like the UMS textbooks had trained them to address race relations and foreign policy. This new terrain for White women's missionary interests became the basis for a revised Christian imperial feminism that tied White women's role in church work to their expertise on managing race and religion in their diverse communities and in a postcolonial world. White churchwomen also defined their new organizations and activism as an instrument to mobilize Protestant women as an interest group that could shape public opinion. In this capacity, local churchwomen's councils like Rochester's Council of Church Women and the coordinating structures of the national organizations articulated a White Protestant moral argument for normative arrangements of race and religion. As the next chapters examine in more detail, while these mostly White women were "learning to cooperate" among themselves, the White supporters of foreign missions would actively live out cooperation locally in their Christian Americanization programs seeking to assimilate immigrants and in interracial cooperation efforts intended to improve White-Black race relations.

4

Christian Americanization and the Tri-Faith Movement

A week after World War I ended, Protestant women spent the first "Home Mission Week" meditating on "Christian Americanization." Wartime nationalism had driven native-born Americans to call for the "Americanization" of the millions of immigrants from the past several decades, and Protestants adopted the same language in their missionary call to unify "the American people under Christian standards." Bearing an image of the American flag and the Christian flag, the Home Mission Week pamphlet published by the White-led Council of Women for Home Missions (CWHM) provided local women's groups with ideas for a meeting, a prayer service, and plentiful quotations and reading recommendations on different immigrant groups. Churchwomen might "visit a foreign settlement, section, or home," or "a church for foreign-speaking people," or they could more easily "read at least one autobiography of an immigrant." Katherine Bennett, the CWHM's president, called on Protestant women to teach immigrants "the best ideals of American womanhood" so that they could become part of "a fine and Christian citizenry." Yet immigrants were not the only target of Christian Americanization. The CWHM also advised churchwomen to make sure their neighbors had the right attitude toward immigrants. They had a Christian duty to shape public opinion on the ongoing debate about immigration law, and they should volunteer to speak at women's clubs meetings in their towns, organize a concert with immigrant musicians, or put on a "pageant using groups from all sections of the community."[1]

Americanization was, as historian Nicholas Pruitt notes, an "amorphous term."[2] It has been used to describe coercive policies targeting non-English speakers while immigrant groups and pro-immigration progressives also used Americanization to refer to their voluntary outreach efforts. Beginning in the late 1910s, the Bureau of Education within the US Department of Interior enlisted teachers and voluntary organizations to fund and run English and civics classes, vocational training, and recreational centers for immigrants to aid them in becoming English-speaking, law-abiding, loyal, and productive citizens. Ecumenical Protestants' "Christian Americanization" programs had these same goals with the additional objective of bringing these immigrants into their Protestant fold. While Protestants' cosmopolitan vision for the United States resonated with contemporary visions of cultural pluralism as defined by the Jewish sociologist Horace Kallen, Protestants developed their vision of a diverse nation out of the Christian imperialism of the foreign and home missionary movement.[3]

Ecumenical Protestants' Christian Americanization programs were in many ways a continuation of decades of home missionary work intended to assimilate and evangelize "New Americans." Foreign missionary leaders also saw the potential of the United States becoming the "land of all nations." Christian Americanization also served as White Protestants' programmatic response to restrictive immigration policies, intensified nativism among their fellow Protestants, and broader debates about the meaning of race, religion, class, and nationality in the 1920s.[4] For reorganizing Protestant women, the cosmopolitan practices of Christian Americanization helped bridge the divisions new churchwomen's councils faced while also giving all churchwomen first-hand experience managing the empire of Christ in their own local communities.

Christian Americanization took place against a backdrop of intensified anti-Black, antisemitic, and anti-Catholic nativism exemplified by the re-formation of the Ku Klux Klan. On the West Coast, White people formed anti-Japanese and anti-Chinese organizations. Ecumenical Protestants spoke out strongly against nativism and "racial hatreds," and they countered such views with a cosmopolitan conception of American identity. Using the Protestant and secular language of goodwill, friendship, neighborliness, and brotherhood, they called on native-born churchgoers to make their communities into a model for a universal church and the global kingdom of God.[5] At the same time, they partnered with Jewish and Catholic leaders who closely aligned religious freedom with American democracy.[6] Yet White ecumenical Protestants' warm words and goodwill work could also mask the ways they exercised their power in Christian Americanization work and more broadly. As Christina C. Davidson notes, White Protestant foreign missionaries in the Dominican Republic had also adopted the language of "friendship" and "neighborhood," and this "shielded them from the imperial and racial violence intrinsic to their evangelical enterprise."[7] A similar dynamic was in play in the United States. Relying on the slipperiness between racial, religious, and national identities at this time, they elided accusations of proselytizing by describing their outreach efforts to Jews and Catholic and Orthodox Christians as racial inclusion. In other cases, they defended religious liberty, albeit as defined in the racially hierarchical terms of the missionary movement.[8]

By focusing on the racial as well as the religious dimensions of Christian Americanization, we can uncover the resonances between Christian imperial feminism and Christian Americanization in the 1920s. We will first examine White Protestant women's mission study materials related to Christian Americanization and the varying ways they defined "race" in relation to nationality and religion. Historians have discussed the complexities of identity in the 1920s and the fluid meanings of racial, religious, and national identity, and White Protestant women were encouraged to learn the nuances of "racial groups" and to evaluate their "cultural gifts" and cultural defects especially as related to gender norms.[9] We will then turn our attention to Protestant women's Americanization programs, including friendly visits, neighborhood houses, and Daily Vacation Bible School programs.[10] Protestant women interpreted these projects as beneficial to immigrants and the larger community and as spiritually formative for White native-born women. Additionally, the Protestant neighborhood house manifested an inclusive and cosmopolitan Protestant Christianity that Protestants used to bolster their universalism through comparison with the provincialism of "immigrant colonies." Finally, we will examine the complexities of churchwomen's entry into interfaith work in the 1930s and as "Christian Americanization" departments of churchwomen's councils became "Race Relations" departments. While this period is often broadly described as one in which Jewish and Catholic European immigrants "became White," a close look at the Rochester Council of Church Women and the Church Woman's Committee on Race Relations within the Federal Council of Churches suggests a less straightforward story.

Managing American Diversity

As Congress debated and eventually passed restrictive immigration laws in the late 1910s and early 1920s, the Federal Council and missionary leaders argued that racist and nativist nationalism hindered their missionary work and undermined their imperial vision of the kingdom of God. White Protestants generally supported what historian Mae Ngai called the United States' "laissez-faire immigration policy," and home missionary organizations had spoken out against the earlier Chinese Exclusion Act (1882) and so-called Gentleman's Agreement (1907) limiting Japanese immigration. They also criticized the racist basis for the national origin quotas put into place in an emergency measure passed in 1921 and firmly established in the 1924 Johnson-Reed Immigration Act.[11] While they did not oppose all limits on immigration, they rejected the quota system as racist. Ecumenical Protestants argued that American economic and agricultural development depended on a steady supply of laborers, and narratives of immigrants' success fed into their deeply Protestant settler-colonial myths of the United States as a refuge for persecuted and industrious people. White Protestants also interpreted immigration through their missionary objectives. Migrants collapsed home and foreign missions by bringing "the world" to American shores. Foreign missionary leaders also worried that restrictive US laws would lead other countries to reciprocate and potentially deny US missionaries entry to other countries.[12]

Although it had plenty of earlier precedents, a formalized "Americanization" campaign began just before the United States entered the First World War and coincided with immigration restriction. A host of Americans including government agencies, teachers, social workers, librarians, public health nurses, and, of course, Protestant missionaries took part.[13] This progressive Americanization movement rejected English-only laws and other punitive measures as "negative Americanization" that they saw as more damaging to assimilation than helpful. Americanization committees instead arranged for voluntary English and civics classes and trade schools, and in some cases they conducted studies of immigrants' working and living conditions.[14] As one government-published handbook on "Community Americanization" put it, Americanization "is a difficult and a delicate art, for we are dealing with human hearts, with primal passions, with inherited prejudices," and the Americanization worker must "possess a spirit of respect, tolerance, and sympathy."[15]

Embracing the new terminology, Protestant home missionary leaders and the Federal Council of Churches renamed their many missionary operations targeting "New Americans" as "Christian Americanization." They even began to apply the phrase to their well-established evangelical and educational efforts among Native Americans and African Americans, a move that indicated that "Christian Americanization" concerned imperial governance as well as providing European immigrants with resources.[16] Yet in terms of "New Americans," ecumenical Protestants saw Christian Americanization as an instrument for managing a seemingly unstable post–WWI social order. Insular "immigrant colonies" seemed like seedbeds for anarchists and socialists with no loyalty to the United States. White ecumenical Protestants believed that because millions of immigrants had come to the United States in such a short period of time, they had not been successfully "absorbed" into the American body politic and therefore necessitated a more intensified Americanization program.

At the same time, White liberal Protestants also worried that the hateful and ignorant nativism of other White Protestants made the situation even worse by alienating immigrants even further. In her 1924 mission study book, *An Adventure in Brotherhood*, Dorothy Giles drove home this point, writing "the greatest obstacle to the Americanization process is the ridicule and prejudice against foreigners on the part of native Americans."[17] Baptist home missionary leader Charles Alvin Brooks took this even further in his mission study textbook when he defined nativism as a "primitive instinct, unworthy of modern civilization," adding that only "the savage regards the savage as an enemy."[18] Comparing White nativists to the Chinese Boxers' anti-western rebellion, Brooks illustrated what Kathryn Gin Lum describes as the "barometric" applications of "heathenism" in White Protestant discourse.[19] Both White nativists and immigrants alike could be considered "savage," meaning that only the civilized and civilizing forces of White liberal Protestants and their Christian cosmopolitan nationalism had the answer.

Handbooks discussing "Americanization" abounded in the early 1920s, and these offered descriptions of American and other "traits" of racial, national, and religious groups. The Council of Women for Home

Missions also produced mission study textbooks on Christian Americanization that put a distinctly Protestant spin on those social scientific texts.[20] In 1919, Charles Brooks's book, *Christian Americanization*, introduced the topic to missionary women. Christian Americanization was also a major part of the home and foreign mission study programs in 1924–1925 under the joint theme "The Way of Christ in Race Relations." That year, women's groups read Dorothy Giles's *Adventures in Brotherhood*, on Americanization specifically, Robert E. Speer's *Of One Blood* and a more general analysis of the Christian solution to the "race problem," and young people read Margaret Seebach's *Land of All Nations*, another Americanization text. The next year, the CWHM selected Kenneth Miller's *Peasant Pioneers*, which provided a more focused study of Eastern European immigrants. Local leaders could find suggestions on how to teach the books in missionary magazines and at the interdenominational missionary summer schools. In some places, like Rochester, New York, Protestant women attended workshops on both the home and foreign mission study books at the annual Missionary Institute each autumn. Notably, the authors did not presume that their readers had favorable opinions of immigrants, and the books sought to win over the mostly White Protestant women readers to a Christian cosmopolitan nationalism at the same time that they laid out plans for Christian Americanization projects.

In their textbooks, the proponents of Christian cosmopolitan nationalism began with a history of the United States that emphasized cooperation among different immigrant groups. Like earlier and other forms of Christian nationalism, Christian cosmopolitan nationalism presented the United States as a chosen nation, and one with a "missionary destiny." But its specialness derived from the fact that it was a nation of immigrants.[21] Mission study histories focused on Americanization usually discussed race as it related to Europeans, and sometimes Asians. They omitted or only briefly mentioned Black and Indigenous Americans. Instead, these histories focused on the diversity of early European colonists, and next turned to the American Revolution and the early republic, highlighting how cooperation among Europeans had produced the basis for democracy that later Americans had inherited. They drew attention to the contributions of later immigrants to American agriculture, industry, expansionist infrastructure, culture, and politics, as well as their enlistment as soldiers in the First World War. Their sacrifices had made the nation and the world better and had even sanctified the nation. As Brooks wrote, "America is a sacred trust which has been bequeathed to us by those who have gone before."[22]

As Christian Americanization supporters narrated a history of the nation, they also reflected on the relationship between nationality, race, and religion in the context of the United States. Specifically, what did it mean to become Americanized? Brooks wrote that "a nation is more than land area. It is a spiritual entity."[23] The ideal at the core of this "spiritual entity" was "an assimilation of newer elements, which would result eventually in complete spiritual identity both with America at large and with the local community." For Brooks, this spiritual conversion is what formed the "American race." Along similar lines, Lutheran home missionary worker Margaret Seebach asked: "what is America? and whom do we mean when we speak of Americans?" to which she replied, Americans were those who "have the spirit and ideals of America." This "did not come from any one race alone, but are made up of the ideals of many nations."[24] Christian Americanizationists like Brooks and Seebach wanted to detach nationality from racial identity in order to imagine a racially diverse nation bound by spiritual bonds instead of blood.

Both authors also took aim at the supposed superiority and purity of "Anglo-Saxons" and those nativists who described the United States as an Anglo-Saxon country. For her part, Seebach noted that the Christian principles underlying American democracy actually came from "a Man who went about long ago in a little country called Judea" rather than from the "Anglo-Saxon race."[25] Brooks pointed to the centuries of intermarriage that had produced a "hybrid people," an "American race."[26] As they imagined a Christian cosmopolitan nationalism, mission study authors argued that one could belong to the American nation regardless of race. For Brooks, becoming an American was almost identical to becoming a Christian, and he put the diverse kingdom of God in parallel to the diverse United States. Following the dark night of the First World War, assimilation was a "miracle," he wrote, and the assimilated immigrant was "born again of the American spirit."[27]

Americanization might be a spiritual process, but just as missionaries had to prepare for their work, so too did Christian Americanization workers. Mission study textbooks and pamphlets described and analyzed different "racial groups," and invited White Protestant women to consider the meaning of race and racial and religious differences as they related to Americanization. Much like earlier foreign missionary literature that chastised missionary women's vague prayers for the undefined "heathen," home missionaries emphasized the importance of specificity. A 1919 article in the Baptist magazine *Missions* asked readers: "Do we have a tendency to classify all foreign-born in one large group? Or have we seen the contrasts?"[28] Mission study textbooks reinscribed and weighed religious, racial, and national differences as well as their entanglements. After summarizing the findings of the federal government's recent Religious Census that showed the sheer variety of people coexisting in American cities and towns, from "Buddhist day schools" to the Yiddish language instruction of "the Polish Jews" in New York to the "Magyar of Hungarian Catholics," Dorothy Giles declared that race could not be separated out from religion, and that "the race problem of America is a religious problem as well."[29]

Mission study authors both relied on and questioned the validity of "race" as a meaningful category. "Race" was used widely in the 1920s to signify national or what we might now describe as "ethnic" identity. Because its meaning was widely understood, race provided an easy method of categorization, and in 1922, the Home Missions Council and the CWHM published a series of "racial studies" that focused on "Czech-Slovaks, Russians and Ruthenians, Poles, Italians, Greeks, and Magyars." The Council planned future books on Syrians, Bulgarians, Armenians, Jews, and others. Like the longer home mission study textbooks, these shorter books were intended to teach readers about the "spiritual wealth" of immigrants and to prepare them for the work of Americanization. Specificity was key, and the committee's report explained that in order "to deal with a particular race, knowledge must be acquired of the national background, the Old World religion, the mental attitude and aspirations."[30] In other cases, mission study materials used the "scientific" schema for categorizing race. For example, a bibliography published in 1925 organized its suggested texts by races, with a page-long list of the many kinds of "Caucasians" that included Pre-Aryans (the Basques), two columns of Indo-Europeans, and much shorter lists of "Semites" and "Malays."[31]

Yet White Protestants also warned their readers that these "scientific" racial categories were deeply flawed. In his 1924 book, *Of One Blood*, Speer summarized numerous theories of "race" from Madison Grant and Lothrop Stoddard to those race scientists' critics, including Franz Boas. Speer sided more with the latter, and he offered his own view that "in a strict scientific sense there is no sure racial classification" but rather there was "a broad division of human groups marked with more or less vague general characteristics of color and habitat and culture, or inheritance and social standards and ideals."[32] Dorothy Giles repeated Speer's definition in her own section dedicated to defining race. The next year, Kenneth Miller included a chart of the "old—if unscientific" divisions of the human family, and located the "Slavic" race alongside the "Latin" and "Nordic" branches of the "Aryan" race. He also added a caveat that "although we are to study the 'Slavs' in America and 'Slavic' life abroad . . . there is, strictly speaking, no such person as a Slav."[33] By using and criticizing the terminology of race science, mission study textbooks positioned Protestant women readers as knowledgeable authorities of shifting academic discourse and as disinterested analysts of racialized people.

The authors of mission study textbooks put forward their own opinions on race science, but the guides provided to mission study leaders turned these into questions for White Protestant women to answer for themselves as they responded to the textbooks' material. The Methodist *Woman's Home Missions* magazine offered several different lesson plans for mission study classes for those reading Speer's *Of One Blood* and Giles's *Adventures in Brotherhood*. One prompt simply asked the group to "define race."[34] Writing for the Presbyterian magazine, *Women and Missions*, Eva Clark Waid set out a program that would focus on Jewish immigrants in particular. Her list of discussion questions included, "Are the Jews a race?" If those discussing the idea said no, it mattered little since one of the follow-up questions asked, "Do the Jews feel themselves a superior race?" The class could also discuss "the 12 causes of ill will and prejudice between Gentile and Jew," a list that included "sheer misunderstandings" to "bad manners" to "economic competition."[35] To further develop their knowledge of race and racial differences, Waid urged mission study leaders to collect "racial maps and photographs" from *National Geographic* as they discussed the different chapters of

Speer's textbook. They could also consult a variety of articles on race from "scientific journals" and "the publications of the American Museum of Natural History."[36]

Deflecting Criticisms with Racial Inclusion and Religious Liberty

The mission study textbooks' proscriptive Christian cosmopolitan nationalism did not address the persistent criticism from Jews and Catholics especially that Protestant Americanization programs were actually evangelical missions. For many decades European immigrants had organized their own communal outreach efforts, including mutual aid and benevolence organizations and through groups like the Hebrew Immigrant Aid Society, the National Council of Jewish Women, and the National Catholic War Council (later the National Catholic Welfare Council).[37] Protestant Americanizationists worked alongside some of these agencies at Ellis Island, and in some cases, Protestants offered positive assessments of the work of Catholic and Orthodox churches and Jewish synagogues. Yet in Giles's mission study book, she criticized those "racial" and "national" churches as "deliberate segregation" that amplified "an acute racial consciousness" that cosmopolitan Protestants saw as detrimental to Americanization.[38] For their part, Jews and Catholics sought assurances that Protestants would not use Americanization to separate Jewish and Catholic immigrants from their religious communities. When Protestants joined Catholic, Jewish, and other civic organizations at a four-day conference on Americanization organized by the US Department of the Interior in 1919, a Catholic priest in attendance brought up the subject of proselytizing with respect to Protestant Americanization work. This led the government official running the meeting to state "very frankly to church people" that using "the work of Americanization to win converts for their own religious creed" would damage the entire enterprise. The Protestants representing the Federal Council who were in attendance agreed, and their statement on Americanization put Protestant efforts alongside those of Jewish and Catholic Americanization work.[39]

That same year, the Central Conference of American Rabbis formally protested the language of "Christian Americanization" and its implication that only Christians could be legitimate American citizens. Leo M.

Franklin requested that the Episcopal Church change the name of its Bureau of Christian Americanization. As Franklin would later explain, "a huge sum of money was to be devoted to missionary work among the Jews as part of the 'Americanization' program of the church." The insult was not only proselytizing but "the implication that Jews are not and as Jews may not be loyal Americans." After discussions with Franklin, the delegates from the Diocese of New York put forward a successful resolution, changing the name to the "Department of Religious Work Among Foreign-Born Americans." Franklin's efforts did not stop there, and he and other rabbis organized a March 1920 meeting with representatives from the Federal Council and the Home Missions Council. The Jewish leaders asked their Protestant interlocutors to communicate to "the preachers of Christianity that they must desist from using such terms as would imply the limited patriotic loyalty of the Jew." The meeting ended with several resolutions, including one that declared that "Americanization" should not be used with "Christianization" in order to imply "that Jews, or other people of other religions or other races are not good Americans. No church should use the term 'Americanization' as a cloak for proselytizing to its distinctive religious views."[40] That the resolution defined religion as a matter of "views," however, reflected a distinctly Protestant definition of religion.

Ecumenical Protestants pursued two different and sometimes contradictory initiatives in relation to Jews and Catholics in the 1920s.[41] The Federal Council's Goodwill Committee fostered dialog between Protestants and Jews and would be instrumental in the creation of the "tri-faith" National Conference of Christians and Jews in 1927, while the Home Missions Council continued to operate missions evangelizing Jews, and the subject of Jews as potential Christians (racially Jewish but religiously Protestant) arose often in Christian Americanization literature.[42] While those in the Goodwill movement would eventually come to define Judaism as primarily a *religion* once Catholics became a part of Protestant-Jewish leaders' discussions, Protestants involved in missions were still more likely to describe Jews as a race, especially when considering Jews who were seen as unaffiliated with a synagogue.[43] White ecumenical Protestants strongly condemned antisemitism, but often with the presumption that antisemitism was a racist attitude that hindered White Protestants from welcoming Jews into their churches.

In a linguistic turn, White ecumenical Protestants spoke less about converting or even proselytizing Jews and instead reframed those efforts in the seemingly neutral language of "goodwill," "service," and "friendship." Methodist theologian Georgia Harkness captured the prevailing Protestant view that Reform Jews who "believe that Judaism is plastic and should be shaped to accord with the times and country in which they live" was at once most viable as an American religion *and* "most susceptible to Christian influence, and offers the church a great opportunity for service."[44] In 1922, the Home Missions Council offered a similarly softened language that disposed of "missions": "Missions to the Jews are not needed so much as goodwill and friendliness, and that each church should be an agency of neighborliness and service in its own environment."[45]

An allegorical example of this idea could be found in a 1923 Americanization play by Margaret Applegarth called "Color Blind." In the play, an artist uses only White children as models for her painting, and she turns away two scruffy European immigrant children (Jaky and Issy) when they ask if they can also dress up as angels. The two children touch one of the White children and then Issy declares that they are "too dreadful dirty for getting painted into heaven." The artist finds herself unsatisfied with the painting. A voice offstage intones from the Book of Acts that "God hath made of one blood all nations," and the play concludes with the White children leading a group of racially diverse children to the stage. The artist prays for God to forgive her for being "color blind" and for ignoring "these lovely yellow faces . . . These dusky browns . . . These rich deep reds, these deep soft blacks—how lovely!" She concludes the play with a prayer: "Dear Father, keep all of us from ever being color blind again. Help each of us to see that since our country marches forward on the feet of little children, the colors are Thy rainbow of promise for the future of our country."[46] In the play, Applegarth ignores and erases religious identity while celebrating racial difference as essential to a missionary Protestant Christianity as well as to the United States.

In addition to presenting evangelization as a matter of liberal racial inclusion, mission study authors also deflected suspicions of their missionary agenda by celebrating "religious liberty." Even in the emerging tri-faith consensus, White Protestants continued to define religious freedom in ways that advanced racist and imperial missionary hierarchies.[47] Further, their use of the term "religious liberty" harkened back to older nineteenth-century Protestant uses in which "liberty" required "religion" to keep liberal subjects from devolving into licentiousness.[48] This was clearly the meaning for Charles Brooks who, as a Baptist, would have been well-versed in arguments on behalf of religious liberty. He defined "religious liberty" as standing against "ignorance and superstition, blind and unquestioning acceptance of authority" that did not "comport with American conceptions of religious liberty."[49] Words like "ignorance" and "superstition" and "authority" had long been integral to how White Protestants judged Black, Indigenous American, and Asian immigrant religions and people as "primitive," and all three were also deployed in anti-Catholic polemics. Alongside Christian Americanization aimed at European immigrants, home missionaries in the 1920s intensified their policing of Indigenous people's dances and ceremonies, and they criticized many rural and poor Black Protestants' "otherworldly" religion.[50] Asian religious traditions were also viewed as incompatible with Americanism. A 1922 report on Americanization efforts in Hawaii expressed concerns about the "approximately 100 Buddhist priests and eight or nine Shinto priests" on the islands. Buddhism and Shinto were seen as incompatible with a "liberal and constructive American spirit based on the principles of Christianity."[51]

Mission study textbooks provided plenty of evidence that even the "religion" of European Christians came under suspicion. Long-standing anti-Catholic tropes prevailed when Kenneth Miller quoted the sociologist Edward A. Steiner on his view that Orthodox and Catholic Slavs' churches did not encourage "sobriety, chastity, conquering the will, or the cultivation of inner virtues." Instead, their religion was just "prayers, formulas, sacrifices, and pilgrimages."[52] Even with these regrettable traits, these European Christian traditions could be tolerated if they eventually assimilated to a more Protestant style of Christianity. White Protestants could help in this process, wrote Miller. "Many of the leaders of the Catholic and Orthodox churches are recognizing the shortcomings of their church," and they would "welcome the cooperation and assistance of American Christians, even of Protestants," so long as the aid was "tendered in good faith."[53] Such sentiments likely drove one member of the Rochester's Woman's Council to instruct

Americanization volunteers to "urge those who are Catholics to be good Catholics, and invite those who have not church preferences to attend some services."[54]

In addition to emphasizing nationality and racial differences rather than religion, Christian Americanizationists also tapped into a long history of American secularism when they emphasized that proper religion should always be a voluntary choice rather than something attached to a communal racial, national, or even familial identity. White Protestants insisted that religion be a matter of "freedom of choice." Under the subheading, "The Christian's Freedom of Choice," Dorothy Giles illustrated this point with a story about two Czech Catholic boys who start attending a Protestant Sunday school, but they are often late since they attend Catholic mass first. One tells the Protestant teacher that "The parish priest had stopped him on the street and scolded him for going to a Protestant Sunday school." The boy reports that the priest said, "all Bohemians were Catholic, and that John and I must not come here at all." The teacher insists that they cannot continue to attend both churches but they each had to choose "according to his own conscience." As expected, they both choose to become Protestants.[55] Giles believed that a changing understanding of what "religion" was (an identity or a choice) took place as "races" interacted in American neighborhoods: "as the races meet and mingle in American life, religious preference becomes a personal matter, and a man's religion belongs to himself alone, not to state or community."[56]

This Protestant and secular position that religion must be a matter of choice and not entangled with "racial" identities aligned neatly with the Christian imperial feminism of the foreign missionary movement that saw "ethnic religion" as hopelessly provincial. Yet in the United States, Jews and Catholics (like the boys' fictional priest) challenged such claims. Religious studies scholar Finbarr Curtis notes that the Catholic politician Al Smith's formation as a child on the Lower East Side contested a normative Protestant-inflected secularism with a different kind of religious freedom that "overlapped with his defense of the ethnic identities and cultural habits of an immigrant, heterogenous, urban working class."[57] It was precisely this kind of ethnic identity that White Protestant women would seek to combat through their "friendly visits" and Protestant neighborhood houses and Christian community centers.

Friendly Visits and Neighborhood Houses

Women's missionary societies and churchwomen's councils organized Christian Americanization programs in their communities, and some White Protestant women employed by Protestant settlement houses turned Americanization work into a career. The literature promoting Christian Americanization as a worthy cause emphasized the comparisons between sequestered immigrant women and those whom foreign missions sought to liberate abroad. Americanization proponents also focused on the benefits of befriending and interacting with immigrants to White Protestant volunteers. In sporadic "friendly visits" and in the more organized Christian friendship of settlement houses, White Protestant women were invited to take an active role in immigrants' assimilation, a missionary project that would also form them into Christian cosmopolitans.

In 1919, Baptist women home missionary leaders urged their constituents to see the potential in connecting their missions to the current Americanization movement. They must "awake to the fact that we have it within our power to translate the Americanization which Uncle Sam is stressing as a war-reconstruction measure into 'Christian Americanization' for Kingdom Reconstruction."[58] More than just a project for home missionary societies, Christian Americanization called on all Protestants to do their part. At the 1920 meeting of the Home Missions Council, the Committee on City, Immigrant, and Industrial Work put forward a list of recommendations that began with the proposal that "the Church press, the pulpit, and all departments of congregational work" be harnessed to promote "a friendly attitude towards the foreign-speaking peoples generally." Churches should also work to establish "just industrial relations and proper working and living conditions," and to provide services to "foreign-speaking neighborhoods."[59] White Protestant women answered this call not only in their mission study classes but also in launching a variety of Christian Americanization programs, including departments in new ecumenical churchwomen's councils.

In Rochester, New York, White Protestant women affiliated with both the foreign and home missionary movements had launched several outreach programs that existed alongside ongoing Catholic programs. Baptist Helen Barrett Montgomery helped establish the Lewis Street

Settlement House, while Rochester's Methodists and Baptists both set up Italian-language churches.[60] These Baptist churches were a project of Colgate-Rochester Divinity School that in the 1920s briefly housed an Italian Department meant to train Italian-speaking clergy for Baptist mission churches in the United States and Italy.[61] The Catholic Diocese of Rochester established several Italian Catholic parishes in the early 1900s, and Rochester's Italian community established their own community organizations, including the Italian Women's Civic Club formed in 1919.[62]

When Rochester churchwomen formed the Woman's Council in 1922, they immediately set up a Christian Americanization department. It was initially led by Helen A. Young, a public school teacher and a Baptist.[63] Young worked through the Council to encourage women to organize Americanization volunteers at their own churches. She had already trained volunteers to visit "our foreign women" at two of the city's Baptist churches, and she was in conversation with Presbyterian and Congregationalist women's groups to launch their own programs. Young stressed the importance of study to prepare for this work, noting that the volunteers attended a weekly class "taught by an experienced teacher" and had access to a circulating library of Americanization methods and other useful books.[64]

Young's library almost certainly included a 1919 pamphlet from the CWHM that focused on convincing White native-born women to get involved in Americanization. It noted that while "foreigners" may "seem strange" and "uncouth," closer acquaintance would show that they have "still quite as much to give us as we have to give them."[65] Primed by decades of Christian imperial feminism to see "ethnic religions" as the source for women's oppression, Protestant women drew parallels between the conditions of womanhood in Asia and European immigrants in the United States. Rather than openly discuss the need for proselytizing, Helen Young made this point as well from her personal experiences. "One cannot be a visitor in many of these homes without the feeling that many of these foreign women sit in darkness as truly as their sisters across the sea—for one can find the European idea of the place and position of women as prevalent in these homes as before coming to America. If we can bring cheer into their burdened lives and help them to 'realize Christ' in America truly we labor not in vain."[66] An implicit version of these comparisons also appeared in the secular Americanization work of the Department of the Interior, suggesting how much White missionary women's Christian imperial feminism had succeeded in tying women's rights to racial progress. A government-published handbook for Americanization workers described the "women of the races from southeastern Europe" as "shy and timid," noting that they were often "forbidden by their husbands to leave their homes."[67] For churchwomen in Rochester and other cities, Christian Americanization provided a way for them to advance Christian imperial feminism in the US.

In many cases, White Protestant women's Americanization work assumed the need to teach the basics of "civilized" domesticity. To that end, a 1919 CWHM pamphlet recommended that "friendly visits" might involve teaching immigrants how to use "American utensils, embrace American foods, and become accustomed to American ways."[68] To this end, Rochester's Council hosted a Christmas party for "eighteen of our foreign ladies" in 1922. Helen Young reported that the party was the first time that the women had been "in an American home of that type," and she attested that "more real Americanization was unconsciously taught in that evening than could have been taught in many formal lessons."[69]

A joint meeting between Catholic and Protestant women in Rochester in 1926 focused on the need to protect young people from immoral movies. In this case, Italian American Catholic women found common ground with Protestant women on the question of the damaging effects of films on young people. The Council of Church Women held a public meeting with Marietta Gianfranceschi representing the city's Italian Woman's Club on this topic. During the discussion, Gianfranceschi protested the presumption that only Italian American girls were in danger of corruption from racy films. "Because a person is foreign-born, we sometimes get the idea that he or she is on a lower plane morally, intellectually and spiritually," but this was not the case. She also suggested that if Protestant girls realized they were a model to their immigrant classmates, this might lead them to behave differently too. "Americanization in its truest sense is service to both, to the native born and to the foreign born," she explained.[70]

While they remained invested in the production of a kind of Protestant womanhood and middle-class domesticity, churchwomen also viewed Christian Americanization as an opportunity to educate immigrant women to be independent citizens. Laura Dixon, who headed a Presbyterian settlement house in Milwaukee, wrote about successful Americanization work that focused less on table manners and more on women's economic independence and public participation. The Americanized woman Dixon envisioned once signed her bank deposits with a mark but could now sign with her own name. She was able to study and apply for "permanent residence in this country." Successful Christian Americanization produced women who could serve as leaders in their own ethnic-national organizations and who had a "community consciousness," and who might find ways to display and profit from "the artistic handwork they have brought with them from the homeland."[71] Dixon's assessment spoke to how Christian Americanization celebrated certain amenable "cultural gifts" of immigrants and even a degree of national or racial pride.

A popular missionary pageant similarly positioned Protestant churchwomen in the role of rescuing and uplifting immigrant women beyond the home. In her pageant "Other Foreign Women," Alice Brimson, who headed northern Baptist women's Christian Americanization work, called attention to the difficulties that the immigrant protagonist faced as she is "beset by politician and storekeeper, and policewoman, and others" that leave her feeling like she did not belong in the United States. This all changes when a group of Christian women call on her and offer their sympathy and their assistance in navigating these public spaces.[72] In 1926, there were at least eleven performances of the pageant at churches in Rochester.[73] Brimson's pageant illustrated how Christian Americanization could be presented as a combination of sympathetic missionary outreach and as an opportunity for Protestant women to exercise their own moral authority as they chastised the politician, policewoman, and storekeeper who mistreated the immigrant. As the CWHM explained in its 1919 pamphlet, "fellow citizens must share ideals, as far as possible, and combine, for the realization of their ideals."[74] Americanization was presented as a means to Christianize social relations beyond just the assimilation of an immigrant.

Missionary literature promoted the idea that Christian Americanization work would benefit Protestant women in other ways as well. Testimonials of settlement house heads like Laura Dixon and more casual volunteers offered evidence of the ways interactions between churchwomen and immigrant women could be intellectually, culturally, and spiritually enriching for native-born White Protestant volunteers. This was the lesson conveyed through several first-hand letters written by the Methodist women enrolled at the Lucy Webb Hayes National Training School in Washington, DC. As part of the fieldwork component of their program to become deaconesses, some taught English in Americanization classes. "In this work we live Christ rather than preach him," wrote one student. "Teaching in the Americanization school is the most interesting work that I have ever done," wrote Beulah Quinn, explaining that "here the teacher receives perhaps as much knowledge as she gives." She learned "first-hand, correct, and up-to-date knowledge" of her students' home countries.[75] Volunteers also disciplined themselves in cosmopolitan attitudes. They were to approach the work with an attitude of "goodwill" and "cooperation" rather than "a patronizing manner and spirit." This was both a spiritual and political practice, and one that honed Americanization workers' Christian citizenship.

The "friendly visit" was another practice believed to improve both the immigrant and the volunteer. The "friendly visitor" was itself an older construct defined by an unequal power dynamic between middle-class moral reformers and social workers and their poor clients. As one historian of scientific charity writes, the friendly visitor was "friend, moral instructor, snoop, scientific investigator" whose intimate knowledge allegedly enhanced her influence and enabled her to see the truth of what was happening in the family home.[76] When Christian Americanization workers called on White Protestant women to befriend immigrant women, the affective dynamics of friendship were quite different. Laura Dixon noted that immigrant women had "no tradition for education" in their home countries, but "deep in the heart of many of these women was a keen desire to advance." Dixon suggested that White Protestant volunteers would meet with an "eager response from women of all nationalities and groups" when they offered to bring English lessons to these women in their own homes.[77]

In contrast to the ways immigrant women's hearts called out for rescue, Protestant women's emotional interest in immigrant women had to be generated through mission study. As one mission study program explained, "as a result of this six-months' study every member should feel her personal responsibility to be a sincere, kind, friend to every 'foreigner' whom she may meet in any contact whatsoever." The volunteer might then proceed to "call upon" the "foreign families," but "a loving tact must always be exercised in the method of approach—never with a spirit of condescension." Friendliness on the part of native-born Protestants would not only supply "a new interpretation of the spirit of American Christianity to the 'foreigner,'" but it also formed an impression on the friendly visitor as such interactions would lead to the "enrichment of our own hearts and minds by the contact."[78]

Friendship also functioned as the emotional language used to describe the neighborhood houses and Christian centers often run by Protestant women.[79] Modeled on settlement houses like London's Toynbee Hall and Jane Addams's Hull House, the Protestant neighborhood house was typically staffed by laywomen and sometimes deaconesses educated in social work, religion, and education in "social religious courses" at secular institutions like Teachers College or in programs at missionary training institutes.[80] They were usually described as "nonsectarian," a term ecumenical Protestants used to indicate that they did not advance one denominational theology and therefore "had no evangelical purpose." As was true in the case of other uses of non-sectarian, neighborhood houses still aimed to spread a "Christian spirit" through their service.[81] A long and rich history of the settlement movement has interpreted these variously secular, Protestant, Catholic, and Jewish ventures as instruments of social control and as more complex spaces that could be used by working-class participants for their own ends.[82] They have been viewed as an instrumental step in the transformation of social welfare programs in the United States and elsewhere. The Protestant neighborhood houses were also a laboratory of the cosmopolitan Christianity that had been integral to the White Protestant women's missionary movement for decades.

While some neighborhood houses targeted one immigrant group, others boasted of serving a "cosmopolitan neighborhood."[83] At the Campbell settlement house in Gary, Indiana, White Methodist missionary women demonstrated "Christian friendship" in an organized fashion. The steel city had "a motley population of people from many lands," and established in 1914, the Campbell Settlement offered employment counseling, "social and recreational opportunities to both old and young," and ran a clinic that provided medical and dental care to the community. "Music and drama" activities were especially popular for "these people whose lives are so dull and colorless," as well as the basketball and baseball clubs for children and the Croatian and Italian mothers' clubs for their parents.[84] Protestants saw Christian centers like the one in Gary as a "new need in missionary endeavor" and as a much more effective and organized means of "Christianizing America" than "random, scattered attempts."[85]

A settlement house provided the opportunity to create the cosmopolitan diversity that Christian Americanization advocates saw as essential to assimilation. In 1919, Charles Brooks contested the idea that Americanization must turn the United States into a "melting pot" or "the reduction of all to a common denominator," and he instead argued that Americanization functioned as a spiritual transformation as "each race reacts upon the other to the enrichment of all."[86] Protestants saw this diversity as a strength in that it created conditions that contributed to the Christian Americanization process that sought to disaggregate what Protestants saw as the problematically layered identities of race, religion, and nationality. In this sense, the Protestant conception of the multicultural neighborhood challenged the moral geographies of the Catholic parish or Jewish ghetto and the anxiety White Protestants felt about "immigrant colonies."[87] As was the scenario in Dorothy Giles's mission study textbook story about the two Czech boys, ecumenical Protestants viewed certain layered identities as an obstacle to both Americanization and Protestant missions, and they viewed the neighborhood house as modeling a different kind of community. Praising integrative (and Protestant-izing) effects of the cosmopolitan neighborhood house, Kenneth Miller wrote, "the intermingling of various nationalities in a Christian center cannot help but break down the national and racial barriers which prevent a real unification of our people."[88]

Accounts of neighborhood centers also amplified the sense that Protestant Christianity's universal welcome distinguished it and made it superior to "ethnic religions" viewed as exclusionary. One revealing report from a West Virginia Christian center illustrated how Protestant Christianity created the conditions for harmonizing racial and religious differences. People representing "eight nationalities" attended the Weirton Christian Center's English classes, and one Jewish man had also started attending Sunday Bible classes held in the church. That the friendliness found in a secular English class led the Jewish man to seek out more explicitly religious activities was a common theme in reports on Christian Americanization work. In this version of the story, the Jewish man was surprised by what he found in the church's sanctuary. "After looking around he said, 'Why there is nothing in here that would hurt anybody.'" Not only was he pleasantly surprised, he also "invited a Mohammedan to join our classes." The "Mohammendan" turned him down, reportedly saying, "'I cannot go there; that is a Christian Center.'" Then, the report concluded, "our Jewish friend replied, 'It makes no difference about your nationality or your religion. Everyone is welcome.' What a wonderful opportunity to teach all nations."[89]

Missionary magazines promoted neighborhood houses and Christian Americanization work as spiritually fulfilling. As when watching or performing a missionary pageant, the volunteer could encounter "all nations," while also ensuring that they behaved in an orderly manner. In "A Gleam," an article about the Sheffield Neighborhood Center in Kansas City, the author described what she saw when she volunteered to help teach the girls sewing at the Daily Vacation Bible School. Closely emmeshed with Christian Americanization, Vacation Bible Schools became popular among Protestants in the 1920s, and they were largely developed as a way for churches and neighborhood centers to keep "idle children" of working parents occupied during the summer. They were also very explicitly an Americanization operation, aimed at "the children of the neighborhood" rather than the children of middle-class White Protestant women.[90] The Sheffield program was typical in that it began with a prayer service and hymns. The volunteer was amazed to hear the children singing "Praise Him" and "Fairest Lord Jesus." She wrote, "I have heard the children at church sing those same songs, but it has never thrilled me as it did to listen to those children, for there were so many nationalities—Greeks, Jews, Serbians, Russians, Poles, Mexicans, and others—but to think that they were all worshipping our Christ as one was a great pleasure to me." At the end of a morning filled with some playtime and lessons in sewing for the girls and "manual labor" for the boys, the children reconvened for an assembly. Holding both the American and Christian flags, they said the pledge of allegiance and sang the national anthem.[91] In this and other accounts of neighborhood houses managed by churchwomen, Protestant women described the fusion between the imperial Christian cosmopolitanism of foreign missions and Americanism. While resonant with the secular cultural gifts movement and cultural pluralism, the readers of missionary magazines were encouraged to see their own Protestantism as the source for the well-ordered and diverse nation.

White Protestant leaders of the missionary movement believed that the fullness of Christianity would only be realized when it had encompassed all races in something like a cosmopolitan neighborhood house. This view informed how some Protestants approached religious difference. In *Of One Blood*, Robert Speer argued that "the contact of Christianity with other races [will] bring out its own latent fulness more clearly and richly." In contrast to more theologically liberal Protestants who might have appreciated other religious traditions on their own terms, Speer contended that the only benefit of other religious traditions to Christianity was that "those religions have come to embody, above their error, the great racial qualities which are to be the contributions of these people to the spirit of God for His use as the materials of the Kingdom of God, the incarnation of the gospel in the life of mankind." From this missionary perspective, Christian Americanization programs, interracial cooperation, and even interreligious efforts could all be interpreted as manifesting and strengthening Christianity. Speer believed that Christianity's progress would stall unless White Christians (White Protestants) encountered "the actual occupation of humanity by God."[92]

In the 1920s, George E. Haynes, the Black head of the Federal Council of Churches' Commission on the Church and Race Relations, created Race Relations Sunday to encourage White and Black Protestants to meet and to address anti-Black discrimination.[93] Meanwhile, in Rochester's Council of Church Women, issues related to anti-lynching and Black civil rights were handled either by the Missions or Americanization department, a classification that indicated that White women designated Black Americans within home missions. In 1932, Nellie Michelson (Mrs. Lewis Michelson) became the new chairwoman of the Americanization department. She proposed that "Americanization" be defined to mean "Adult Education for Foreign Born People," a move that reflected her background in social work and departure from the explicitly evangelical objectives of her earlier predecessor Helen Young.[94] A couple of months later, Michelson recommended changing "Americanization" to "Race

Relations," given that "the term Americanization is not only limited in meaning but also obsolete in use."[95] When Michelson and her committee (comprised of White women) held a day-long conference on race relations in October 1932, the program showed that she and her associates conceptualized "racial problems" in terms of foreign-born Europeans. The panels at the conference held at Third Presbyterian Church focused on Rochester's social welfare programs, settlement houses, and public education, and for the midday entertainment, three Italian American women and their children performed an instructive play. The only Black woman on the program was Estelle Fitzgerald, who headed the Clarissa Street YWCA, who spoke during the settlement house session. In her report about the conference's results, Michelson pointed out three areas in need of White native-born churchwomen's attention that further emphasized her attention to the city's European immigrants. First, White churchwomen must work on the "elimination of prejudice," something that they could do by reading the books she suggested and in recognizing "the good qualities in other races and stress those instead of their faults." Second, churchwomen could volunteer at evening schools aimed at adult immigrants, and third, they could participate in a parental education program that would teach "foreign-born parents whose children are going to our schools" about "our customs and ways of thinking."[96]

During Michelson's short tenure as chairwoman of the Race Relations Committee, she sidelined Black-White interracial cooperation efforts. In December 1932, she complained that the previous Race Relations Sunday services had been "for the colored people," and she proposed that the 1933 service should be "broad enough to include Italians and Poles."[97] While not addressed directly in the meeting minutes, it seems likely that the Council's Black members (and perhaps some White members) were not on board with this plan. In 1933, Rochester's big February Race Relations Sunday vespers service took place at the Clarissa Street YWCA. It featured Howard University dean Lucy D. Slowe as the guest speaker, and it had been organized by an interracial committee of one hundred Protestant women.[98]

The Tri-Faith Movement as Christian Americanization

While ecumenical Protestants' approach to Christian Americanization often irritated Catholics and Jews involved in their own Americanization work, this shared objective was also a factor in the emerging tri-faith movement. Formed in 1927 by the Federal Council of Churches and the Central Conference of American Rabbis, the National Conference of Christians and Jews (NCCJ) organized conferences in the early 1930s that promoted the idea that religious freedom and religious tolerance were essential to preserving American democracy. They pitted what they crafted as a distinctly American model of pluralism against a "secularism" that they identified with communist and fascist brands of totalitarianism as well as fixed arrangements of religion, race, and nation associated with the Old World.[99] In this sense, the NCCJ's conception of religion was not all that different from the Protestant notions that had animated earlier Christian Americanizationists. As scholars of the tri-faith movement and pluralist models more generally have argued, these constructions are always both inclusive and exclusive. Not only were the included faiths limited, but White ecumenical Protestants also chose to separate their ongoing Black-White cooperation activities from their goodwill programs.[100] For White ecumenical Protestants, the tri-faith movement conveniently lent itself to a layered interpretation. It affirmed long-standing racialized Protestant missionary hierarchies by granting some Jews and Catholics a higher status while presenting a host of other people and religious traditions as ineligible for toleration. Also, White Protestant women interpreted their participation in these interreligious activities as evidence of their Protestant Christianity's distinctive capacity for dealing with difference whether within the nation or globally. Like the Protestant neighborhood house, interreligious organizing, if carefully managed, meant that the different groups acted on each other in positive ways. For churchwomen, interreligious cooperation enabled Protestant women to become more deeply (Protestant) Christian and to both develop and publicly display their tolerant and cosmopolitan Protestantism. Protestant churchwomen rarely sought to convert their Jewish and Catholic allies, and often had meaningful relationships with these women whom they worked with in other civic organizations. At the same time, by emphasizing their own liberality in these scenarios, they often rendered their Catholic and Jewish partners as beneficiaries of ecumenical Protestant largesse. Religious freedom was, for many churchwomen, a gift that Protestants had crafted and delivered rather than a contested discourse fought for by Jewish and Catholic religious minorities.

The tri-faith movement factored into how organized Protestant women conceptualized their own identity as "Protestant women." This was evident in a letter sent to members in 1931 in which the National Council of Federated Church Women's president Frances Ferguson urged Protestant women to see themselves as a unified group in friendly competition with well-organized Catholic and Jewish women. Appealing for donations, Ferguson wrote that "Catholic women are effectively organized through their National Council" and "Jewish women, through the Temple Sisterhood, are no less energetic in the development of their program of activities. Are we, as Protestant women, less concerned for the welfare of our youth and the future of our great Faith?" Instead of speaking in terms of missions, Ferguson wrote vaguely about the "complexities of our every day life" and the "new and difficult problems" and the challenge of "the betterment of human life." If Protestant women wanted to "make our power and influence effective in the solution of these problems," they had to organize. She concluded: "Will you not join with others in making a financial investment in this program of our united Protestant womanhood that we may render a service commensurate with our obligations?"[101]

By claiming the identity of Protestant women, representatives from the National Council of Federated Church Women joined the Women's Committee of the NCCJ and promoted tri-faith activities to their constituency. In 1937, Rochester churchwoman and Episcopalian Georgiana Sibley condemned religious bigotry at a rally organized by the NCCJ in New York City, and she called on women to lead the way in ridding society of its old prejudices. That year, Sibley's husband was often in the news as well as the president of the US Chamber of Congress and a critic of the New Deal.[102] The National Council's official representative on the NCCJ was Golda Bader (Mrs. Jesse M. Bader) of the Disciples of Christ. In her articles for the *Church Woman*, Bader reported on the NCCJ's work and advised local women in exactly how they might achieve what Sibley proposed. In one piece, she wrote about her meaningful experiences talking to Jewish and Catholic women at the NCCJ's conferences, noting that its purpose was to "bring people of various religious cultures face to face." For the tenth anniversary of the NCCJ, she called on all local churchwomen's councils to organize an "inter-group meeting" in 1938 that would address the theme: "Make America Safe for Differences" as part of the NCCJ's Brotherhood Week events.[103] These "inter-group meetings" certainly differed from the power dynamics of the cosmopolitan neighborhood house. Rather than seeking to convert their Jewish and Catholic colleagues, churchwomen would now seek to play a leading role in how they would work together to manage differences, a task they argued was critical for democracy to thrive.

Immediately following Bader's article in this issue of the *Church Woman* (that was, notably, dedicated to the topic of race relations), Louise Wise (Mrs. Stephen S. Wise), the wife of the well-known Reform rabbi, offered a Jewish perspective. In her article titled "How Does the Jew Feel in the World Today," Wise described the German laws that had stripped Jews of their rights and property because of the "racial doctrine of Aryanism." Jews in those "so-called Christian countries" faced violent threats, and they found "the very existence of religion threatened." In the United States, Wise continued, "the Jew resolves increasingly to stand with those forces which would save civilization and democracy." Wise appealed directly to the Protestant readers of the *Church Woman* with a warning that attacks on Judaism were also attacks on Christianity. "The Jew does not feel lonely because he is living in a **Christian** world, but because he is living in an **un-Christian** world, in a world which threatens to become anti-Christian." Wise added that the "fate of Judaism and Christianity is bound up with the saving and fortifying of the democratic ideal."[104] In the typical tri-faith way, Wise's article aligned Christians, Jews, and democracy against the irreligion or even anti-religion of Nazism and antisemitism. While she might not have meant it as such, her words also suggested a strategy to appeal to her readers' belief that a "Christian world" alone allowed religious freedom to exist.

Protestant women conducted interreligious programming in churchwomen's councils because of convenience and civic comity. Rochester's Council of Church Women worked with the city's Catholic Women's Club and Council of Jewish Women on a host of charitable and social service activities. Many of these projects were coordinated by the Council of Social Agencies, an umbrella organization for all the city's clubs and civic associations. Catholic and Protestant women organized a toy depot at Christmas, and both Christian women's groups also sponsored a Thanksgiving service to which they invited Jewish women to participate as well.[105] On a different front, the Council of Church Women and the Council of Jewish Women jointly sent Ida Post (Mrs. Walter Post) as their delegate to the National Conference on the Cause and Cure of War (NCCCW). Founded by White suffrage leader Carrie Chapman Catt in 1924, this moderate branch of the women's peace movement counted most major women's organizations in the United States as members.[106] When Post returned from the Washington conference, the groups held a joint meeting to hear her report.[107] The Council's minutes did not discuss this as an "interfaith" endeavor. Since Post was an active member of Rochester's League of Nations Association, the decision for her to represent the groups was probably just an obvious choice.

In contrast, more attention would be given to the connection between interreligious cooperation as an illustration of American democracy and, for churchwomen, the importance of Protestant women to creating the cooperative conditions for peace. In 1934, the Protestant Council helped plan a "mass meeting" on world peace at the Eastman Theater. The annual report of the International Relations Department reported that this "was probably the outstanding achievement of the year for it demonstrated in a very concrete way how Christians can step over the boundaries of race and nationality and work together for peace."[108] While it might have been an oversight, the statement is notable for describing an event sponsored by Jews, Catholics, and Protestants as one that crossed boundaries of "race and nationality" rather than religion. Events like this one became quite common in the 1930s. In 1937, the three women's councils organized an interfaith luncheon attended by eight hundred women. Georgiana Sibley emceed the event at which Golda Bader spoke along with the Jewish Council's Madeleine Heilbrunn (Mrs. Robert J. Heilbrunn) and the Catholic Council's Blanche Jennings Thompson. Bader repeated much of what she had written in her *Church Woman* article as she encouraged women not just to "tolerate" each other but "to teach good will through cultural and racial groups." In her speech, the Catholic representative Blanche Thompson harkened back to the 1926 Americanization meeting with the Italian Woman's Club when she suggested that the three women's groups' shared common ground was a desire to protect their children's morals.[109] Following this meeting, the three women's organizations became part of a new "Cooperative Civic Committee."[110]

The growing popularity of the tri-faith model also raised some concerns from national leaders that pluralism could lead to "secularism," that is, the absence of any discussion of "spiritual" matters. At a 1937 meeting of the National Council of Federated Church Women, some of those who had attended that year's conference on the Cause and Cure of War praised it as "informative and illuminating to the nth degree" but complained about the insufficient attention to the "spiritual causes of war." They suggested that "church women take a more influential part in the conference" to put these "spiritual causes" on the table for discussion.[111]

Yet it seemed that the primary issue was not one of influence, per se, but one of visibility and identity. The National Council of Federated Church Women voted to request that all Protestant delegates representing Protestant institutions at the NCCCW could be seated together as "Protestant women" so "that our group of church women on the floor may not seem so misleadingly small as compared with other delegations." Further, they agreed to help pay the way of local women's council's delegates like Rochester's Ida Post. They wanted "our most able church women" to go to the conference "as church women and not as members of other groups." By making their identity as Protestant women explicit, they would "permeate the Cause and Cure of War Conference program with a christian emphasis."[112] The chairwoman of the National Council's International Relations department, Elinor K. Purvis, also hoped to organize a separate meeting of Protestant women at the next NCCCW meeting. This, she proposed, would invite Protestant women representing secular groups like the League of Women Voters as well as the representatives of church groups. These recommendations would have demonstrated Protestant women's numerical majority on the floor of the meeting in a way that may have added more force to the requests of Protestant women to emphasize the Christian answers to the problem of war.[113] Notably, not all Protestant women who attended the NCCCW found the experience devoid of spiritual meaning. Mabel Mangano (Mrs. Antonio Mangano) had represented Rochester's Protestant and Jewish women at the conference in 1931. Her description of the event once she had returned home paraphrased the New Testament and the Golden Rule as she hailed the meeting's Christian cosmopolitan atmosphere. It was a "symphony where the theme running through the whole was 'Ye must be born again.' 'As has been done to you, do ye even so unto them.' America can be a good neighbor in a neighborhood of the world."[114]

Other Protestant women in Rochester who played an active role in the National Council of Federated Church Women took a different approach to interreligious relations. Georgiana Sibley was quite theologically liberal, as evidenced by her participation on the Layman's Inquiry, and Alice Walker, the Council's executive secretary, belonged to the liberal Universalist denomination. Further, her active involvement in Rochester's social work sector meant that she had long worked alongside Catholics and Jews. At Sibley's urging, following the reports of Kristallnacht and intensifying Jewish persecution in Nazi Germany, the Council women also sent formal expressions of sympathy to the city's Jewish women. In late 1938, they wrote a letter expressing their "great concern over European events and their enduring friendship for our Rochester Jewish Sisters."[115]

One of Sibley's fellow Episcopalians on the Rochester Council of Church Women was also enthusiastic about interfaith cooperation. Elizabeth Stebbins (Mrs. Edwin Allen Stebbins) chaired the Spiritual Life Department. Perhaps not surprising given that she was an Episcopalian, Stebbins had written a glowing article for the *Church Woman* about the Catholic and Protestant liturgies she had experienced on board the USS *Normandie* as she sailed back to the United States after attending the Faith and Order Conference at Oxford in 1937. She encouraged Protestant women to experiment with different forms of worship, as this was one powerful way to live out the ecumenical ideal discussed at Oxford.[116] In 1942, Stebbins organized an "ecumenical study" for Rochester's churchwomen that included visits to different churches and a synagogue. In November, the Council held its meeting at Temple B'rith Kodesh, effectively reversing Americanization programs that once sought to have non-Protestants come into welcoming churches. After their meeting concluded, they attended the Friday Sabbath prayers and a tea hosted by the Council of Jewish Women.[117]

The work of the NCCJ and local interfaith cooperation did not mean that European-descended Jews had been definitively categorized as a religious group. In the 1930s, persistent and rising antisemitism in the United States and the European refugee crisis meant that neither Jews nor Christians could ignore Jews' racialization. In the 1930s, the American Friends Service Committee and other Protestants affiliated with the Federal Council organized committees to fund the resettlement of Christian refugees from Germany, a category that increasingly included "non-Aryan Christians."[118] At the end of the 1930s, the Church Woman's Committee on Race Relations (CWCRR) housed within the Federal Council's Department of Race Relations also decided to address antisemitism. Committee member Ellen Louderbaugh (Mrs. H. C. Louderbaugh), a White Presbyterian from New Jersey, had just returned from the International Missionary Council's meeting in Madras via Europe. Witnessing firsthand the persecution of Jews during her return travel, Louderbaugh made a convincing case to her colleagues for the need to address antisemitism against Jews in their race relations work, which had almost exclusively focused on Black-White relations among Protestants. George Haynes, who headed the Department of Race Relations, opposed this decision. He recommended that antisemitism be considered an interreligious matter and left to the NCCJ. The CWCRR women were not convinced, and "a feeling was expressed that something might be done" to supplement this work.[119]

At the next meeting, Louderbaugh presented a resolution for a new antisemitism committee because of "the present acute crisis." While the CWCRR lacked the financial resources to support European refugees, they compiled a packet on how local groups could help local refugee resettlement that they distributed to churchwomen's councils. They also discussed the need for articles in the "Negro secular and religious press" that would address what they saw as "Negro fear of economic competition of Jewish refugees and the existing anti-Semitism among Negroes."[120] In this instance, churchwomen were less concerned with parsing categories and more focused on the immediate issues related to antisemitism, Jewish refugees, and resettlement. At the same time, their focus on how they as Protestant women could shape Black and White Protestants' public opinion when it came to Jews reflected the broader shifts taking place in how churchwomen defined their power and purpose. They claimed the authority to manage the challenges presented by racial and religious diversity. They also worked through churchwomen's councils to advance and spread what they would have perceived as their Protestant cosmopolitanism.

* * *

In the 1920s and 1930s, White Protestant women debated the meaning of "missions" as they restructured their institutions, and they invoked "cooperation" frequently as they clashed over combining their different domains. Christian Americanization programs that coexisted with that institutional history offered a site for cooperation among White women. Christian Americanization brought the familiar practices and feelings of mission study and pageants into what was effectively community service work. Christian Americanization also resonated with foreign missionary women's Christian imperial feminist concerns about women oppressed by "ethnic religions," and home missionaries' efforts to Protestantize and Americanize immigrants and the nation. The outreach practices of "friendly visits" and neighborhood houses had the advantage of resonating with those missionary practices while also aligning Protestant women (accurately or not) with liberal secular articulations of cultural pluralism. For White-led Protestant women's groups, Christian Americanization offered a way to stake out their brand of Protestantism as cosmopolitan and racially inclusive. They contrasted their universalist way of being religious with the nativist White Protestants they deemed "un-Christian" *and* with some Catholics, Jews, and others whose religion and religio-racial arrangements were unsuitable for an American style of religion. Ecumenical Protestants' participation in the tri-faith movement worked along similar lines even as some White Catholics and Jews became part of (while still often contesting) ecumenical Protestants' conception of American religion.

The tri-faith movement and White Protestant women's interpretation of it also shows how they defined their Christian imperial feminism in new ways. Without entirely abandoning their rescue efforts targeting immigrant women, they reconceptualized missions and Christian imperial feminism into managing "relations" between different groups. This turn was evident in the CWCRR's approach to antisemitism as a systemic and structural problem rather than just one that concerned individual

Protestants' prejudices. When churchwomen formed the United Council of Church Women in 1941, they created departments of Christian Social Relations and Christian World Relations. Also, in contrast to "Christian Americanization," the names and objectives of these departments demonstrated how churchwomen rejected an exclusive focus on the nation as they viewed local, national, and global "social relations" as always interrelated. As the discussion of the CWCRR concerning antisemitism suggested, and as the next chapter argues, Black churchwomen played a singularly important role in redefining White women's Christian imperial feminism from White women's duty to Christianize racialized others to the much broader Christian imperial goal to Christianize all social and world relations.

5

The Spiritual Feelings and Religious Politics of Interracial Cooperation

In 1934, the ecumenical Church Women's Committee on Race Relations (CWCRR) held a special meeting to discuss its purpose. Formed in 1926 and housed within the Federal Council of Churches' Department on Race Relations, the CWCRR was made up of White and Black women from mission boards, the YWCA, and denominations affiliated with the Federal Council. In contrast to the White missionary societies that had viewed Black people as in need of White Protestants' aid, the CWCRR focused its attentions on changing individual White Protestants and their institutions. Yet at this meeting eight years after the CWCRR's founding, many members felt disappointed by their lack of progress.

Those on the CWCRR thought that part of the problem was that the church "follows community patterns" instead of disrupting the status quo. Also, too many White churchgoers implemented "Christ's teaching in a personal way" instead of thinking in terms of "social goals," and this prevented Protestants' collective action. Another committee member thought that there was a disconnect between the church's teachings and practice. While ministers and laypeople might call for "more liberal attitudes on the part of the government and business groups (hotels, etc.)," churches remained largely segregated. The women on the CWCRR recognized the enormity of the work, but they also found grounds for hope. One of them noted that the Social Creed of the Churches adopted by the FCC at its founding in 1908 had once been "considered highly radical," but its ideas were now commonplace. So even if the "ultimate goal may be so far from reality as to seem in the millennium," their work still counted, and they should focus on "what steps we can take in our generation." As a result, the CWCRR discussed a new statement of purpose: "Believing as Christians that churches should not be divided because of race or class, the Church Women's Committee states as its objective complete mutuality in the life of the church."[1]

While they agreed on the goal of "complete mutuality," White and Black Protestant women experienced interracial cooperation differently. Most White Protestant women continued to see interracial cooperation as missionary outreach toward less fortunate Black people. As they had done in their missionary societies and in neighborhood houses, White Protestant women tended to interpret interracial cooperation as an educational and spiritually fulfilling experience for White participants. Many Black Protestant women had been active supporters of foreign missions as well, but they had frequently mobilized this imperial feminist discourse to condemn the "barbarism" and "heathenism" of supposedly Christian White American enslavers and lynch mobs and the creators of Jim Crow segregation.[2] For Black women, interracial cooperation with White Protestant women could be more frustrating than spiritually fulfilling. Writing about the earlier experiences of Black women in the YWCA, Judith Weisenfeld argued that they remained committed to such fraught interracial efforts because they were willing "to organize in any and all arenas that would prove productive avenues for achieving justice and ameliorating the harshness of many African Americans' daily living conditions."[3] Black women played an instrumental role in directing their White colleagues' cosmopolitan spiritual feelings about interracial cooperation into political action. Additionally, before the Federal Council of Churches stated its formal opposition to segregation in 1943, the CWCRR no longer focused solely on remedying individuals' "race prejudice" and instead shifted to structural changes through political action.[4]

George E. and Elizabeth Ross Haynes were at the center of how White-led Protestant institutions came to understand interracial cooperation. Born in Arkansas, George Haynes graduated from Fisk University in Nashville. After a short stint at Yale Divinity School, he decided to study sociology instead and pursued his doctorate at Columbia University. Haynes's research in the 1910s focused on the conditions facing Black migrants to northern cities, and he would be aided in this research by his wife and fellow sociologist, Elizabeth.[5] The Alabama-born Elizabeth Ross Haynes worked briefly as a teacher before becoming one of the first Black women employed by the YWCA as a "special worker" to organize Black southern college students. After marrying, the Haynes's moved to Washington, DC, where George had been appointed as the head of the new Division of Negro Economics at the Department of Labor. Working with her husband, Elizabeth began her own line of sociological research on Black women workers that she would complete as a master's thesis at Columbia after the couple moved to New York in 1922. George had by then begun work as the executive secretary of the Federal Council's new Commission on the Church and Race Relations, a post he held until his retirement in 1947.[6] As the head of the Federal Council's Commission on the Church and Race Relations, George Haynes helped coordinate the formation of the CWCRR along with White home missionary leaders, Elizabeth Ross Haynes, Eva Bowles, and other Black women active in the YWCA.

George Haynes's 1923 mission study book on Black-White interracial cooperation introduced many northern White missions-supporting women to the idea that their churches should be taking a stand on anti-Black racism. While Haynes approached the topic in the Christian cosmopolitan language and feelings familiar to White readers, he also drew on his wife's research on Black domestic workers to challenge White women to consider their own role in upholding intersectional class, race, and gender hierarchies. Such fissures between Black and White experiences also appeared during the CWCRR's meetings and in the many interracial conferences and other meetings Protestant women attended in the interwar years. By examining how White and Black women experienced the CWCRR's national conferences in the 1920s and two conferences that took place in 1937 as well as the dynamics of churchwomen's councils' local "race relations" programming, we can see that Black churchwomen pursued an intersectional Christian feminism intended to make White churchwomen recognize that their cultural and religious norms were not necessarily the universal ideal to which Black women aspired. While such arguments from Black women often fell on deaf ears, White women could be moved to political action when Black women invoked the celebratory and aspirational language of Christian cosmopolitanism. The CWCRR's political mobilization campaigns in the 1930s appealed to White women's enthusiasm for a diverse Christian community by urging them to "Christianize" race relations in their communities and the nation through demanding Black civil rights.

The Origins of Northern Interracial Cooperation and Mission Study

The demographic changes of the Great Migration of Black southerners to northern cities in the 1910s and 1920s led White ecumenical Protestants to quite suddenly see "race relations" as a concern beyond their home missions institutions in the South. Black and White men competed for jobs and White women hired Black domestic workers, and Black neighborhoods in northern cities became as troubling to White Protestants as "immigrant colonies." White northerners feared so-called race riots in East St. Louis and Chicago as harbingers of further unrest if Christians could not solve the "Negro problem."[7]

In many ways, the northern Federal Council was playing catchup to earlier interracial efforts in the South where White Protestants, and especially Southern Methodists, had already organized the Commission on Interracial Cooperation (CIC). Led by Will W. Alexander, the CIC helped organize state and local interracial councils to address Black living conditions, healthcare, and educational and work opportunities. Notably, these "interracial" councils were not racially integrated. White southern churchwomen played a key role in the grassroots efforts of the CIC and through the Association of Southern Women for the Prevention of Lynching founded by Jessie Daniel Ames.[8] Earlier interracial efforts in the North looked somewhat different. The NAACP, formed in 1909, and the National Urban League, founded the year after, had White Protestant and Jewish founders and members but were Black-led institutions.[9] The Federal Council included historically Black denominations as affiliated members in the 1910s, and the historically White Home Missions Council and Council of Women for Home Missions (CWHM) and the Foreign Missions Conference and Federation of Woman's Boards of Foreign Missions (FWBFM) similarly expanded their membership to include Black denominations' mission boards. Yet Black people remained a very small minority in these White-led organizations.[10]

When the Federal Council created its Commission on the Church and Race Relations, it was initially conceptualized as a northern version of the CIC, but with Black men in leadership positions alongside White men. Early on, George Haynes shared the executive secretary role of the Commission with the CIC's Will Alexander.[11] Chaired by

Bishop George C. Clement of the AME Zion Church, the members of the Commission included representatives from the Federal Council's member denominations. The group's purpose was, according to a 1921 statement, to show that Christianity alone provided "the solution of race relations in America." Mostly White-attended churches would be urged to host interracial conferences and educational programs and to ensure members' "accurate knowledge of the facts regarding racial relations and racial attitudes." Church members could also influence the "public conscience" on matters of "education, health, housing, recreation, and all other aspects of community welfare."[12] In 1922, Haynes created the publicity-attracting Race Relations Sunday, an annual event scheduled on the Sunday closest to Abraham Lincoln's birthday. Black and White ministers across the country were encouraged to preach on race relations and to swap pulpits. The Commission also published pamphlets and books, co-sponsored an Interracial News Letter with the Friends' General Conference, and in the 1940s began to host interracial clinics where Protestant clergy and laypeople examined issues of local concern, including housing rights, medical access, and employment.

It is likely that few White Protestant women in the North thought much about Black-White interracial cooperation as a Christian practice until they read George E. Haynes's *The Trend of the Races* in 1922–23. Chosen by the Council of Women for Home Missions (CWHM) as its home mission study textbook, it was read and discussed in women's missionary societies and churchwomen's councils. With three printings and close to 60,000 copies sold by that November, *The Trend of the Races* and Haynes's call for churches to take the lead on interracial cooperation reached a significant audience of predominantly White Protestants.[13] In the book's preface, White CWHM leader Edith Allen provided a missionary seal of approval. After quoting the commandment to "love thy neighbor," she wrote, "obviously, if our neighbor is to be loved, he must be known." Allen also explained how, in studying the conditions of Black life, readers (who were assumed to be White) should "seek to know ourselves in respect to our limitations, achievements, and goals in the building of the social order."[14] Learning about Black history and Black life was both spiritually productive and essential to training White women to take an active role in managing race relations in their communities.

Haynes began the book with a brief foray into the nineteenth-century history of emancipation, notable Black leaders, and a sufficiently grateful account of White northerners' noble efforts to fund Black schools and colleges. But the bulk of the text drew on his and others' research on the conditions facing Black people in the early 1920s. Haynes provided a sociological and economic analysis of the costs of White supremacy on Black people and the damage done to White people as well. The answer that would save both resided in mutual understanding rather than material changes alone. He wrote that the "relations of the two races finally rest, not upon wealth or poverty, not upon things or lack of them, but upon the mental, social, and spiritual attitudes and habits of conduct of life that grow out of the feeling experiences of the two races as they have contact in agriculture, industry, education, government, religion, and the like." The solution rested in "the ideals of Jesus" that must "determine the conditions of these experiences and the conditions of these contacts."[15] Yet Haynes insisted that "real cooperation" only occurred when Whites gave up a measure of power that manifested in their treatment of African Americans "as less than freemen or as children." Haynes was clear: "where one race or the other thinks more highly of itself or of its interests than it ought to think, such joint operation is practically unworkable." Haynes optimistically stated that "White Americans are gradually coming to see that race relations in the future require that they work not simply *for*, but *with* Negroes."[16] He argued that a solution rested in the simple, spiritually profound, and pleasurable work of interracial cooperation.

Haynes examined the consequences of racism, political exclusion, and discrimination on African Americans' feelings and sense of self as well as on family life, wages, housing, healthcare, education, and the justice system. Perhaps aware that his book would reach White women in mission study classes, Haynes focused on White women's homes as a site for action. He cited Elizabeth Haynes's research about northern Black domestic workers and suggested how White women could address these racist structures in their own homes.[17] In *Trend of the Races*, George Haynes picked up her argument that the power inequity between White employers and Black domestic workers made gender or religious solidarity difficult if not impossible. The White woman employer "usually asks how much work she can get out of her and how cheaply, while the

Negro woman usually figures how little she can give in return. The personal interest of each in the other as cooperators in the greatest of enterprises, the home, seems to be a diminishing part of their bargain, quickly made and easily broken."[18] Borrowing from Black churchwomen's discourse of respectability, Haynes also addressed White women's role in a White supremacy that put Black women and their families in danger. "How many white men who think and speak of protecting, even with lynch law, their own homes and women ever give serious consideration to the inroads made by white men upon Negro homes and the pressure put upon defenseless Negro women and girls?" Haynes put a similar question about a double standard to White women readers. "How many white housewives know the surroundings or see the inside of the homes of their faithful servants upon whose health and skill the comfort of their own families depends?"[19]

Haynes and his Protestant colleagues, including the women on the CWCRR, recognized that middle-class and wealthy White churchgoers had a degree of power in their communities when it came to changing White public opinion regarding the respectability of interracial cooperation. White women (and some Black women) especially had translated decades of grassroots activism that included educational programs around temperance and women's suffrage into constitutional amendments. Haynes noted that if they wanted to change the "machinery of government and law," they must first change the attitudes of the "individuals and groups" that "lie back of government and control the machinery of law." Haynes promoted interracial cooperation as the method for changing "conventional 'public opinion,'—'folkways' and 'mores.'"[20] This is where White churchgoers entered the picture, not only in terms of their own individual attitudes but in fostering interracial cooperation in their institutions. In integrated organizations, clubs, and events, "individuals and groups and races" would learn to "avoid the ways, attitudes, and feelings that have proven harmful and to cultivate those that have proven truly pleasurable and helpful" such as "good-will, tolerance, justice, and cooperation." While interracial cooperation might take place in many venues, its best hope was in "the Church, where justice, mercy, and communion with Jehovah are visioned."[21]

For its 1922–1923 mission study program, the CWHM paired Haynes's textbook with *In the Vanguard of a Race* by the White Southern Methodist writer Lily H. Hammond. Hammond's book's perspective shows how a racist and sentimental Christian imperial feminism was still very much in play alongside Haynes's quite different analysis.[22] Hammond's *In the Vanguard of the Race* was comprised of biographical chapters on Black men and women, from Booker T. Washington to educator Nannie H. Burroughs and businesswoman Maggie L. Walker.[23] Besides the stylistic choices, Hammond presented a totally different reading of the White home. While Haynes described White women's homes as demoralizing and potentially dangerous spaces for Black women, Hammond, a White southerner, romanticized the relationship between White slavers and enslaved Black women. She described how the "Christian white women of America" had "kindled in the Negro women's souls" the "capacity for God" that they had carried from Africa. Slavery was wrong, Hammond wrote, but even so Black women had "found God through their mistresses' lives and took up their predestined task of making Him real and lovable to their own people by living in His spirit from day to day."[24] Hammond's analysis echoed others who viewed slavery as a White missionary project that God had ordained for the conversion of Africans.[25] Hammond recognized that the times had changed, at least to a degree. Now, she concluded, "Negro women are entitled, not only to our sympathy, but to our respect and cooperation."[26]

The White Protestant press greeted Haynes's *The Trend of the Races* and the interracial cooperation argument it represented with caution. The *Missionary Review of the World* dedicated most of an issue to the topic of race relations, which included contributions from Black men and women. The editorial introducing the special issue took pains to clarify exactly what interracial cooperation entailed to the imagined White reader. The issue's intention was not to "exalt the Negro, to discount his limitations, or to advocate closer social fellowship between the races."[27] "Social fellowship" led to interracial marriage, a point that the Protestant promotors of interracial cooperation avoided discussing in virtually all their publications and even in internal deliberations. In the 1920s, numerous states passed or strengthened anti-miscegenation laws, and real or false charges of interracial sex between those involved in interracial cooperation would be a primary scare tactic deployed against the proponents of racial liberalism and later civil rights activists.[28]

Meanwhile, White Protestant women proceeded to organize their usual mission study classes for *The Trend of the Races*. In Rochester, New York, an audience of mostly White women attended the Council of Church Women's one-day missions institute in October 1923. James E. Rose, a Black clergyman and husband of Council member Carrie Rose, gave the lecture on the Haynes's textbook. Perhaps because of the mission study theme, Council leaders invited Buffalo clubwoman Mary Burnett Talbert to speak at their next meeting. Talbert was known for helping found the Phyllis Wheatley Club in Buffalo, and she had most recently worked as a Red Cross nurse in France during the war and belonged to the Women's Committee of National Defense. She spoke to the ninety Rochester churchwomen about her family history, on Black women's organizing "to defend our people," her recent wartime experiences, and what she had witnessed in her travels in the South, where she taught before marrying and moving to Buffalo. She condemned lynching as contrary to the democratic ideals the country had fought for during the war, and she urged the churchwomen in the audience to send telegrams to Washington urging support for the Dyer Anti-Lynching Act. The meeting concluded with a vote in support of sending a telegram to their senators and representatives on just this point. The lecture was also significant enough to get a full writeup in the *Democrat and Chronicle* under the headline "Democracy Sham If Lynchings Persist."[29] More than just a textbook, women's practice of mission study made *The Trend of the Races* into an opportunity for Black women to gain White women's support for a political program, specifically the NAACP's long-desired federal anti-lynching law.

The Church Women's Committee on Race Relations

Several years after Haynes's *Trend of the Races* introduced White-led women's missionary organizations to the Christian work of interracial cooperation, a group of White and Black Protestant women held their first interracial conference. In September 1926, the Federal Council of Churches and the YWCA sponsored the conference on race relations in the mountain resort town of Eagles Mere, Pennsylvania. When the conference's Continuing Committee met later that November, they formed the Church Women's Committee on Race Relations. The Black women on the CWCRR worked to make long-standing Black women's political issues central to White women's religious politics. This would be a challenging process as White women more often approached interracial cooperation through the same missionary lens as they had Christian foreign missions and Christian Americanization, that is, their "friendship" relied on a Christian imperial feminist power dynamic that was rarely named but keenly felt.

From the beginning, the CWCRR members' race and class identities mattered as did their organizational backgrounds. Many of the White and Black women on the CWCRR had worked for the YWCA at some point, and these women came to the CWCRR with many more years of experience with interracial work compared to the White women who had been situated in segregated home missionary societies. Notably, both Elizabeth Ross Haynes and Eva Bowles had fought to gain resources for "colored" YWCAs, and especially their own local 135th Street YWCA in Harlem. Working alongside White women on the Committee on Colored Work, Ross Haynes, Bowles, and other Black YW women achieved a measure of success, and by 1930, there were sixty-five YWCAs for Black women, up from just four in 1907, and Black women served on the boards of directors in twenty-five cities.[30]

As founding members of the Church Woman's Committee, Bowles and Ross Haynes would have to work with other Black women and the White executive secretaries and representatives of the White-led missionary organizations, the CWHM and the FWBFM. A core group of around twenty women living in New York City and its suburbs regularly attended the Church Woman's Committee's bimonthly meetings and guided its agenda, which primarily focused on spurring the newly organized White-led churchwomen's councils to embrace interracial cooperation as a Christian imperative and to make the moral case for Black civil rights to their communities.[31]

Initially, the committee members debated whether the new CWCRR should try to reach White women through missionary organizations or the small but growing number of churchwomen's councils. Eva Bowles suggested that the CWCRR channel its work to the women's missionary societies of each denomination, likely due to the organizational breadth compared to the fledgling councils. George Haynes disagreed and instead pushed for the Federal Council's interests in the new ecumenical churchwomen's councils. Perhaps he was also skeptical about the willingness of White missionary women to treat Black women as equal partners. "The whole project should not be regarded as a missionary project," George Haynes noted, according to the meeting minutes. Interracial work should instead be "a responsibility of the church women of all the denominations." He set the course of the committee to "go out to the church women with the hope of laying these problems on the hearts of each of the women."[32]

The lingering questions about how missions fit with race relations persisted when the CWCRR's newly appointed secretary, Katherine Gardner, a White Presbyterian, wrote an article expressing her view that interracial cooperation marked a departure from White women's missionary work and all its assumptions. Gardner did not have an especially strong affiliation to the women's missionary movement herself. After she graduated from the New York School of Social Work, she ran the Social Service Federation in Englewood, New Jersey, where she also helped organize a local chapter of the Urban League.[33] The article plainly articulated her views on the missionary movement. "Recent years," wrote Gardner, "have shown that mission work is only the first step in the development of a Christian attitude on race relations; that while it is very fine to do things for another race, the time has come when the word must change from **for** to **with**—when Christians must face the world as 'workers together with God,' irrespective of race and color."[34] Over the course of the late 1920s and early 1930s, White churchwomen interpreted interracial cooperation programs in different ways, and despite the CWCRR's wishes, for many White women this work remained tied to both home and foreign missions and the Christian imperial feminism those movements inspired.

The CWCRR's efficacy relied on its ability to mobilize organized Protestant women, and it did so with mixed results. The CWCRR published its first pamphlet, *A Clearer Vision of the Race Problem*, in early 1928, with the intention of encouraging local churchwomen's councils to launch interracial cooperation committees and programs. The pamphlet encouraged the White churchwomen who led these new councils to study the conditions of Black people in their communities, and it included a list of questions and prompts as well as suggested readings on topics ranging from housing conditions and barriers to Black people renting or buying homes, employment conditions for Black and White women, access to hospitals and clinics, educational disparities, popular perceptions of Black people, and how churchwomen had or had not organized interracially. The CWCRR strongly recommended that churchwomen build racially integrated councils and work to organize opportunities for interracial discussions and collaborative social outreach. Churchwomen could participate in their local Race Relations Sunday activities, but they could also organize lecture series and study groups for White and Black women to learn about and discuss issues like "Race and Industry" or "Race and War or Peace."[35] Emphasizing a key objective of the Haynes's vision of church-based interracial cooperation, the CWCRR affirmed "that the one solution to the race problem is living out in daily life and action the prayer of their Saviour Jesus Christ: 'That they may be one even as we are one . . . that the world may know that thou has sent me.'"[36]

The CWCRR modeled this kind of interracial work in their national conferences held in 1928 and 1930. Building on the earlier 1926 conference that had led to the CWCRR's formation, these conferences brought dozens of churchwomen together with the hopes of jumpstarting interracial cooperation across the North. At these meetings, White participants focused on their feelings and their spiritual experiences. Like playing a part in a missionary pageant, attending an interracial meeting generated a similar thrill of inhabiting God's diverse kingdom while also leaving the White participant confident in her superior Christian virtue and liberal cosmopolitan attitude. Black attendees had more varied responses. Many attended these meetings for strategic political reasons. While they might appreciate the conference discussions, Black women had no need to prove their cosmopolitan bona fides.

Sixty women representing thirty-one organizations had attended the September 1928 conference at Eagles Mere Park. In her opening address, the CWCRR's White chairwoman and YWCA leader, Mary Westbrook (Mrs. Richard W. Westbrook) explained the origins of the committee and its growth to forty-four members. She also introduced Katherine Gardner, the committee's new executive secretary. The first session was an "open forum" in which six women spoke about their experiences with interracial work. The panel included three Black women: the CWCRR's future chairwoman Josephine Humbles Kyles from Washington, DC,

Methodist Florence Sterling Randolph from New Jersey, and YWCA secretary in Indianapolis, May B. Belcher. Joining them was White Episcopalian Clelia McGowan (Mrs. C. P. McGowan), who led South Carolina's interracial commission. Speaking from the missionary and church council points of view were Edna Slutes (Mrs. Merril C. Slutes) from Cincinnati, representing the northern Methodist home missions, and Adeline MacFarlane (Mrs. William MacFarlane), the chairwoman of the Americanization Committee of Rochester's Council of Church Women. McGowan gave practical advice about how interracial groups could conduct surveys regarding education, health, housing, public school access, and other issues in order to bring them to the attention of a wider public. Most of the sessions focused on what White people could and should do. To this point, Addie W. Dickerson, a Black lawyer from Philadelphia, urged the White women in the audience to "mould public opinion without fear."[37]

The post-conference reviews of the 1928 meeting offer a window into the dynamics of interracial cooperation among churchwomen. When southerner Clelia McGowan weighed in on the conference to the CWCRR along with other attendees, she praised the opportunities it gave women to get to know each other, but she also said that "it is necessary for there to be a very free expression of things which are wrong in order that action may be taken to right them."[38] McGowan may have been expressing what one historian has described as White southern women's dislike for Black northern women whom they found "aggressive and less accommodating."[39] Some other White attendees were also frustrated that the sessions repeated much of the same information presented at the earlier conference in 1926. Perhaps reflecting this, the general consensus of those who attended was that the event would have been better had there been more social time, "longer periods for informal contacts," and "a strong emphasis on the spiritual part of the conference."[40] Black women agreed with the calls for more informal time for conversation and socializing, but they also expressed a familiar frustration with some of the White women organizers.

By 1926, Elizabeth Ross Haynes and Eva Bowles had gained more than a decade of experience with ways to work with patronizing White women within the YWCA. Although she had helped found the CWCRR, Bowles had been unimpressed with many of the White churchwomen she encountered at the first interracial conference at Eagles Mere in 1926. She reported back to the YWCA's Council on Colored Work that the YWCA women were "far in advance of the methods used at this conference."[41] At the 1928 conference, as in 1926, many of the White participants had little to no knowledge of the issues Black women like Haynes and Bowles had been working on for decades. In her tempered comments to the CWCRR after the 1928 conference, Florence Randolph from New Jersey put this delicately. She was "enthusiastic in her appreciation of the conference and what it had meant to a number of people who had never previously been in touch with the problems."[42] Black author and suffragist Alice Dunbar-Nelson also attended the second interracial conference, and was more openly critical in her column in the *Washington Eagle*. Dunbar-Nelson praised the "colored women" in attendance who had kept the event from devolving into a "mutual admiration society." In her private papers she was more candid, describing Mary Westbrook, the White YWCA president and the CWCRR's chairwoman who had once headed the YWCA's Committee on Colored Work, as one of many "churchly ladies" in attendance who were "all smug and satisfied and too smiling."[43]

After the Eagles Mere conference, the CWCRR put out a new pamphlet, *Church Women at Work on the Race Problem*, and Gardner wrote articles touting the conference as a success and emphasizing its impact on White participants. The 1928 pamphlet *Church Women at Work on the Race Problem* presented interracial cooperation as a solution to White women's apparently diminished spirituality as they poured themselves into activities. "American woman's religion today lacks spiritual depth and a sense of eternal values," began the first paragraph, and in many cases, "service has replaced the ideal of a growing knowledge of God," and "organization has taken the place of the spirit of goodwill." Then, using a quotation from Howard Kester, the White southern Christian Socialist and labor organizer, the CWCRR presented the new front of race relations as a spiritual awakening for White participants: "those of us who have been emancipated from the bonds of race prejudice feel that a great light has suddenly fallen upon us and that a liberating force has opened us to treasures of new experience."[44] For Kester and for White churchwomen, interracial cooperation played with the Christian imperial feminist script. On one level this seemed like a change, as it positioned White women as the objects of the emancipatory and "liberating force" of Christianity. Yet in other ways it echoed the cosmopolitan feelings generated in missionary pageants and mission study as White women found enchantment in imagining themselves as part of a larger world Christianity.

The 1928 pamphlet also connected familiar cosmopolitan practices to social activism. The suggestions encouraged local groups to "use Negro spirituals and Indian folk songs" at interracial meetings and prayer services to help (White) participants "learn the achievements of members of other races that there may be a sympathetic appreciation of their contributions to American life."[45] At the same time, they should also investigate "discrimination and segregation" at public schools and other public spaces, and at private businesses.[46] As Gardner wrote in an article for the *Church School Herald* bearing the same title as the pamphlet, "there is no more effective method of solving racial problems than by bringing together the leaders of the groups in close fellowship for periods of heart-to-heart discussion and planning. And oftentimes the informal contacts at these conferences have the most far-reaching results."[47]

Practicing Protestant Interracialism

One did not need to travel to one of the CWCRR conferences to be enchanted by interracial cooperation. The broad umbrella of race relations often incorporated the Black-White interracial cooperation of the CWCRR and Christian Americanization work targeting mostly European immigrants. "Race," for many White Americans and others, remained a fluid category used to mark various social differences. A closer look at the Rochester Council of Church Women's "race relations" practices shows how the ideas of the CWCRR women were applied at the local level. As illustrated here, their programs and politics were contingent on the preferences of individual White women, as well as the existing networks that connected Black and White women. Yet the messaging from the national organizations did break through, as the evolution of Rochester's programming demonstrates. Further, the media coverage of Rochester's Council of Church Women's events suggests how prayer services or presentations could work to shape public opinion. As reported in the city's newspaper, Protestant women worked to make their racial liberalism a morally sanctioned and normative racial regime.

In 1928, the Council of Church Women in Rochester held its first Race Relations Sunday vesper service. The prayer services featured guest speaker Addie W. Hunton, a Black suffragist and clubwoman from Brooklyn. Over a thousand people attended, according to the Council, and a photo of the racially mixed planning committee appeared in the Rochester *Democrat and Chronicle*.[48] The planning committee exemplified how networks created through the Council of Church Women, the YWCA, and the NAACP had already forged an interracial group of reform-minded citizens. The Council of Church Women's White secretary, Alice Walker, was on the committee, as was YWCA leader Helen Pomeroy, the Woman's City Club founder Helen Probst Abbott, and well-known local activist Mary L. Gannett. Abbott and Gannett both were members of the NAACP, and Gannett's deceased husband, William C. Gannett, had been one of the northern missionaries to freedpeople in Port Royal, South Carolina during the Civil War, after which he led a long career as the minister at the First Unitarian Church. The Black committee members included Council members Carrie Rose (Mrs. James E. Rose), Anna Lee (Mrs. John G. Lee), and Ernestine Burks (Mrs. George Burks), and the head of the Clarissa Street YWCA, Estelle Fitzgerald. While Rose's husband was a prominent minister, the husbands of Anna Lee and Ernestine Brooks had more modest jobs as porters at banks. Yet with James Rose, the two men were prominent leaders in the city's Black community. John Lee was the master for the Prince Hall–affiliated Eureka Masonic Lodge, and it had been George Burks who initiated the creation of Rochester's chapter of the NAACP in 1919.[49]

In 1929, however, the vespers service's approach to "race relations" included speeches from a Black minister, a Seneca man who was also the director of Rochester's Municipal Museum, and a Reform Rabbi. The 1929 service took place in the downtown Baptist Temple Building's auditorium, which was adorned with flags representing the nations of the world. The Council's vice president, Mrs. Robert E. Beinselman, began with the call to worship, and Mary Gannett, who had helped plan the 1928 service, led the responsive reading. The Italian Baptist Vittorio Aghetto's wife, Carmela, was invited to say one of the prayers. The AME Zion preacher James Claire Taylor, the pastor of the AME

Zion church, spoke about Black people's successes in literature, the arts, and in business, highlighting Black-owned business enterprises. He also pointed out the barriers Black people faced in the North as they were shut out of industrial jobs by the Whites, who feared their success. His speech exemplified what the CWCRR hoped these vespers services might accomplish. In contrast, Arthur C. Parker, a member of the Seneca Nation who was an anthropologist and the director of the museum, focused on the past and, in a conciliatory fashion, he "spoke of the Indian's qualities of patience, hospitality, and loyalty."[50] Finally, Rabbi Jeremiah Berman of Temple Beth El gave a more general address on the importance of tolerance. He criticized those "who would solve the [race] problem by obliterating the races" since "uniformity" would be "drab and colorless." People were "interesting in that they are different," he argued, and "the race problem does not exist because of differences but because there is that pathological state of mind that cannot tolerate differences. We must learn to live together side by side in a true brotherhood of man."[51]

The Rochester's Race Relations vespers services in the 1930s often departed from the intentions of the CWCRR as they highlighted European "races" in ways that minimized the participation of Black Protestants and Black civil rights demands. The ebb and flow of the emphasis on the sins of White supremacy and the striving of Black Protestants points to the unsettled definitions of race and the ambivalence toward the CWCRR's goals on the part of White churchwomen. In a 1938 pageant Rochester's Council put on for that year's service, missionary pageant aesthetics and a focus on native-born White people's European heritage took center stage. Churchgoers from Brighton Reformed Church played Dutch colonists and members of Emmanuel Lutheran played more recent immigrant Germans. With a nod to Americanization work, members of the Polish Baptist church and the Methodist and Baptist Italian churches dressed as "ethnic" Poles and Italians. Black members of James Rose's Mt. Olivet Baptist Church also took part, presumably without special costumes. Meanwhile, White women dressed as Welsh, Arabs, Chinese, Armenians, and Turks.[52] The decision to continue to interpret "race" broadly to refer to European nationalities allowed the Council of Church Women to sustain their Christian imperial feminism as they depicted and celebrated a cosmopolitan world consumed

Rochester *Democrat and Chronicle*, February 10, 1938, 19. © Democrat and Chronicle – USA TODAY NETWORK

by Protestant Christianity. They ignored the anti-Black racism of their White churches, White-led Protestant institutions, and broader society that the services were intended to address, while at the same time feeling as though they were truly exhibiting racial diversity.

Perhaps because of the conflicting interpretations of "race relations" being shared among White-led churchwomen's councils, the CWCRR prepared a pamphlet in 1933 entitled *Suggestions for Interracial Gatherings* that provided specific guidelines. The pamphlet also spoke to how the CWCRR members believed local churchwomen could make a difference. "Just one really interested woman can set the ball rolling," and working with other women's groups including the YWCA would ensure widespread support. "Be sure that racial representation is as equal as possible" on all committees, the CWCRR advised. The pamphlet outlined possible agendas for a one-day conference, an afternoon tea featuring a "program of cultural interest," and a combined conference and tea. At an afternoon tea, the goal was to bring Black and White churchwomen together in a pleasant setting, and an atmosphere of sophistication was essential. The pamphlet's description of the afternoon tea drew from a 1932 event held at Riverside Church in New York City featuring a poetry reading from Countee Cullen and a performance by soprano

Ruby Elzy. To organize a similar event, churchwomen should select "a meeting place of charm and dignity," and the tables should be set with freshly cut flowers and "candles and linen." The CWCRR had special invitation cards made for the tea at Riverside to indicate to potential guests that this was a dignified event.[53] The emphasis on appearances and etiquette was not only a signal of the planners' class and social mores, but it also underscored the moral soundness and respectability of interracial events.

Along the same lines as their attention to aesthetics in these suggestions, the CWCRR members had also become involved in efforts to promote the Black arts. Not unlike the United Mission Study program that promised missionary women cosmopolitan credentials, the CWCRR's administration of the William E. Harmon Award for Distinguished Achievement Among Negroes invited White Protestant women to see interracial cooperation as culturally refining instead of a social drag. The Harmon Award was a joint project between the Harmon Foundation and the Federal Council's Department of Race Relations, and the prizes were awarded to Black writers and artists who were featured in several exhibitions hosted by the CWCRR. In the mid-1930s, White Protestant women also directed their Race Relations departments to plan activities around the popular trend of African art. In April 1936, the Council of Church Women in Rochester took advantage of the arrival of the "African Negro Art" exhibit to the city's Memorial Art Gallery. James Johnson Sweeney's vast collection of "masks and fetishes," textiles, and sculptures from across Africa had been welcomed with rave reviews at the Museum of Modern Art in New York City the previous year, and the women from the CWCRR had visited the exhibit together.[54] Rochester residents might have read about it in a piece in their own city's paper that described the "radical artists, society women, and collectors" who had flocked to see the bronzes from Benin among other objects.[55]

In the 1930s, the African "masks and fetishes" and Polynesian and African "primitive textiles" were in vogue as inspiration for avant-garde European artists, as an article by the museum's director pointed out in the Rochester *Democrat and Chronicle*.[56] When the exhibit arrived in Rochester, the Rochester Council organized a "tea and lecture" for women on one day, a gallery tour and party for children on another, and "an evening at the gallery for colored people" with a musical program featuring Nathaniel Dett, the renowned Black composer who had recently earned an MA at Rochester's Eastman School of Music.[57] Before coming to the gallery, the children watched a film about "native life in South Africa" and heard a presentation from the gallery's director, Isabel Herdle, and then they would either watch or participate in "a dramatization" directed by Council member Carrie Rose.[58]

Interracial cooperation took many forms in the 1920s and 1930s, from vesper services with elements of missionary pageants to conferences to artistic events like these. Writing for White Protestant women, the CWCRR emphasized the spiritual and cultural benefits of such experiences that made interracial cooperation a pleasure rather than a chore. A collection of anonymous quotes in the 1933 "Suggestions" pamphlet both promoted such activities and endorsed their moral purpose. "We all carried away a lasting and inspiring memory," wrote one woman, and another declared that "it gave me a broader outlook on life" and that "every colored person I see now makes a different impression on me than before." One woman described the event as if it was a conversion experience. "I want to confess to you that I went into the conference with much misgiving, skepticism, and doubt. But, I came away thrilled." Another illustrated her Christian cosmopolitanism credentials after the Countee Cullen poetry reading. She thanked the CWCRR "for having opened the door for me to see a poet whom I thought was truly great. He had only been a name to me before—now I have bought his books of poems and will put him on my favorite list with Tagore and Keats and Whittier."[59]

Even as the CWCRR became more involved in taking concrete political and economic actions in the 1930s, the committee's members continued to present interracial cooperation practices as enchanting. After pausing its national conferences after the third interracial conference in 1930, the CWCRR planned two conferences in 1937, a feat made possible in part because of financial support from the National Council of Federated Church Women. The CWCRR invited the renowned English social worker and pacifist Muriel Lester to be the keynote speaker at both the "western" conference in Evanston, Illinois, and the "eastern" conference in Asbury Park, New Jersey. As a member of the International Fellowship of Reconciliation, Lester gave frequent lectures about Christian attitudes toward race relations and colonialism in addition to having founded Kingsley Hall, a settlement house in London's East End. As part of her Fellowship work, Lester visited India, where she met Gandhi, whom she hosted at Kingsley Hall during his visit to England in 1931.[60]

A *Church Woman* article about one White woman's experience of the Asbury Park conference shows how the leaders of the National Council and CWCRR aimed to present these events as spiritually powerful and respectable. Sarah Trowbridge was no stranger to interracial gatherings as she and her husband, a physics professor at Princeton, had lived in a residence for international graduate students.[61] In the article, however, she adopted the demeanor of a less worldly woman. When she told some friends about her plans to attend the conference, they responded, "of course you wouldn't be mingling with those colored women socially." It was, however, exactly this "rare privilege" that attracted Trowbridge to the conference. Trowbridge's article stressed the class status of the Black women involved. She reported that the seventy White and seventy Black women in attendance were all "attractively dressed and distinguished looking" and that they were "a group of smart and modern looking women." They included "Presidents and Deans of women's colleges, professors and teachers, wives of successful physicians, lawyers, and ministers" as well as YWCA secretaries. Notably, such assessments, likely meant to assuage White anxieties, could also draw attention to Black women's achievements and, more generally, draw a strong association between ecumenical Protestantism and women's professional success. This was, in a sense, the idealized outcome imagined by earlier Christian imperial feminists.

At the conference dinner, the participants were assigned tables and Trowbridge found herself dining with Florence Randolph, the longstanding CWCRR member, AME Zion minister, and domestic worker organizer. Randolph told Trowbridge about her church in Summit, New Jersey, and how the members had scrimped and saved in the hard years of the Depression so that their donations answered their prayers for a new church and parish house. Trowbridge was deeply moved by Randolph's story and the conversation, but she was "ashamed I felt that out of my experience I had so little to contribute."[62] Upon returning home, Trowbridge reflected on how she might "nurture and develop" the friendships formed at the conference. The owner of her apartment building would not likely welcome any Black guests, and she feared that if they were to meet at a restaurant, they would encounter similar challenges. In a rhetorical style that perfectly captured the middle-class moral righteousness of White churchwomen, Trowbridge concluded that "this brought home to me the appalling need of education along these lines among Christian white women and of the stand we must take in demanding the same social opportunities for people of the same social standing of whatever race."[63]

If Trowbridge's article made interracial gatherings less daunting to White women and centered on modest changes in attitudes instead of more controversial political activism, Katherine Gardner took a different tack. Gardner praised both the New Jersey and Evanston conferences, but she also noted that Black churchwomen had been left with questions "about the sincerity of white churches." One unnamed Black woman had spent the previous year on a lecture tour of sorts and had spoken to seventy-nine different White church groups and wondered "if action could be expected as a result of her talks on local conditions or if mission study is carried on in a vacuum."[64] The cheerful testimonial of Trowbridge paired with Gardner's mention of Black women's disappointment illustrated a common dynamic in the promotion of interracial cooperation to White audiences. Trowbridge's remarks vouched for the respectability and enjoyability of interracial cooperation while Gardner's article centered on the unfinished business that called women to action.

Religious Politics and Racial Justice

The CWCRR took up different political actions and protests in the 1920s and 1930s. Some of these came from the very pragmatic issue of locating accommodations and a meeting place for interracial organizations' conferences. Black delegates might not be able to stay in the same hotels as White delegates or dine at restaurants depending on where the Federal Council, Home Missions Council, or Foreign Missions Conference meetings were held. Some White CWCRR women initially sought a work-around by identifying YWCAs or Girl's Friendly Homes willing to house Black conference goers, but others rejected this plan, noting that "it is important for us not to let organizations establish the plan of giving up hotel headquarters, as that is simply begging the question."65 Katherine Gardner worked with other Protestant groups to stage polite but direct inquiries into hotel policies. In 1930, Gardner traveled with CWCRR chairwoman Caroline Chapin and two White leaders of the Home Missions Council to Washington, DC, where they met with the management of four hotels concerning the upcoming Home Missions Council and CWHM annual meeting.66 The CWCRR also formed a subcommittee to issue a statement on the necessity of "fundamental courtesies" toward all members of an interracial group. They recommended that organizations form an interracial arrangements committee, and that this planning group would ensure that all delegates had adequate and equal accommodations and access to dining areas and meeting rooms. The CWCRR voted to send the statement to the Federal Council's Administrative Committee to be disseminated to its member organizations.67

Hotels' discriminatory policies and the ongoing work of Black committee members drew the CWCRR into larger discussions about state civil rights laws. After the National Urban League's conference was shut out of New York City hotels in 1935, Gardner sent out a survey to other interracial organizations asking how they managed this issue. Summarizing the response at the January 1936 meeting, Gardner noted a "keener interest than was formerly evidenced and quite wide acceptance of the policy of insisting on the same arrangements for all members of conferences and conventions." At this meeting, the churchwomen also heard from invited guest speaker Roy Wilkins of the NAACP. Wilkins had been asked to address the status of state civil rights laws as the question of the legality of hotels' discriminatory practices had come up at a previous meeting. Wilkins stressed the importance of Black activists in the passage of civil rights laws. When asked what an interracial group like the CWCRR might do, Wilkins replied that "the initiative must come from the Negroes who suffer the restrictions but that it is of great help to have witnesses from the white group." He recommended that churchwomen form an interracial committee to meet with hotel and restaurant managers to "thoroughly discuss the civil rights laws with them," noting that it was better when private business owners conceded than "forcing the issue through recourse to the law."68

While the push for integrated hotels amounted to one kind of pressure, Haynes and Gardner also allied with the NAACP and other Black activist groups on a host of issues in the 1930s. In some cases, the CWCRR responded to events that directly affected its members. Following the tragic death of CWCRR member and YWCA secretary Juliette Derricotte, who was denied emergency medical care at a White hospital following a car accident in Georgia in 1932, the CWCRR formed a Hospitalization Committee that addressed segregated hospitals and that later advocated for Black nurses to be hired by "White" hospitals in New York and New Jersey.[69] In other cases, the CWCRR supported the work of the NAACP and grassroots activists focused on economic disparities that hit African Americans harder than Whites. For example, Gardner joined other Christian and Jewish religious leaders who met with the new Social Security Board's head, John G. Winant, to discuss how churchwomen might advocate on local and state levels for the fair implementation of "old age pensions, mothers' allowances, etc." She called on churchwomen to "seek to bring the benefits of Social Security Law to racial minorities."[70] At another meeting, the CWCRR heard from representatives from several interracial economic cooperatives, including future SNCC leader Ella J. Baker, who at the time represented the Milk Cooperative in the Dunbar Apartments in Harlem.[71]

While members of the CWCRR took up this range of issues, partnerships between the NAACP and local churchwomen's organizations proved inconsistent. In Rochester, New York, for example, the local chapter of the NAACP requested that the Council of Church Women join their opposition to a contract to continue University of Rochester's Strong Memorial Hospital's oversight over the city's public municipal hospital. The NAACP contended that the University of Rochester's School of Medicine and hospital refused admittance to Black medical and nursing students. At their December 1937 meeting, the Executive Committee of the Council of Church Women voted to acknowledge receipt of the request but not to take a position on the issue.[72] While the minutes did not give the reason for the decision, Black council women who were also active in the NAACP remained committed to the churchwomen's organization.

Yet other local women's councils were far more proactive with regard to local civil rights issues. The Council of Church Women in Oakland, California, became one of the more consistently vocal organizations in large part because one of its Black members, Delilah L. Beasley, wrote a regular column for the *Oakland Tribune*.[73] Although Beasley was Catholic, she belonged to the Protestant Council as well as many other Black and interracial women's clubs in the Bay Area. After her untimely death in 1934, the president of the Council of Church Women wrote a letter to the editor of the *Tribune* endorsing Beasley's successor, Lena Wysninger, noting that the Council, "as a group of women deeply interested in bringing about such conditions in our city as shall make it a place where all people may find happiness," appreciated the column. "Your column is read by many of our church women and is sought for each week as a source of information for those items of National interest and importance."[74]

Beasley's advocacy had been the reason the Oakland Council had invited Black women to join a year after its founding in 1928.[75] As Beasley wrote in a December 1929 article, her "one object" in the column was to "create a better understanding between the races."[76] In April 1930, Beasley organized a "mass meeting" on race relations featuring Mrs. J. W. Emerick, the secretary of the Federal Council's Commission on International Justice and Good Will.[77] She was also elected to serve as the Council's chairwoman of race relations and international relations.[78] Until her death in 1934, Beasley publicized ecumenical Protestants' interracial work as a way to make the moral case for civil rights. For example, in November 1930, Beasley's column dedicated most of its words to the employment challenges faced by Black workers during the first year of the Great Depression, citing a statement from George Haynes of the Federal Council. She also reported on the recent meeting of the Council of Church Women at which she had spoken briefly about the upcoming exhibit of Black art sponsored by the Harmon Foundation.[79] It seems likely that Beasley also encouraged the Council to take a stand against a proposed state law to segregate public playgrounds and pools by limiting Black children's access to certain hours. To emphasize that White women also opposed the law, Beasley included a "(white)" after the Council of Church Women's name, even though the organization did include Black members like herself as well as Asian Americans. They declared it "un-Christian" and a "backward step" in race relations.[80] At one of her final Council meetings in February 1934, Beasley was unanimously reelected to her position as chairwoman, and in her column, she remarked on the large number of Black women in attendance. The

Council's president also recognized Beasley's important work toward the passage of a state anti-lynching law, while Beasley's own remarks focused on the anti-lynching Costigan-Wagner bill, a law drafted by the NAACP that was making its way through Congress.[81]

Back in New York, the CWCRR joined the NAACP and other civil rights groups to mobilize their constituency in support of the Costigan-Wagner bill. A federal lynching law had been a central concern of the committee from the start. The Church Women's Committee issued anti-lynching statements and sent telegrams to governors and other politicians when lynchings took place in their jurisdiction. The CWCRR endorsed the work of the Association of Southern Women for the Prevention of Lynching that the CIC's Jessie Daniel Ames had formed in 1930.[82] But the CWCRR would be more progressive on this issue than the White southerners when it came out strongly in support of the Costigan-Wagner anti-lynching bill in 1934–35. After earlier attempts to pass the Dyer anti-lynching bill had failed in the early 1920s, Black activists had renewed hope that the Roosevelt administration would be more supportive of federal anti-lynching legislation, especially given the support of many Black voters in his 1932 campaign. In 1934, New York Senator Robert F. Wagner and Colorado Senator Edward Costigan, both Democrats, co-sponsored a bill written largely by the NAACP. The bill redefined "mob" to mean only three to five people, it made local law enforcement officials who participated in lynchings subject to federal trials and prison, and it also offered compensation to families of lynching victims.

Opponents challenged the bill as an unconstitutional overreach of federal power, and in a shift that anticipated later opposition to federal civil rights laws, few White southerners attacked the bill with a defense of lynching but rather as a violation of state's rights. It was also a moment of political fracture as Democrats had sponsored the bill. In any case, Roosevelt refused to support the bill out of deference to his White southern Democrat allies and fears of losing White southerners' support in the 1936 election, and the much-discussed bill was never even brought up for a vote.[83] For churchwomen on the CWCRR and in some local councils, their campaign for the Costigan-Wagner bill alongside legislative items concerning disarmament and peace issues helped crystallize their moral politics. It also demonstrated how women who may have been reliably Republican as temperance voters did not operate primarily as partisans but rather as issues-oriented activists.[84]

First announced in 1934, the Costigan-Wagner bill was continually put off by Congress and would ultimately be withdrawn in early May 1935 after a filibuster led by southern Democrats. Throughout this period, the CWCRR sent out word for local churchwomen to write letters to their representatives and to otherwise make a moral argument on behalf of the bill in their communities. The filibuster's success was a blow, but Gardner had not given up entirely. When she prepared the CWCRR's May 1934 meeting minutes to be sent to committee members, she added a note to the top of the document: "We are counting on you to enthusiastically continue the fight for the anti-lynching bill," and she asked those receiving the minutes to "spread this information broadcast." At the May meeting, Gardner updated the CWCRR on its ongoing efforts to support the bill, including a few petitions sent to "key people" as well as a document that listed each senator and his current position. She had spent two days in Washington meeting with senators as well.[85] She also offered a succinct civics lesson, explaining that when Costigan had tried to introduce the bill for debate in April, "it was possible for a small group of Senators to prolong the discussion for seven days" during which its opponents tried to "adjourn the Senate, instead of recessing, thus displacing the bill." While four such efforts were defeated, the constant filibustering led a majority to vote to adjourn for a half hour on May 1, and the bill was moved to the end of the calendar. Gardner was disappointed, and she wrote that "many of us feel that if a few more Senators had held firm for a day or two longer the rising tide of displeasure in the South itself, as well as in other sections of the country, would have forced the opponents to stop their filibuster, or perhaps would have induced the president to say the long-hoped-for word in favor of the bill."[86]

While this version of the bill would not be reintroduced, Gardner remained hopeful, and she laid out the steps churchwomen should take. First, they should exert pressure on the president, and write to Roosevelt "expressing your deep disappointment that he has failed to speak out in favor of the bill." Second, she advised them to send letters to their senators and coached them on what to say depending on their position. For women writing to senators who had not backed the law,

Gardner suggested that an antagonistic stance be avoided and instead, the writer should "assume that they want to end lynching just as much as you do and let them know that you, your organization and thoughtful students of the subject all over the country are convinced that a federal law is imperative for this purpose." Those churchwomen who held leadership roles in other organizations should write to senators as well, although, Gardner cautioned, only national organizations or those with significant southern membership should write to the senators from the South.[87] In January 1935, Rochester's Council of Church Women took a vote in support of the Costigan-Wagner bill and wrote their legislators. Oakland's Council of Church Women, as noted, had been discussing the statute for many months earlier. Churchwomen once again took up the anti-lynching legislation cause in 1937 when yet another attempt was made in Congress by Wagner and Frederick Van Nuys from Indiana. An article in the *Church Woman* offered much the same action items as could be found in the NAACP's *Crisis*, including advice on what to write to senators to encourage them to stand up against a likely filibuster.[88]

By 1937, the leaders of the National Council of Federated Church Women were training the various legislative committees whether within a group like the CWCRR or a local church women's council to see themselves as essential to the preservation of democracy and as an important front against false propaganda. "We are living in a fearful time," and "we must determine to *know facts* to *face facts* and to *deal with facts* in the light of the ethical and religious teachings of Jesus and under the guidance of the Holy Spirit," wrote the leaders of the National Council's Department of Government. They offered tracts examining "Social Security Legislation" and "The Wagner-Steagall Housing Bill," both of which opened new ways for state legislatures to deny Black Americans federal aid. For their part, the churchwomen heading the Department of Government declared that churchwomen should be prepared to receive an "S.O.S." when "united action" was required. They would then proceed to "get information to the rank and file of church women," to make sure that women were warned "against 'wishful' thinking," to avoid "prejudice and hate," and to refuse "to be influenced by slogans or epithets."[89]

* * *

The Church Woman's Committee on Race Relations disbanded in 1942, and Katherine Gardner and other members would help to organize the Christian Social Relations department of the newly formed United Council for Church Women (UCCW).⁹⁰ At the inaugural meeting of the UCCW in December 1941, Christine Smith, the future president of the National Association of Colored Women and an AME leader, addressed the convention after being elected as one of the UCCW's vice presidents. In her speech, which was later printed in the *Church Woman*, she pointed out the inconsistencies between what she heard White women leaders say and what they did. As she addressed her mostly White audience, she reminded them that their own policy was "to work *with* and not *for* people." Smith told the audience about the condescending attitudes and the hypocrisy she had experienced firsthand, and she then asked the audience: "I wonder if the women of the United Council of Church Women have backbone enough to return to their communities and put into action the many fine statements that have been made in all these conferences."⁹¹ After Smith left the podium, the UCCW's White president, Amy Welcher, declared that it was "a shame it was the negro [sic] who said it, and not the white." Welcher then pivoted away from the substance of Smith's comments and refocused the mostly White audience on their moral failings and their need to repent. Welcher also paused the meeting for the singing of two hymns and a "most effective fervent prayer."⁹²

Smith's political point became Welcher's opportunity for a soul-searching reflection. Like other White racial liberals, White churchwomen called out racist practices, primarily when they affected middle-class Blacks, and they acknowledged their complicity. But at the same time, White churchwomen involved in interracial projects sought to protect themselves from what they saw as overly harsh criticism. They excluded so-called radicals who found fault in the patronizing tone of White liberals and instead looked for Black allies whom they believed would address racism "without rancor or bitterness."⁹³

The Protestant interracial movement begun in the 1920s and focused on practices like integrated committees and interracial prayer services had grown into a central concern of organized Protestant women. The missionary origins of White women's part in interracial cooperation grew more subtle over time. Many White women had initially found spiritual meaning in the thrill of meeting with Black women in the 1920s and 1930s and described their participation as evidence of their modern and liberal attitude. Black women had approached interracial work more as a means to an end as they explained to White women the value of gaining White churchwomen's moral support for policy demands and civil rights legislation. These dynamics did not fully disappear in the liberal antiracism of the UCCW even as the organization's leaders joined a broader coalition of similar groups focused on institutionalizing racial liberalism in the Cold War era. Liberal Protestants would link the religious freedom developing in the National Conference of Christians and Jews and racial liberalism as they defended what they often explained as the Christian basis for American democracy against fascism and communism. White and Black ecumenical Protestants made a moral case for postwar American power even as they also rendered judgment on what they saw as its moral lapses. Like the Christian imperial feminism of the early twentieth century that wanted to unify Christian and American empires, churchwomen who envisioned themselves as Christian citizens and world citizens would mobilize behind a Pax Americana they believed could create a Christian world order.

6

Christian Citizens, World Citizens

Before the 1944 election, the editors of the *Church Woman* took advantage of recent polling data suggesting that this would be the first election in US history with a majority of women voters. The September issue of the magazine was focused on "Christian citizenship." In her article on the topic, Indianapolis churchwoman Mabel Jordan Hudelson wrote that churchwomen's priorities were "world cooperation and interracial relations," and she implored Protestant women to study the platforms of both parties and educate themselves about individual candidates. She asked, "Was ever a graver responsibility placed on womanhood, especially on Christian womanhood?"[1] In the November *Church Woman*, Millicent Foster argued that churchwomen must vote to compensate for the fact that Protestants voted less than any other religious group. The Denver National Research Center's recent poll showed that only 66 percent of Protestants voted compared to 84 percent of Jews, 72 percent of Catholics, and 67 percent of "non-church members." Churchwomen showed "unflagging devotion" to their churches, but too many of "these consecrated women have not seen that Christian citizenship is another way to carry out the works which must be combined with their faith."[2] Both Hudelson and Foster used "Christian citizenship" and the relatively new phenomenon of polling data to mobilize churchwomen to take political action and to make them feel united as a political constituency.[3] Foster borrowed from the tenets of White women's Christian imperial feminism when she urged all churchwomen to see themselves as responsible for managing Christian social and world relations. She concluded, "the leadership in the country cannot succeed without the stabilizing and energizing work of the women of conviction." By informed voting and political activism, they would "bring to actuality the new world in which the Christian criterion will more nearly coincide with the public life."[4]

White Protestant women were not the first nor the last to describe themselves as "Christian citizens." Protestants of different political stripes and in different eras have deployed the term to underscore their belief that Christianity ensured the creation of virtuous citizens that made democracy possible.[5] The White Protestant leaders of the UCCW encountered the appeal of Christian citizenship most often in the campaign for woman suffrage and in the women's peace movement. In many cases, these advocates of Christian citizenship implicitly or openly called for educated and middle-class White Protestant women's votes to protect the White nation from anti-temperance Catholics, racialized immigrants, and Black men.[6] To this end, White suffragist leaders were ambivalent and often opposed to Black and colonized women's voting rights. Yet Black Protestant women also developed related but distinct ideas of Christian citizenship within the temperance and peace movements that stressed Black women's suffrage as critical to securing Black enfranchisement and broader civil rights.[7] It would be Black women like the UCCW's vice president Christine Smith and UCCW staffer Louise Young and others on the Church Woman's Committee on Race Relations who asserted their civil rights–oriented religious politics into the UCCW's conception of Christian citizenship of the UCCW.

Additionally, these ecumenical Protestants' envisioning of a postwar Christian world order imagined women's Christian citizenship beyond the nation. Christian citizenship preserved some aspects of White Protestant women's Christian imperial feminism while broadening the constituency of Protestant women that the UCCW's White leaders considered qualified to create and manage this Christian world order. In the discourse and practices of Christian citizenship, organized Protestant women helped shape a postwar liberal politics supportive of civil rights, women's rights, and human rights that they attributed to their Protestant Christianity.

Protestant women's conception of Christian citizenship operated in two registers. First, Protestant women employed "Christian citizenship" as a unifying discourse to foster a sense of shared identity and political unity among Black and White Protestant women in the United States while also rendering them members of a larger global Protestantism. As Christian citizens, churchwomen interpreted voting and other political activism as a cosmopolitan religious practice that would strengthen their sense of collectivity and direct churchwomen to bring about the kingdom of God. The malleability of Christian citizenship also enabled them to imagine themselves as citizens of the nation, the world, and a sacred Christian community. Along with ecumenical Protestant men, Protestant women imagined Christianity as "a form of unity independent of the nation-state system with its own nonstate ways of relating people to one another," a feature of what historian Gene Zubovich calls "Protestant globalism."[8] Protestant women's task as Christian citizens was to bring that Christian community into alignment with the earthly world as much as possible, and they saw this as their goal when they supported the League of Nations and the World Court, the United Nations, and campaigns for civil rights, and human rights. They also continued to call attention to the educational and professional achievements of women around the world, including women's ordination to the ministry, a feature of the UCCW that connected this interracial organization to the Christian imperial feminism of the missionary movement. In most cases, their advocacy for a *Christian* world order was identical to liberal imaginings of a postwar internationalism overseen by the United States. Yet their persistent anti-militarism would on occasion make churchwomen into sharp critics of US foreign policy, although those moral arguments had far less success than their more frequent efforts to incorporate the history of benevolent Protestant missions into justifications for beneficent US power.

The second register of Christian citizenship takes inspiration from Lauren Berlant's analysis of early twentieth-century women's political culture as an "intimate public." What was the affective character of the community produced through the idea of Christian citizenship, and how did it shape churchwomen's religious politics? Missionary literature and rituals mediated how organized Protestant women in the United States and around the world formed an intimate public. In most cases they were "strangers" to one another, but in different ways, they believed themselves to be "emotionally literate in each other's experience of power, intimacy, desire, and discontent."[9] White women "knew" others through missionary literature, while Protestant women on the other side of missionary institutions also "knew" their would-be benefactors. Protestant women grappled with the tension between hierarchical missionary power dynamics and a common identity as Christian citizens in juxtapolitical spaces. By focusing on the World Day of Prayer services written during World War II, the 1944 biennial Assembly of the UCCW, as well as a wartime pageant written by Chinese Protestant women, we can see the variety of religious feelings that Protestant women brought to their political activism. These and other examples illustrate how Protestant women believed that the righteous politics of Christian citizenship were not only based on studying the facts and practical strategies but by producing the right kinds of emotions. The UCCW's formation in December 1941 and the despair of the war years were always paired with the hope that women Christian citizens could transform the world. This was the attitude on display at the 1944 UCCW Assembly when the Los Angeles Council of Church Women asked: "Can women prevent a third world war?" Their answer: "We can IF!"[10]

From Prohibition to Peace

In the early 1920s, the twin victories of the Eighteenth and Nineteenth Amendments reoriented White Protestant women's political activism from an intensive focus on temperance and, for many, woman suffrage to Christian internationalism. In 1915, the Baptist and ecumenical foreign missionary leader Lucy Peabody launched the Christian Woman's Peace Movement as a corollary to the more radical Woman's Peace Party that would become the US branch of the Woman's International League for Peace and Freedom following the war.[11] In the early 1920s, both the Federation of Woman's Boards of Foreign Missions and the Council of Women for Home Missions became institutional members of the National Conference on the Cause and Cure of War (NCCCW). While still invested in bolstering "law enforcement" when it came to Prohibition, White Protestant women made Christian internationalism a political priority.

Christian internationalism and the later World Order Movement both describe how ecumenical Protestants developed an ethics of international relations and a way to bring a Christian influence to bear on a bourgeoning "foreign policy public." As historian Michael Thompson explains, Christian internationalists believed a universal Christianity must serve as "a check against nationalism rather than a boon for it," and they lobbied politicians and sought to educate Americans to support internationalist institutions like the League of Nations and the World Court.[12] They also presented Christian internationalism as the eventual replacement for European and US imperialism, and they envisioned a colonial Protestant elite guiding their gradually independent nations into cooperative relationships with their former colonizers. Although White ecumenical Protestants in the United States proved strong critics of empire—and especially European imperialism—and White supremacist racial segregation, they could also be critical of non-White nationalist movements that they interpreted as opposed to "cooperation." Their Christian internationalism and their later articulation of a Christian world order was in competition against older empires, White ethnonationalism, and some radical anti-colonial movements alike.[13]

For White Protestant women, Christian internationalism formed in practices that reshaped the Christian imperial feminism of the missionary movement into a vision of "world friendship." These practices often replicated rather than reassessed the racial imperialism of the missionary movement. One of the more well-known cosmopolitan practices was a doll exchange program with Japan. In the mid-1920s, Lucy Peabody and other national missionary leaders set up the Committee on World Friendship Among Children within the Federal Council of Churches' Commission on International Justice and Goodwill. Peabody organized annual gift-giving projects, and in some cases, gift exchanges. After the passage of the restrictive 1924 Immigration Act, Peabody and the Commission's chairman, Sidney Gulick, worked with Japanese Christians in Japan to organize an exchange of "friendship dolls" between the two countries to foster goodwill. As historian Rui Kohiuama has argued, the American dolls also became a relatively inexpensive stand-in for human missionaries at a time when the women's missions boards faced declining budgets. The materiality of the dolls enabled American churchwomen to have a tangible sense of the abstract ideals of Christian internationalism and the new missionary motto, "World Friendship." Foreign missions, humanitarian aid, and friendship were all tied together with the Christian vision of internationalism and US foreign policy. Other projects followed the doll exchange, including sending schoolbags to Mexican children and "treasure chests" with toys to the Philippines.[14] Notably, in Rochester, New York, the World Friendship projects fell to the Council of Church Women's Legislative Department rather than the Missions Department, and the chairwoman reported that the most recent collection of school supplies to send to Mexico was "convincing us that Rochester folks have a truly Christian International consciousness."[15]

Churchwomen also attended carefully to foreign policy debates taking place at the national level. The Rochester Council of Church Women's Legislative Department kept members informed on issues of local governance as well as domestic and foreign policies. The chairwomen updated members on anti–child labor laws, the enforcement of Prohibition, and good governance, in the 1920s, and the Legislative Department also tracked interwar disarmament conferences and lobbied for the Senate to ratify the United States' membership in the League of Nations and the World Court. Like others in the women's peace movement, they also strongly endorsed the quixotic Kellogg-Briand Pact that outlawed war, a campaign that, historians note, mirrored the earlier temperance campaign to outlaw liquor.[16] It is also notable that they gave little to no consideration to American colonies in their conception of "internationalism." The work of the Legislative Department often overlapped with the activities of the Missions, and, newly created in the 1930s, the International Relations and Race Relations departments. The fluid categorization of internationalist concerns illustrates how these issues could be used to connect seemingly different spheres of churchwomen's interests. In the late 1930s, foreign and domestic policies would be combined as churchwomen's councils created new departments of Christian Citizenship. In Rochester, Mabel Mangano served as the first chairwoman of International Relations even though her background was in home missions. The White Baptist had been raised in Connecticut and attended Vassar, and after college, she worked as a home missionary to Italians in Brooklyn, where she met and married Antonio Mangano, an Italian immigrant and Baptist convert who taught in the Italian Department of Rochester-Colgate Theological Seminary. After Mangano moved back to New York City, the White Presbyterian Ida Post (Mrs. Walter Post) took over the International Relations Department. Post was also active in many of the city's peace and civil rights organizations and was instrumental in ensuring that political issues were included on the Council's agenda.[17]

In their work for the Council's Legislative and International Relations Departments, Mangano and Post elaborated on "Christian citizenship" as it was being discussed in missionary literature and at White churchwomen's national meetings. Of course, as temperance women and suffragists, most churchwomen were not political novices, but Mangano and Post would ask them to see foreign policy as a woman's issue and a Christian issue. This shift could be seen in the 1921 United Mission Study textbook, *The Kingdom and the Nations* by Eric North. Perhaps reflecting North's limited understanding of White Protestant women's pre-suffrage political activism, he urged the "missionary-minded women of America" to do more than simply raise money for missionary salaries. They needed to use their newly granted right to vote to elect peace-minded representatives and to recognize that they "are part of the public that expresses 'public sentiment.'" North explained that "opinions are made, confirmed, or changed in ordinary conversation," and it was a simple matter to "assist the expression of sound opinion" by speaking up when others besmirched other countries or "the foreigners who live among us" and to write to newspapers to correct the record when "speeches of your local politicians are prejudiced or misrepresent the facts." Women could also write to their senators, especially those serving on the Committee on Foreign Relations, to "block un-Christian proposals relating to foreigners and foreign affairs."[18]

Churchwomen viewed their ecumenical women's councils as a hub in an expansive network of Protestant women, and they engaged in the kinds of political activism North proposed. In 1928, Ida Post described the Legislative Committee that she chaired as "a political centralization terminus for Civic activity and legislative service." She recruited "key women" who were leaders in their churches and in other community organizations to be members, and she praised them for shaping "public opinion" by "disseminating their influence to interest other women."[19] The International Relations Department of the National Council of Federated Church Women distributed similar guidelines to other local councils in the early 1930s. Churchwomen should "become intelligent as to the world situation" in order to generate "the Will to Peace" in their communities. They should train women to "take [their] right place" as advocates for peace in their churches and other women's organizations. They should also each send delegates to the annual meetings of the National Conference on the Cause and Cure of War.[20]

As Christian citizens, Rochester's churchwomen sent telegrams, organized letter-writing campaigns, and otherwise weighed in on policies being debated in Washington. For example, in February 1928, the Council called a special meeting to discuss a request from the Federal Council's S. Parkes Cadman concerning a bill to allocate more money to the construction of naval ships. After discussion, those attending the special meeting voted in support of sending a telegram, noting that "this movement on part of U.S. would make disarmament an utter impossibility." They also voted to send copies of their telegram to other women's clubs in town and to the Council of Jewish Women.[21] Newspapers reported on the wave of telegrams and letters from "bombarding pacifists" that poured into congressional mailboxes in February, giving churchwomen, among others, a sense of their political import.[22] The House's Naval Committee drastically reduced the number of requested new vessels from seventy-one to fifteen, though this move was less a result of the pacifist petitioners and more due to the fact that Great Britain had stopped production of its own shipbuilding program.[23]

Organized Protestant women's political activism ranged from the more traditional feminine modes of politics like petitions and education to grassroots voter mobilization campaigns. As Christian citizens, they saw it as their duty to educate voters. In 1932, Rochester's International Relations department distributed "many hundred pieces of literature" and the chairwoman and vice-chairwoman gave a total of sixty-one talks around Monroe County on topics like "Peace, Disarmament and International Affairs."[24] The Council's literature and programming associated internationalism and anti-militarism with the city's respectable Protestant women. In 1936, Rochester's churchwomen also organized a "get out the Christian vote" campaign. The new head of the Legislative Department, Mrs. Scott E. Lyon, had made posters listing the names of all of the previous year's voters (names that willing Protestant churches apparently had supplied). Hung in stores and churches around the city, the posters were meant to encourage churchgoers to vote. Lyon was aware that this was a controversial idea, but she defended the project by contextualizing it in the prophetic books of the Bible. Since "the very beginning, religion and politics have been extricably [sic] mixed," she wrote in her annual report. The prophets had interpreted God's will "in terms of political and social order" that was "founded upon justice, and righteousness," and she argued that Christian citizens now also must see God's imminent presence in the structures of society.[25]

In the two decades before the United Council of Church Women formed in 1941, missionary and churchwomen had worked out a relationship between personal faith and social and political activism that was exemplified in the concept of Christian citizenship. *Church Woman* columnist, Jean Beaven Abernethy, addressed this topic by comparing Christian citizenship and its related religious politics with "Humanism." The humanist argued that changing the world did not require something "outside of and beyond ourselves." Humanists dismissed "such ideas as supernatural nonsense" and argued that "revealed religion cannot satisfy intelligent people today." Yet Abernethy defended revealed religion as important for the "modern woman" and as necessary for any kind of social change. She concluded that people required a "functioning personal faith in a power greater than us humans, either individually or collectively, if we are ever going to change or transform the world."[26] If organized Protestant women shifted away from evangelical missions and the Christian imperial feminist project of emancipating women by spreading Christian civilization, they remained committed to the missionary objective of Christianizing the world through their political activism.

From Failure to a Christian World Order

In November 1939, the National Committee of Church Women released a statement acknowledging the "failure" of the League of Nations and other international measures to prevent war. Throughout the past several years, many articles had appeared in the *Church Woman* addressing the alarming rise of National Socialism in Germany and describing terrifying accounts of the Japanese invasion of China. Ecumenical Protestants who had committed themselves to peace and Christian internationalism had split into the idealistic pacifism of most Federal Council leaders and Union Seminary professor Reinhold Niebuhr's interventionist Christian realism. Organized Protestant women remained committed to the Cause and Cure of War conference and its statements that the United States should remain neutral.[27] On behalf of the Protestant women's organizations on the cusp of forming the UCCW, the *Church Woman* published a list of "imperatives" that instead directed churchwomen to "pray without ceasing and in all prayer be free from hatred or from prejudice against any people," especially their enemies or those perceived as such. The statement also called on churchwomen to support refugees and less restrictive immigration policies, to oppose any who sought to profit from the war, and to ensure that their own communities were "free from all racial discrimination" since the local community served as "a laboratory for building a Christian democracy." Local churchwomen were also advised to think ahead. Believing that this war would be different from the last one, they must "commit ourselves to the task of urging the American people to accept their responsibility as citizens of the world to build anew a society of nations and share in the obligations which accompany membership in an international organization."[28]

One of the more heated moral and strategic debates between pacifists and realists took place in 1940–1941 on the question of whether the United States should violate the British blockade and send food relief to civilians in Nazi-occupied Europe that winter in a plan proposed by former president Herbert Hoover.[29] Accounts of starving women and children were pitted against claims that the relief brought by the supplies might quell any internal uprisings against the Nazi regime. The editors of *The Church Woman* printed articles on both sides of the debate with the introductory note "the Christian citizen will have to decide."[30] The English pacifist Muriel Lester urged American women to support relief aid to Europe. "Women are the practical half of the human race," she wrote, and women "want children to live and not to die." Women could act as voters, and "can speak about food ships wherever we go. We can put notices in shops, announcements in churches, schools, and colleges. We can present the idea at clubs, put it before labor unions."[31] Lester paired what she presented as women's innate sympathies for other women and children with a practical program of mobilization. Henry P. Van Dusen, a theology professor at Union Theological Seminar, strongly opposed the relief plan. His article, "Food or Freedom," drew from joint statements of other ecumenical Protestant leaders. While recognizing that this choice was a "dilemma of heart-searching difficulty" for Christians, Van Dusen urged Christians to secure other means of aid to these "needy peoples" that would not prolong the war and "their present sufferings by strengthening their oppressors."[32]

The circumstances that led to these "both sides" articles tell a more complicated story of where churchwomen's sympathies rested. The decision to publish Lester's article fostered a sense of distinctive feminine

Protestant politics that differentiated churchwomen from ecumenical men like Van Dusen. As Susannah Crowe, the editor of the *Church Woman*, later recounted, it had been "one of the high moments for the magazine." The article reflected the *Church Woman* committeewomen's decision that "we as Christian women should continue to love our 'enemies of war and advocated the feeding of women and children during the war period.'" Before they went to press, however, "leading churchmen" wrote to Crowe "begging" the editors not to take this position, as it would "sever the unity of the church and certainly ruin the circulation of the magazine." Crowe refused and, with the support of the oversight committee, they decided that Lester's article expressed a "Christian principle and we dare not be false to it." She did, however, agree to run an article explaining the anti-aid position in the same issue. In the end, it was a moral victory that put churchwomen in the forefront of the shifting opinions about peace and war relief. Ever eager to impress their secular peers, Crowe wrote that "later other far better known magazines came out advocating the same thing but it was THE CHURCH WOMAN which had fearlessness [sic] lead out in an unpopular cause—and instead of hurting the circulation, we had dozens and dozens of letters from women across the country who said in effect 'Thank God that one magazine dares to stand for the right.'"[33] In the December 1940 issue, the editors included a number of articles for women to read as they studied this question, along with a note from Lester: "Perhaps women really are going to begin to stand up to the 'old guard' in church leadership. . . . Maybe we will take our stand on this. Thrilling!"[34]

In the years before the United States entered the war, churchwomen extended their interwar activism into new and pressing areas. The *Church Woman* printed articles calling for readers to mobilize on behalf of legislation permitting more refugees entry into the United States and for women to organize aid efforts in their communities.[35] The *Church Woman* also published numerous articles warning against propaganda stoking antisemitism and ran articles condemning Japanese internment.[36] At its January 1941 meeting, the National Committee of Church Women comprised of representatives from the three Protestant women's organizations heard from Elinor Purvis, the chairwoman of the Committee on International Relations. She listed one of the committee's purposes as providing literature and other materials that would "help church women to cultivate attitudes of mind which are in accordance with the principles of the Christian faith upon the acceptance of which the ultimate peace of the world depends." Further, she sought to teach churchwomen that "the missionary task of the church and the cause of world peace are so closely related" that they were effectively "two phases of the one great task of bringing the kingdom of God to earth."[37] The National Committee sent delegates to the February 1940 Conference on the Churches and International Situation organized by the Federal Council's Department of International Justice and Goodwill, where they weighed in on immediate matters ranging from supporting conscientious objectors to more long-term issues for building a "Christian world order." The latter demanded the "curtailment of national sovereignty" and Protestants who belonged to churches that "transcend national frontiers" were well-suited to help Americans come to see that their "loyalties" were to "the whole number of the children of our Heavenly Father."[38] Yet the question of the United States' obligations to the war fronts in Europe and Asia loomed. The National Conference on the Cause and Cure of War cancelled their usual January meeting in 1941, and the *Church Woman* continued to advocate for the United States to work with other nations to mediate an end to the war and to develop a plan for a postwar world order.[39]

By October 1941, however, the United States' entry into the war was a question of if rather than when, and Protestant women prepared to do their part in a war they had prayed to avoid. More than a hundred churchwomen met at a conference on "Church Women in the Emergency" in New York City. Organized by the Women's Cooperating Commission of the Federal Council of Churches, the conference's speakers discussed military chaplains, conscientious objectors, and the social changes taking place due to military mobilization. The organizers emphasized that "arms alone are not enough to beat Hitler" or to "defend our nation." The press release announcing the conference explained, "there can be no victory over oppression unless the spiritual resources of the people are equal to the task of preserving democratic institutions in the midst of emergency measures, moral objectives in the midst of war efforts."[40] Churchwomen had come to agree that their missionary goals were one and the same as building a Christian world order, a point that speakers at this meeting drove home. Theologian Georgia Harkness insisted that Protestant women must play a key part in wartime work at home and postwar planning. This work could not be left "to the Women's Club, or some propagandist secular agency" who might "provide all the education the community gets on international relations, labor conditions, trade unions, social security, cooperation, public health, housing." Harkness was surely preaching to the choir when she told her audience of organized Protestant women that "Christian work ought to be more social, and social work more Christian," and "to bring this about is part of our job as church women."[41]

In December 1941, Protestant women on the National Committee of Church Women formally established the United Council of Church Women at a meeting in Atlantic City. The organization grew out of years of meetings and negotiations, and the new president, Amy Welcher, wrote that it was the "result of consecrated thought and study, of unselfishness and a deep devotion to that which is greater than any one of us or any one of our fine societies." Cognizant of the meeting's unexpected timing, she asked if "future historians" would note that this momentous event took place the same week that the United States entered the war, hoping that they would show how the "spirit of the church women of the United States" who made the UCCW would make their organization "an instrument of the Spirit of Christ in the world."[42] Whether or not Welcher felt that the UCCW lived up to her vision, the war and ecumenical Protestants' concurrent imagining of a Christian world order had a profound effect on shaping how organized Protestant women understood themselves. The early UCCW Assemblies, the wartime World Day of Prayer services, and a pageant written by Chinese Protestant women demonstrate how the feelings of despair and hope mingled in the religious lives of Protestant women as politics structured their cosmopolitan practices.

Juxtapolitical Practices: Prayer, Conferences, and a Pageant

The persistence and reformulation of White women's Christian imperial feminism into Christian citizenship could be seen in the UCCW's practices. In contrast to their more direct politicking, practices like the annual World Day of Prayer services and the UCCW's biyearly Assemblies allowed Protestant women to imagine and enact an idealized

Christian world order among themselves. These practices honed a common sense of Protestant womanhood largely defined by White women (but not always uncontested) at the same time that they displayed Protestant Christianity's racial and national diversity. Through these practices, churchwomen took on the same political questions debated in the *Church Woman* and in local councils, but rather than seeking specific answers, they instead became outlets for expressing a host of political feelings. In these practices, churchwomen drew on feminized emotions of motherhood and a universalizing feeling of shared womanhood, as well as on the familiar iconography of Christian cosmopolitanism that had been formulated in missionary pageants for decades. They combined these emotional resonances with a missionary past and women's new forward-facing and unified Protestant project to create a new world.

As the war escalated in Europe and Asia, the World Day of Prayer committee worked harder to integrate current events into the service and to consider new ways that prayer addressed global politics.[43] The prayer service, held on the first Friday of Lent each year, went back decades to the White women's foreign missionary movement. The first *World* Day of Prayer, as the Day of Prayer for Missions was renamed in 1926, took place in 1927. In the 1920s and 1930s, the popular event had motivated local Protestant women to organize ecumenical committees that often laid the groundwork for more regularized churchwomen's councils. The service's liturgy that was often prepared by non-US women also reflected the broadening sense of international Protestant womanhood. In 1930, the service was written by Helen Kim, a Korean national who was a student in the United States at the time. Throughout the 1930s, the committee commissioned liturgies from women from China, Chile, Holland, South Africa, New Zealand, and England. While the service themes were taken from the Bible, current politics often played a direct role in the service in the prayers for peace, for morally righteous governments, for just race relations, and for a more equitable society.[44]

The chairwoman of the World Day of Prayer Committee in the 1940s was a White Baptist, Margaret Applegarth. Applegarth rightly predicted that there would be greater interest in the World Day of Prayer as American Protestants uninterested in the foreign missionary movement suddenly found themselves thinking about "the world." In 1944, she wrote, "in the good old days . . . the world had a certain medieval flatness for many of us, but nowadays, this flatness is bulging up to global proportions so vaulting and alarming that whole families, even on the most isolated farms in America," had begun to put "a finger on the globe in eager, anxious prayer."[45] New opportunities to expand the event appeared as well. During the war, secular (if largely White Protestant) women's organizations like the Junior League and General Federation of Women's Clubs had become interested in participating in WDP services. In some cities, the World Day of Prayer had become an opportunity for interfaith gatherings that expressed the wartime feeling that the United States' racial and religious tolerance is what differentiated it from the Axis powers. At a 1943 service in Cincinnati, 1,500 people reportedly attended, and the women ushers included "Negroes, Jews, and other church women." The choir was "interracial and interfaith." Other services that had participation from non-White Protestants continued the missionary tradition of pageantry. In Washington, DC, that year, one service included "a Seneca Indian of the Iroquois tribe, the Chinese wife of a Chinese minister, and a Negro woman from the Juvenile Court Staff" in a dramatic presentation. In Columbus, Ohio, the ushers wore "costumes of other nations—China, Korea, India, with three Scandinavian women in Danish, Swedish, and Norwegian dress." These women found in the World Day of Prayer a response to what they experienced as "a constant 'pull' toward the ends of the earth," Applegarth noted, a feeling that she believed "should be broadened into the spiritual realm also."[46] A prayer service could "haunt the memory," she wrote, and when it combined "spiritual beauty and stern facts," a ritual might "form a new opinion" by "erasing old prejudice."[47]

For Protestant women, prayer must lead to social and political activism to be meaningful in the world. In one of her regular columns for the *Church Woman*, Jean Beaven Abernethy explained that prayer was "a supplement, not a substitute for, our action," and she told women that "we must think more in terms of asking God to help us see clearly **what we should** do, and how we should do it, rather than of asking Him to do it Himself." She observed that it was "easy" and even "presumptuous" for Christians to take "five minutes off every day to ask God to do certain things—to bring peace on earth, for example, or to help a person in sorrow." Instead of praying for a list of demands, or "telling God what to do," Abernethy argued that prayer was a way to bring "us under His inspiration in order that **we may do**."[48] Along these lines, the World Day of Prayer services articulated multiple relationships between prayer and action that would come to define the motto of the UCCW: informed prayer and prayerful action. Applegarth also believed that conceptualized prayer was a form of spiritual discipline and a way to broadcast one's values to an outside audience. Through praying at a publicized event like the WDP, women "discipline ourselves into neither hurting nor hating nor discrediting anyone on earth," a practice that would lead women to be living examples. "Everyone," she wrote, "sees that our religion is world loyalty."[49]

Prayer could also generate feelings of community and connection across distances. The World Day of Prayer chairwomen often stressed the fact that women around the world prayed together in their different languages beginning in New Zealand and spreading from time zone to time zone as the earth turned. In looking at prayer through this lens, the committeewomen described prayer not only in terms of motivating women to act or to be exemplary Christian citizens, but as producing mystical bonds of sympathy and spirituality. As an example, a 1942 radio program aimed at rural audiences guided the listeners through the difficult circumstances facing farmers in other countries, including war-torn Russia, China, and Eastern Europe. Then, the narrator switched to the second person and coached the listener through the proper physiological and emotional responses she experienced as she heard these stories. "Suddenly your heart widens hospitably with a new concern and a deep tenderness for all these unknown women who must shoulder such tragic burdens of sowing and weeding and reaping . . . your heart sends up an instant prayer." The script then explained the transcendent power of prayer. While warring nations erected barriers between God's people, "a volume of prayers" moved "over every borderline and over every national boundary—without passport or visa." Prayer was an "instant tie" that bound "us all together with that Eternal Spirit to whom there is neither time nor space, neither east nor west."[50] Indeed, in other WDP materials, prayer itself was compared to radio waves. The prayers that went up into the air as thousands of people listened simultaneously to radio broadcasts could be described as "a story of the mingling of prayer and other waves." On the Day of Prayer, wrote committeewoman Myrta

Ross, "the very air was saturated with the earnest petitions of Christian women around the world."[51] Margaret Applegarth presented prayer as a positive energy that replaced the negative news usually transmitted over the air. On one day a year, the World Day of Prayer replaced the usual "malice and misery beyond belief" into "something more deliberately mystical" that "fills the air of 51 different countries with hope for tomorrow."[52]

On a more terrestrial level, Protestant women imported the aesthetics and materiality of missionary pageants into their prayer services. Interracial prayer services were seen as a microcosm of the diversity of world Christianity: The congregation became "the Kingdom in miniature."[53] Many liturgies included a short dramatic skit or had other suggestions about using international flags or costumes during the service. More broadly, the World Day of Prayer committee put out an annual booklet, the "Account of Observances," that compiled short descriptions of the services across the United States and around the world. The Account of Observances' lists produced a sense of community in print, and the narration of these local services also highlighted the kinds of cosmopolitan expressions that the White American women on the committee valued. In some cases, the Account of Observances was turned into a part of the World Day of Prayer liturgy. At one 1945 service, the local planners had women in each pew represent a different country, and at the appointed time in the service, each row stood up, lit a candle, and then read in unison from the "Account of Observances" about the WDP observances in "their" country.[54] A Chicagoan reported that she had found a similar ritual to be deeply moving, writing that she had "never felt such a strong sense of *belonging* to a world-wide church family as in that stirring roll-call of the nations."[55] Additionally, maps, globes, candles, and flags became ritual elements and symbols of the world community during the service. At a service in Indiana, as the descriptions of the "four needy areas of the world (Migrants, Service Men, War Torn Areas, New Missionaries)," were read aloud, a woman lit "four candles around the globe" to direct the participants' prayers and to symbolize the light that their humanitarian donations would bring to each problem.[56]

The existential crisis of the Second World War amplified the poignancy of the World Day of Prayer for many American women, and it also tested their commitment to the kingdom of God as they had to find a way to pray for their enemies. Missionary reports about prayer services held in war-torn regions affirmed readers' understanding of the spiritual power of the WDP while also urging Protestant women to be agents of peace. An article on the 1937 WDP service in Shanghai pointed out that the service "was filled with women whose faces proclaimed that they were of many nations." Chinese women, Koreans, Indians, Germans, Russians, Dutch, Swiss, Americans, and Britons worshiped together. "We sang the hymns together, each in her own tongue, and this unique experience in a city set in the midst of nations fired our spirits with new purpose and filled us with new strength."[57] Similarly, a story about Chinese and Japanese women ushering together at a service in Oakland demonstrated how the "dire conflict between their peoples" did not prevent Christian fellowship.[58] The author of the 1943 service, Georgia Harkness, contemplated the problem of "how to pray in wartime without praying against our fellow-Christians." By including a prayer from the Japanese Christian leader, Toyohito Kagawa, alongside much older prayers from Wesley, Luther, and the Book of Common Prayer, Harkness illustrated her conclusion that a "service of world prayer ought to transcend both time and space."[59]

The wartime anxieties of affluent White American Protestants were on full display in the liturgical drama of the wartime prayer services. When the World Day of Prayer committee met to read and edit the 1942 prayer service, several women complained that the draft of the service had no "climax," and Florence Tyler worried that the service "did not 'hurt' enough."[60] Entitled "I Am The Way," the 1942 liturgy guided participants through the many ways of following Christ. The final draft of the service provides an example of how World Day of Prayer liturgies were written to invoke emotions like guilt, shame, and fear in addition to the soaring feelings of fellowship and belonging. The service began with a note explaining that it was different from those of past years because of the frequency of periods of silence. Silence would help "in opening our wills to His will," wrote Applegarth in the introductory note, and "any group feeling restless under such silence is in all the deeper need of learning that the real beauty and usefulness of prayer lies in *listening*." After an opening Quaker prayer inviting participants to open their hearts "to realize the Divine Presence," the leader continued, let us "stretch our imaginations to the ends of the earth to take in those other groups of women who, even as we slept, were gathered together in prayer.... Conscious of oneness, whatever our nation or race, let us ask the blessing of God upon this day of prayer." The service then progressed through a number of different "Ways" to reach out to God—"The Way Men Have Lost" included the confession and "The Way Back to God" entailed prayers for forgiveness. The third segment, "The Way of Self-Surrender," began with the hymn, "O Sacred Head Now Wounded," set to J. S. Bach's mournful chorale.[61]

From the seasonal Lenten meditation on Christ's crucifixion and broken body—a body that also represented the broken church and the war-torn world—the service then moved toward a ritual of reconciliation and healing. The intercessory prayers during "The Way of Peace" included prayers for both the aggressors and victims of war, "for those who are consumed in mutual hatred and bitterness" and "for those who groan under cruelty and subjection." A poem from Georgia Harkness served as the main feature for the next section, "The Way of Love." Notably, one woman on the planning committee had wanted to remove this poem in the versions of the service sent abroad because she thought it to be "too dangerous politically." In four verses, Harkness contrasted the life of a person living in comfort with images of starving, homeless, and dead children. Ultimately, the poem ends with the startling claim that only those who truly suffer from hunger, deprivation, and persecution can really understand Christianity. From this place of unease (especially among the worshippers who had not faced acute suffering), participants then recited St. Francis's prayer, a prayer that offered them another spiritual path instead of suffering—a path that called them to serve others. "Grant that I may not so much seek to be consoled as to console . . . for it is in giving that we receive, it is in pardoning that we are pardoned, it is in dying that we are born to Eternal Life." At this point, the ushers passed the collection plate. The ecumenical prayer services never included a communion rite, but in the 1942 service, the offering ritual became the service's ceremonial sacrifice. Instead of affirming their membership in the body of Christ through taking communion, women ritually bound the wounds of a broken world through the act of sacrificing money that would connect them to others. Finally, the service led the attendees out of their despair as it concluded with a millennial vision of the coming Kingdom of God through prayers about love and Christian unity in sections entitled "The Way of Light" and "The Way of Power."[62]

While most Protestant women could attend a local World Day of Prayer service and feel themselves a part of this wider unseen community, far fewer were able to attend the UCCW's first National Assemblies. The first National Assembly met in 1942 in Cleveland, Ohio, and the next two in 1944 and 1946 both met in Grand Rapids, Michigan. The UCCW's meetings took place over several days, and included speeches, worship services, business meetings, debates and votes on resolutions, and small group discussions meant to help local leaders in their planning and work. At these and later Assemblies, churchwomen focused intensively on defining their vision for a Christian world order and the means of realizing it. These political questions that generated prayers and elicited resolutions made the National Assembly into a juxtapolitical space in which organized Protestant women developed their identity. The Assembly, like the World Day of Prayer, *assembled* Protestant women together. Even those who did not attend could read many first-hand accounts of the gathering in the *Church Woman* along with committee reports and the resolutions passed.

The 1944 National Assembly in Grand Rapids had as its theme: "Our Responsibility in our Christian World-Wide Fellowship." The meeting itself became an opportunity to enact the interracial community that had been on churchwomen's agenda for at least a decade. While White women still made up the vast majority of speakers, discussion group leaders, and attendees, the UCCW's Black vice president Christine Smith presided at one business meeting, and staff member Louise Young chaired another session. Throughout the sessions, Black churchwomen participated as leaders and "resource leaders" in small groups as well. This included some who had been active on the Church Women's Committee on Race Relations, including the former chairwoman, Josephine Kyles. In addition to discussion groups that addressed "racial tensions" directly, the presence of Black women in groups discussing topics like "Housing and Family Life, "Education in the Post-War World," and "Post-War Employment" made it likely that those issues would also be addressed from Black as well as White women's perspectives.[63]

Earlier in the year, Smith had written about these objectives for the *Church Woman* with a White audience in mind. Her explanation of

Black civil rights as a fulfillment of the kingdom of God coopted the Christian feminist imperialism of the White women's missionary movement and its earlier insistence that women's emancipation must be part of building God's kingdom. "I firmly believe in a Divine plan for the ultimate government of this world," she wrote. "We can and have delayed the purposes of God by our own willfulness and the question to be decided is whether we will work with God or whether we will follow the pattern we have made around racial superiority." She then pointed to women as "the ultimate solution of this whole question." In an appeal to their shared identity as Christian women meant to cut across race, Smith focused less on churchwomen's political organizing and suggested that they had a more powerful resource at their disposal as they educated and trained a rising generation of future Christian citizens. "Politicians may have their secret meetings, diplomats may gather in various corners of the globe and make decisions, governments may promise to cooperate in constructive world building and deliberately act in another way," yet all of these men were "ineffective when it comes to the power of the home and the training of youth from the cradle upward."[64] As a Black woman, Smith was surely aware of how White women's "power of the home" had been deployed against Black men especially, but she chose to use this symbolic imagery to win White churchwomen to see racial equality as part of their Christian world order.

The organizers of the 1944 Assembly also chose to highlight the organization's world purpose even if it was primarily a national organization. They invited several foreign women to lead the short devotional services each morning. In an article published just before the meeting, the UCCW's staffer Myrta Ross wrote about the organizers' intentions. "Christian nationals of many lands will be in our midst to make more real the invisible fellowship with Christian souls about the world," she explained. She hoped that their mere presence would be spiritually transformative and conducive to action. She prayed, "may there leap from heart to heart the flame of reconsecration, born on a current of determination to change our actions until they bespeak our Christian professions."[65] In 1946, the end of the war had made international travel more possible for civilians, and the Assembly featured speakers from the Philippines and Puerto Rico, and from Korea, China, India, and Japan as well as from France, Holland, England, Denmark, and Italy.[66] With much broader attendance than the White missionary women's interwar committee meetings, the UCCW Assembly was where churchwomen practiced cooperation. The resolutions developed at this spiritually poignant event defined the UCCW's political agenda for its Christian citizens that was then disseminated widely to local churchwomen's councils' departments of Christian Social Relations and Christian World Relations.

The final illustration of how politics and emotions combined in Christian citizenship is a missionary pageant of sorts—except this pageant's authors were Chinese Protestant women and their subject was an anti-war nativity pageant rather than women's emancipation. Originally written in Mandarin and performed at Ginling, the pageant was later translated and staged at some US churches. The original version of the pageant, "Mothers of the World," had four main characters representing different nationalities: Finland, Germany, Japan, and China. As each nation-character met a weary Mary and Joseph, she explained why they could not offer refuge and then proceeded to fight with each other. The Finn told the Holy Family that no one will take them because they are Jewish, and the Japanese woman declared that her island is too small, which is why they invaded China. The Chinese woman answered by refusing to help the Japanese woman locate the graves of her soldier sons. The international quarreling continued until "It Came Upon a Midnight Clear" played, and the women fell asleep. Finally, Mary and Joseph came back on stage with baby Jesus, and Mary reluctantly left him with the four argumentative women because "Joseph says there is no other way if she really wants to show her love—that love alone is willing to be dependent on others." When the women awakened, each explained why she could not accept Jesus, and the play ended with the women turning to the audience and imploring: "if any place is to be safe, then all places must be safe." The women then knelt on either side of the baby, and, holding hands, they "pledge themselves to build a world where all babies will be safe from poverty, fear, war, and sudden death, and where all babies will be brought up to love and not to hate, and to realize that only by sharing can all have enough."[67]

The play was translated into English and expanded, and it was staged by women of First Presbyterian Church in Englewood, New Jersey, in 1941. The play's maternalist and Christian pacifist message certainly appealed to churchwomen, but even more meaningful was the fact that it had been written by Chinese Protestant women. The pageant's familiar emotions and form represented the successful fruits of the White women's missionary movement and offered White American women a chance to learn from Chinese women even if the lesson mirrored their own values. The translator, Amelia Joseph Elmore, added a new prologue making this point: "We of the West have so long regarded ourselves as guides and givers in our relation to the Orient that we have been slow to recognize the growing extent to which we should ourselves look eastward for light and leadership."[68]

Interestingly, it seems that Elmore also added a North American and South American character to the pageant. Americans were, in fact, not part of the original pageant at all. In Elmore's English version, the North American character interrupts the other countries as they fight over Jesus. Then, the other countries jump in to criticize her. The South American mentions that she is also an "American," an American whom North America ignores. Then the other characters ask why North America insists that "it is wrong for the strong to take advantage of the weak" when racial segregation is the rule in the United States. "God forgive us!" the North American cries, "that in my own country all these things have happened—and are happening today. I know what is wrong; but I do not know how to make it right."[69]

In the English version, the North American character also gave the longest speech at the end of the play as the women each pronounce themselves unworthy to care for Jesus. She notes that North Americans had wanted to "to welcome to our homes the endangered children of the world" and had long thought of themselves as "those appointed to be the helpers, the beautiful givers, the fortunate who relieve the need of others." But she now recognized that "our own need . . . is greater than we know." Addressing the German, she says, "we are not guiltless of the sin that has left such a scar on your spirit," and points out that "we have reared between human beings barriers that we call race and class, saying all the time that we are created free and equal."[70] Unlike earlier missionary pageants, "Mothers of the World" did not present American missionary women as agents of peace or even for women's emancipation. In the Chinese version, the United States is absent entirely, and in the English translation, North America is proven to be ignorant and unable to save the day. Instead, the only hope comes from a not-yet-realized effort on the part of women everywhere. They must move apart from their national, racial, and class pride as well as their hopelessness to instead work for change. In the play, Jesus was present, but his power came from being a helpless baby; his weakness is what stimulates the women's Christian devotion and maternal instinct to create a different world entirely. The mothers initially reject him as they are complicit in their sins of racism, nationalism, greed, and cruelty, but the common devotion to God manifested through the mother instinct toward the infant Jesus allows the possibility of escape from those sins in the end. The play makes the daring theological point that Jesus lies vulnerable, unable to save anyone in this time of immense trial unless human beings—and especially women—work to make the world a better place.

Churchwomen's Postwar Mobilizing for Peace

World Day of Prayer chairwoman Margaret Applegarth described the founding of the United Nations as "the world's most momentous event since the Prince of Peace came."[71] In late May 1945, the UCCW's executive committee passed a resolution calling on its members to write letters of support for the UN charter to President Truman and their senators. The resolution concluded, "after the ratification of the charter, responsibility must be fostered in church women for developing the attitudes necessary for getting the international machinery to work."[72] The UCCW appointed Mabel Head as its observer at the UN, and she wrote monthly columns for the *Church Women* outlining the main issues under discussion. At the UCCW's Third Biennial Assembly, held in Grand Rapids in 1946, the Department of Christian World Relations called upon churchwomen to keep up to date on Head's columns about the new UN, and use this information to "help create public opinion in every community in this country."[73] The next year, the UCCW offered a case in point in an article entitled "A New Way to Be Christian." The article described exactly how grassroots relational organizing worked. A churchwoman calls a busy housewife, Mrs. Richardson, and asks her to write a letter to her senators in support for international controls over nuclear weapons. Gazing upon her children just returned from school, Mrs. Richardson agrees, but asks her friend, "Do you think it's really all right for church women to be getting into these political questions?" The other woman responds, "Taking action on the great moral issues before Congress is as much a part of putting our Christian principles into practice as supporting missionary work or sewing clothes for relief. It's a new kind of Christian service."[74]

In the immediate postwar years, the UCCW rallied behind the civilian control of nuclear energy, refugee resettlement, reciprocal trade agreements, multilateralism, and the newly created United Nations as well as the UN Declaration of Human Rights. They downplayed or ignored criticisms of the UN's trusteeship arrangements that more radical activists protested as perpetuating colonialism. They opposed Universal Military Training (the draft) and declared that "in the human family under God there should be no such thing as an Iron Curtain." They also called for churchwomen to pay attention to motion pictures and radio programs to promote "character building elements." In terms of domestic policies, they condemned segregation in all areas of American life and called on churchwomen to study the 1948 Report of the President's Commission on Civil Rights. In their discussions about home ownership loans, the need for a minimum wage, and other "basic economic rights," they always qualified their discussions with a demand that policies apply to all people equally regardless of "race, sex, creed, or national origin."[75] In advocating for these and other policies, churchwomen expanded their interwar efforts to define Christian citizenship and enact their hopes for a Christian world order. Not unlike Ida Post's imagining of churchwomen's councils as information hubs, UCCW leaders would work through the growing network of churchwomen's councils to try to influence public opinion and mobilize women to vote as Christian citizens and world citizens. The UCCW organized Leadership Training Workshops to help local leaders recruit new members (especially working women, whom they viewed as "a great pool of potential power") and work effectively.[76] The "ways" of leadership, outlined at the UCCW's Fifth National Assembly in 1950, listed the growing number of activities churchwomen coordinated and performed: conferences, institutes, seminars, workshops, clinics, a town meeting, a rally.[77]

At the same time, churchwomen often couched their arguments in the language of motherhood, a gendered moral politics that differentiated their arguments from those of ecumenical Protestant men. As UCCW leaders testified before Congress and as local leaders organized public rallies, their activism illustrated a socially engaged form of Protestantism. They rejected a Protestantism that centered primarily on personal faith and continued to try to "Christianize" the world around them. Their gendered and activist Protestant approach to politics echoed the social ambitions of the White women's missionary movement's Christian imperial feminism *and* the quite differently oriented prophetic religion of the Black civil rights movement.[78] To be sure, churchwomen did not lose sight of issues related to family life and "the Christian home," but like the fictional Mrs. Richardson, they connected those private-sphere matters of domesticity to politics and public life.

To this end, a 1945 statement by the UCCW encouraged local councils to study the relevance of missionary programs to the work of the UN human welfare agencies, and to "ask Church women to welcome courageous ideas in missionary thinking as much as the use of missionary experience in United Nations planning." Another avenue was prayer, and it was often recommended that individual churchwomen add five or more minutes of prayer on international issues each day. Building on the FCC's World Order Day, the UCCW had its World Community Day, begun in November 1943. In 1948, the annual World Community Day service took up the familiar missionary message of sacrificial giving of both material supplies and money for Church World Service and UNICEF to help war survivors in Europe and Asia. The theme in 1948, "Peace Is My Responsibility," emphasized what American women could and had to do as mothers and Christian citizens. The World Community Day service in 1956 turned the preamble of the UN's Universal Declaration of Human Rights into a call and response liturgy in combination with the religious freedom clauses of the First Amendment of the Bill of Rights and Jesus's two commandments to love God and your neighbor.[79]

The UCCW and the Federal Council of Churches both became strong advocates for more generous immigration policies, especially as they related to the war's displaced persons (DPs). Through an executive action in 1945, President Truman had reinstituted State Department outposts near DP camps in Germany and had modified immigration quotas to allow around 40,000 mostly Jewish DPs to enter the United States. By mid-1946, however, a new wave of people fleeing communist regimes in Eastern Europe flooded into the western-occupied zones in Germany, creating a new crisis. Over the next several years, this "last million" would become the central focus of American refugee relief organizations. This population included 400,000 Poles, 150,000–200,000 Estonians, Lithuanians, and Latvians, and more than 100,000 Ukrainians. Approximately 25 percent of the "last million" were Jews (mostly the Poles), 50 percent Catholics, and 25 percent Protestants.[80] As had been the case in refugee aid before the United States entered the war, the Jewish, Catholic, and Protestant agencies continued to focus on supplying sponsors for "their" people at the same time that religious leaders joined together with immigration activists, academics, and Eleanor Roosevelt to form the Citizens Committee on Displaced Persons in 1946.

In 1947, the UCCW joined the Federal Council of Churches to support the Stratton Bill that the Citizens Committee had a hand in writing. The bill called for the admission of 400,000 displaced persons to be admitted over four years. It would die in committee due to conservatives' objections that it effectively ended the national origins quota system. The more conservative Displaced Persons Act passed in 1948 allowed just 200,000 people entry and included restrictions that would have effectively limited the number of Jewish admittees.[81] After the Stratton Bill died and the more restrictive Displaced Persons Act was signed into law, the UCCW voted unanimously in disapproval of this more restrictive measure and called for the "hampering administrative provisions" that limited Jewish refugees to be eliminated.[82]

In their effort to rally Protestants' support for the Stratton Bill in 1947, Federal Council leaders sought to emphasize Christian DPs so that Protestants would not see this issue as primarily a "Jewish problem." In their letters about how to "sell" the issue to Protestants, these men thought that the effective messaging of Jewish relief groups had unintentionally created apathy among Protestants.[83] To counteract this perception, both the nonsectarian Citizens Committee on Displaced Persons and the FCC would frequently state that only 20 percent or 25 percent of DPs were Jewish, and that it was the responsibility of the FCC to aid the Protestant and Orthodox DPs.[84] At least some Protestants took issue with this approach. Churchwoman Lily Wendel of Ames, Iowa, raised concerns about the antisemitic implications of this argument when she read an editorial in the Federal Council's *Bulletin*. She wrote the Federal Council's leader, Samuel McCrea Cavert, to ask why the Federal Council "is only speaking about one kind of DP." These Christians were likely

Germans who had collaborated with the Nazis and who feared retribution, and, she wrote, "Why have you to soothe your readers by saying, no fears, 'only a small percentage are jews [sic]?'" Wendel chastised Cavert, arguing that the famed anti-Nazi pastor Martin Niemoeller would not approve of an article "about being a good neighbor to (a certain kind of) displaced persons."[85]

Cavert defended the article in his response to this Iowa churchwoman. He explained "the incidental reference to the fact that approximately three-fourths of DPs are Christians was for the purpose of correcting the widespread misimpression that the Jewish community was taking and could be expected to take the whole responsibility for caring for the DPs. In other words, the whole purpose of the editorial was to build up support in Christian circles for a much more vigorous program which would care for all of the DPs."[86] His response seems to have satisfied Wendel even as she warned him in her reply that the FCC's focus on Christian DPs was still a mistake since "misrepresentation could easily happen."[87]

UCCW president Georgiana Sibley was one of several national Protestant leaders who testified before the House Committee on the Judiciary in support of the Stratton bill. In her testimony, Sibley did not emphasize the religious identity of DPs but rather focused on the fact that more than 50 percent of DPs were women and children. In doing so, she used gendered strategies that had long been part of Protestant women's activism. "Do we turn our backs on 150,000 displaced children, half of them under 5 years of age, all of them homeless, many of them orphaned and unclaimed?" Even more powerfully, she indirectly addressed the anti-refugee positions of the conservative national VFW and American Legion who had argued that refugees would take jobs from returning GIs, emphasizing that she and the members of the UCCW were "mothers of veterans" and of young men who had died in the war. Finally, Sibley connected this maternal interest in future Christian citizens by shaming congressmen for their failure to apply the United States' democratic values to the larger world. "The experience of the war has reaffirmed our fundamental American belief in liberty and freedom for all—has taught us that we can no longer live in several worlds but must work toward one world," she explained. "Accepting 100,000 displaced refugees from totalitarianism in each of 4 years is the very least we can do to demonstrate that as a world leader we are realistically concerned about the freedoms for which we fought World War II."[88] Sibley used maternalist rhetoric to forward a liberal position on immigration and a liberal definition of "liberty and freedom for all" that echoed Protestant women's cosmopolitan Christianity and their certainty that they could make the United States into their agent in creating a Christian world order.

Can the UCCW be considered a feminist organization? The women who led churchwomen's organizations in the 1940s and 1950s may not have aligned with second-wave feminist's style and liberatory sexual politics, but they did advance a liberal feminist agenda that supported women's equal rights in terms of political representation, employment, and pay. Church Women United would later support the Equal Rights Amendment, and after initially supporting the repeal of restrictive abortion laws in 1970 at the state level, they ultimately decided not to take a formal position on *Roe* as some member denominations remained opposed to abortion.[89] More revealing, however, is the way that the UCCW promoted international women's rights, a position that continued the Christian imperial feminism of the White women's missionary movement and reimagined it as the basis for a transnational community of women who, it was implied, shared a common progressive politics if not always a common Christianity. Beginning in the late 1940s, the *Church Woman* opened with a regular feature called "Catching Up with the News for and about Women," that listed brief notices about different women's accomplishments and changing laws and policies concerning women. This included notices about women's educational achievements and professional advancement as well as women who had been ordained to the ministry and elected or appointed to public office, and the annual notice of who had been named "American Mother of the Year." The notices often included Black and White women involved in civil rights in the United States and updates on interreligious cooperation. In June 1940, for example, the notices included a short biography of Mrs. Vijaya Lakshmi Pandit, the newly appointed Indian ambassador to the United States, a notice about the new mayor of San Juan, Puerto Rico, Mrs. Felisa Rincón, a mention that Lebanon would be the first Arab state to allow women to vote, a rundown of the diversity of foreign students in the United States, and a short summary of the differences between the

Equal Rights Amendment proposed by the National Women's Party and a different measure endorsed by Eleanor Roosevelt and the League of Women Voters.[90]

The UCCW also kept a steady eye on women's progress, which they defined in terms of political rights and representation. In March 1950, one notice stated briefly: "In the early part of the 20th century, only three countries had given women the vote. By 1949, 59 nations had recognized women as citizens."[91] Without making direct connections between women's emancipation and Protestant Christianity as Helen Barrett Montgomery had done a century earlier, the editors of the *Church Woman* rooted their identity as cosmopolitan Protestant women and based their vision of a Christian world order in this ever-unfolding progress narrative expanding women's rights.

* * *

For Protestant churchwomen, the coincidence of the United States' entry into the Second World War and the creation of the UCCW could seem providential. Organized White Protestant women's religious politics had realigned in the 1920s and 1930s from their almost singular focus on Prohibition to a wider array of issues that included Christian internationalism. When we attend to the continued influence of the foreign missionary movement within White-led Protestant women's organizations, however, this shift is less surprising than it might at first seem. White and Black Protestant women had both been active in the women's peace movement following the First World War, and they interpreted larger programs for a Christian World Order through their missionary lens. Like the White Protestant women who once insisted that Christianity would bring about women's emancipation the world over, Black and White Protestant women believed that they could secure racial equality and women's rights together by "Christianizing" social relations at home and world relations abroad. Christian citizenship's usefulness for political mobilization worked in large part because of the religious feelings and spiritual experiences of Christian belonging generated in the services of the World Day of Prayer and, later, World Community Day. In these and other juxtapolitical spaces Protestant women in the United States came to think of Christian citizenship as world citizenship as they felt mutual belonging to a global community of Christians that could motivate them to critique what they perceived as their nation's failings. By conceptualizing churchwomen as Christian citizens with loyalties to the world, the UCCW adopted a stance that was not unlike the Christian imperial feminist view of American empire in the early 1900s. As Georgiana Sibley's testimony before Congress suggests, churchwomen often endorsed the United States' growing power. Churchwomen viewed the United States, governed by liberal Protestant mores, as best equipped to govern the world order along Christian lines even if its own domestic record on racial and economic inequality still required their attention.

Conclusion

Christianity and Women's Rights

Sixty years after the UCCW's founding, Americans heard a new appeal to Christian imperial feminism when First Lady Laura Bush gave a radio address about women's rights in Afghanistan. In just under four minutes, Bush framed the United States' military attack on Afghanistan as a humanitarian crusade to rescue women and children from oppression. "Civilized people throughout the world are speaking out in horror—not only because our hearts break for the women and children in Afghanistan, but also because in Afghanistan, we see the world the terrorists would like to impose on the rest of us."[1] The events of September 11, 2001, dissolved into the background as Bush focused on the suffering of Afghan women to rally bipartisan support for their rescue. On this Sunday morning in 1995, at the United Nations' Fourth World Conference on Women, the Republican (and Methodist) Bush echoed the words of her predecessor, the Democrat (and Methodist) Hillary Clinton, who voiced the famous refrain that "women's rights are human rights."

For feminist and postcolonial scholars, Laura Bush's radio address, and to some extent Clinton's earlier Beijing speech, have become symbolic of the links between an earlier imperial feminism and the US feminist movement's international turn. Many scholars have examined the resulting and conflicting liberal ideals of religious freedom and women's rights.[2] Both speeches also exemplify the long legacy of the White women's missionary movement's Christian imperial feminism. For example, a brief notice in a 1948 issue of the *Church Woman* commented positively that "western influence" brought "radios, telephones, and American movies" to Afghanistan. "Progress is the new watchword," in a country they described as a "zealously Mohammedan land," and they hoped for a ban on the veil.[3] For White and western Christian and secular feminists in the 1940s and 2000s both, Afghanistan served as a symbol for a racialized religion and its inherent gender disorder. It was also a problem that White women were used to mobilize American women as both rescuers and members of what was imagined as a universalized community of women.

By examining how churchwomen's cosmopolitan practices sustained Christian imperial feminism and translated it into political liberalism, we see how organized Protestant women bridged a (Protestant) Christian feminism and secular women's rights. Christian imperial feminism did not remain constant as White and Black churchwomen redefined it and their feminine authority to manage the challenges presenting by diversity by applying Christianity as the solution to these "problems," whether local, national, or global. Indeed, for churchwomen, geopolitical boundaries and spatial differences mattered little as they believed that the seemingly small actions taken in one's own community relatedly strongly to wider world events. They created cosmopolitan practices to render "the world" on the pageant stage or in their prayer services, generating often complex feelings of belonging as they considered the challenges a diverse Christian community presented. In those practices, White Protestant women honed an identity as the managers of an often-conflicted diverse Christian community, an identity and responsibility they also applied to their Americanization programs and interracial cooperation efforts, and that infused their maternalist cosmopolitan politics in support of a Christian world order.

A focus on Christian imperial feminism's continuities from the missionary movement to liberal ecumenicalism challenges the view that White Protestants' growing support for religious pluralism and civil rights stands as a liberal progress narrative that is also a secularization narrative. It is, of course, a demographic fact that the mainline denominations affiliated with the National Council of Churches (which replaced the Federal Council in 1950) have shrunk dramatically in the late twentieth and early twenty-first centuries.[4] But it is a missed opportunity for scholars of American religious history to center our inquiries only on explaining this phenomenon. Those accounts are valuable, yet an exclusive focus on change over time that is most interested in contrasting (White) liberal Protestants with (White) conservative evangelicals can gloss over other inquiries. In other words, we might study liberal Protestants as something more than just the staid and vaguely secular background to a more dynamic twentieth-century evangelicalism. In this book, my aim has been to put the ecumenical movement and Protestant women in a new perspective. By focusing on the imperial logic of Christian imperial feminism in both the missionary movement and churchwomen's liberal activism, I have offered a reminder that Christian nationalism coexisted with Christian imperialism. As self-declared cosmopolitans, churchwomen often critiqued and even challenged nationalism as "un-Christian," while at the same time, their conception of a global empire of Christ and a Christian world order typically endorsed a model of US power on the global stage.

The imperial objectives of ecumenicalism also played out within the borders of the United States and in cities and towns that White Protestants described as filled with "immigrant colonies" and with Black migrants from the South. While ecumenical Protestants often pushed for fewer immigration restrictions and envisioned their cities and towns as models of cosmopolitanism, they sought to manage these processes of including (sometimes coercively) these "diverse" people into the body politic. They believed that their cosmopolitan neighborhood houses would disabuse mostly Catholic, Orthodox, and Jewish immigrants of their un-American notions about racial, religious, and national identity, and that White Americans would also be transformed through the experience of mingling with different groups who embodied the fullness of the body of Christ and the kingdom of God. When ecumenical Protestants grew more engaged with the new tri-faith movement, they helped to define and articulate a new American way of being religious. They promoted a Protestant-friendly notion of religious freedom along with programs for civil rights, women's rights, and human rights that affirmed rather than challenged the liberal social order. As White and Black Protestant women, as well as mostly White Catholic, and Jewish women joined forces in some interfaith programs, they shared a common understanding of women's role in pursuing the liberal goals of tolerance, cooperation, and goodwill that was suspicious of the conservative gender ideologies of other Protestants, Catholics, and Jews and of other racialized religions. The interracial cooperation programs of ecumenical Protestants insisted that racial understanding and integration offered a Christian approach to race relations in contrast to other civil rights campaigns that issued more of a threat to the status quo.

Despite many scholarly books written with arguments to the contrary, "religion" and "feminism" are still too often seen as opposing forces, especially when the subjects are White women.[5] At the same time, historians of ecumenical Protestants often downplay the role of ecumenical churchwomen because they are not seen as advancing a particular form of gender equality along with their other political and social interests. This book speaks to this work in its analysis of an early twentieth-century articulation of Christian feminism that was related to but distinct from a more familiar second-wave White feminist movement. In this case, White and Black women criticized many aspects of what they deemed to be patriarchal religion and the marginalization of women. They also saw the possibilities in collective women's organizing when it came to politics. While these women might very well have rejected the label "feminist" by the 1960s and 1970s, they had a quite well-developed understanding of women's power and engagement in the public sphere. Their Protestant women's organizations also seem to have provided a fruitful space for interracial cooperation. Certainly, Black women did not always find fellowship or support in White-led Protestant women's councils, but in contrast to the normative segregation of most secular women's organizations, the UCCW demanded interracial organizing of its affiliates and assessed US economic and other policies with race as a factor.

If Protestant women's organizations addressed intersectional feminism as early as the 1920s, this does not mean that these religious organizations were somehow anti-racist feminist utopias. As we saw in relation to churchwomen's Americanization efforts and their interreligious and interracial cooperation, they created hierarchies of racial groups and forms of religious expression attributed to those racialized people. As Christian imperial feminists, they classified people and traditions considered more modern by virtue of their position on women's rights as superior to those believed to be oppressive to religion. Moreover, they connected a Protestant missionary–related cosmopolitanism and diversity, tolerance, and "religious liberty" with women's rights and used them to critique and condemn both other kinds of Christianity and "ethnic religions." There is perhaps not a direct line from churchwomen's Christian imperial feminism to Laura Bush's 2001 address, or for that matter, to the renewed feminist concern for Afghan women after the

2021 departure of US troops. Yet churchwomen's organizations exist and existed in most American cities and towns, and these women played a singular role in normalizing and disseminating these layered arrangements that shaped American secularism. This book has shown what can be missed when we think about feminism(s) as a secular project and religion as inevitably endorsing a conservative gender ideology.

Every four years, Church Women United sets out its "quadrennial priorities"; for 2021–2024, these include inequities in healthcare and wellness, climate stewardship, social justice (focused especially on mass incarceration), and hunger and poverty. The explanation for the social justice priority declared that "Church Women United realize that for the Church to be (and represent) the House of God—it must not collude with social systems which create and protect injustice. Rather, all social oppressive systems must be 'flipped' in order for the real work of Kingdom building to occur." Along with this bold statement, the practical activities recommended are familiar. They include reading books about "people of different racial and ethnic groups" and inviting people who "are part of a specific lineage ethnic group to learn about groups' lineage, history, culture, and challenges facing them." This information-gathering should then motivate local women to rewrite their bylaws so that they are "an anti-racist organization" and then to decide how they might change other institutions in their communities.[6] With a Black woman (Mira J. Washington of Rochester, New York) serving as its president during the setting out of the 2021–3024 priorities, and with Black women as majority members of many local affiliated groups, Church Women United is quite different in many respects from what it was in its first few years of existence. Yet its practices and methods show the continuities with organized White Protestant women from a century ago. Churchwomen then and now formed their identity as organized Protestant women in waging battle against forces they saw as unjust and oppressive as they worked instead to manage what they insisted would be a more equitable and liberatory kingdom of God.

ACKNOWLEDGMENTS

Research and writing a book is hardly a solo endeavor, and I have benefited immeasurably from the conversations, advice, criticism, and friendship of many people throughout the process. The questions and feedback of the North American Religions series editors David Harrington Watt, Laura Levitt, and Tracy Fessenden helped shape the book into what it is, and I am indebted to them for their advice. These editorial interventions came at a critical time in the revision process, and it is a far better book because of them. Jennifer Hammer of NYU Press deserves a great deal of thanks for her guidance and attention to the book, and I am grateful for the work of Veronica Knutson and all of the others whose work made the book possible.

I am also thankful to my colleagues at Barnard College and Columbia University. Without Janet Jakobsen's regular encouragement and advice, this book might have remained in a state of perpetual revision. I am profoundly lucky to have her as my official Barnard mentor. Writing this book was also made easier by the support of my Barnard Religion Department colleagues: Elizabeth Castelli, Beth Berkowitz, Jack Hawley, Najam Haider, Tiffany Hale, and Timothy Vasko. Their encouragement, good cheer, and collegiality have created a vibrant intellectual community. I would also like to thank both Tynisha Rue and Anna Hotard for good cheer and generally getting things to run smoothly. I have learned much from my colleagues in the Columbia Religion Department, especially Courtney Bender and Josef Sorett. Thanks also go to Ellen Morris, Severin Fowles, Thea Abu el-Haj, Elizabeth Hutchison, Jennie Kassanoff, Lisa Gordis, Monica Miller, Debra Minkoff, Rachel McDermott, and Celia Deutsch, some of whom have commented on parts of this book along the way and all of whom have been terrific colleagues. Current and former Columbia graduate students Liz Dolfi, Andrew Jungclaus, Kit Hermanson, Connor Martini, Sarah Hedgecock, Sam Stella, and Gabriella Lee generously listened to me talk about this book ad infinitum, and I cannot thank them enough. Undergraduate students in my course, Religion in the Archive, deserve thanks for bringing the Ginling College pageant to my attention.

I am also indebted to those who have been interlocutors as the book took shape. A very special thanks goes to my writing group, Emily Conroy-Krutz and Ben Wright. Emily's friendship and continued excitement for this project helped remind me why it mattered when I doubted, and I benefited from both Emily's and Ben's thoughtful comments of draft chapters and "so what" questions. At conferences and workshops, I learned much from conversations with Tisa Wenger, Hillary Kaell, Heather Curtis, Jodi Eichler-Levine, Jen Graber, Dana Robert, Peggy Bendroth, Gene Zubovich, Matthew Hedstrom, Heath Carter, Judith Weisenfeld, Cara Burnidge, Anthony Petro, Noriko Ishii, Jonathan Ebel, Melissa Borja, Kathryn Gin Lum, Lauren Turek, Mark Edwards, Alison Greene, Luke Harlow, Connie Shemo, Samira Mehta, Matthew Sutton, and Kate Bowler. The members of the American Academy of Religion's Religion and US Empire seminar invited me to present on a chapter at a critical time and provided valuable feedback. I also owe thanks to the members of Columbia's University Seminar on Religion in America for their feedback on a draft of one of the book's chapters. Early in the process of research, Barbara Parmenter very kindly sent me a stack of family newsletters written by her grandmother, Myrta Ross.

It is safe to say that it would have been impossible to write the book without the resources and generosity of librarians and archivists. Matthew Baker, Jeffrey Wayno, Caro Bratnober, Leah Edelman, and Betty Bolden at the Burke Library always made me feel welcome. Matthew went above and beyond by meeting me at the door with books from the Union Stacks when the library was still closed during the Covid lockdown, and Betty, a churchwoman herself, provided a host of stories about the World Day of Prayer, her international travels, and participation in myriad social justice programs. At the University of Rochester, Liz Call and Melinda Wallington proved exceptionally helpful, and Liz went out of her way to make me feel welcome during my time in Rochester. I am also appreciative of Dani Marsella, who helped facilitate the reproduction of the image that appears on the book's cover. I am grateful for the able assistance of Frances Lyons-Bristol at the Drew University Library and Lisa Jacobson and the staff at the Presbyterian Historical Society in Philadelphia.

Finally, I would like to thank my fellow lap swimmers and especially Naomi Kleinberg, whose steady encouragement helped keep me motivated. I am ever grateful for the friendship of Nazia Malik, Joyce Cheng, Jeremy Cleveland, Sonia Omulepu, Amy Gentry, Laura Trice, Erin Williams, and Shirin Baskey. My parents, Barbara and Mike, have always been supportive and encouraging, and my sister Lizzy and brother-in-law Jeff, and my niece Harper, offered a regular and welcome home away from home. Finally, two decades of conversations with Jackie Schmitt about religion, social activism, race, and church institutions undoubtedly shaped my interest in churchwomen and politics in the first place, and it is to her that this book is dedicated.

NOTES

INTRODUCTION

1. Leila Avery Rothenburger, "Needed—A Racial Cartography," *Church Woman*, Oct. 1940, 13–15.
2. Rothenburger, "Needed—A Racial Cartography," 13–15. See also: "Mrs. Leila Avery Rothenburger, Wife of Christian Church Pastor, Dies," *Indianapolis Star*, March 28, 1942, 9.
3. The term "missionary ethnology" comes from Brumberg, "Zenanas and Girlless Villages," 355.
4. Instead of the more accurate "Protestant," I have opted to use "Christian imperial feminism" and "Christian cosmopolitanism" as a reflection of how White Protestant women claimed this more capacious (and imperial) term. They used "Christian" and "Christianity" to underscore their ecumenical theology and its universalist idea of Protestantism and to counter the global reach of the Roman Catholic Church. Notably, by the 1950s, ecumenical Protestants had begun to include Orthodox Christians in their organizations, and some Catholic women would later become part of Church Women United.
5. Brumberg, "Zenanas and Girlless Villages"; Hill, *The World Their Household*.
6. Exemplary of this distinction in relation to missionaries is Hollinger, *Protestants Abroad*. This typically laudatory approach to White liberal Protestants has also been criticized: Preston, "The Limits of Brotherhood."
7. Hollinger, *Protestants Abroad*, 293; Preston, "The Limits of Brotherhood," 1230.
8. This "liberal dilemma" most often arises in regard to western secular feminism and Muslim women. On its roots in American liberal religion see: Fessenden, "Religious Liberalism."
9. Braude, "Women's History *Is* American Religious History," 101–103. See also: Brereton and Bendroth, "Secularization and Gender."
10. Histories of the White women's foreign missionary movement include: Hill, *The World Their Household*; Robert, *American Women in Mission*. On White Protestant home missionaries see: Pascoe, *Relations of Rescue*. More recently see: Reeves-Ellington, Sklar, and Shemo, eds., *Competing Kingdoms*. On ecumenical Protestant women see: Bendroth, *Good and Mad*; Yohn, "'Let Christian Women Set the Example'"; Brereton, "United and Slighted"; Beaver, *All Loves Excelling*, 177–209. Scholars focused on Black churchwomen and the civil rights work of organized Protestant women include: Collier-Thomas, *Jesus, Jobs, and Justice*;

Adams, *Black Women's Christian Activism*. See also: Denomme, "To End This Day of Strife"; Wiggins, "United Church Women"; Johnson, "Building Bridges."

11 A relevant analysis of the development of evangelicalism among White northerners in the early 1900s is: Gloege, *Guaranteed Pure*, 7–13. For other scholarship on the different intellectual, economic, racial, and gendered formations of postwar evangelicalism see: Worthen, *Apostles of Reason*; Vaca, *Evangelicals Incorporated*; Hawkins, *The Bible Told Them So*; Du Mez, *Jesus and John Wayne*.

12 For more detailed discussions of the different meanings of "ecumenical," "liberal," "mainline," and "Protestant establishment," see: Coffman, *The Christian Century*; Sehat, *The Myth of American Religious Freedom*; Hutchison, ed., *Between the Times*. On liberal theology see: Warren, *Theologians of a New World Order*. Ecumenical Protestants might also be considered by who they opposed, that is, "anti-fundamentalist," see: Watt, *Anti-Fundamentalism*.

13 Griffith, *Moral Combat*; White, *Reforming Sodom*.

14 Zubovich, *Before the Religious Right*. On the different discourses of religious pluralism among Protestants see: Gaston, *Imagining Judeo-Christian America*.

15 Curtis, *Holy Humanitarians*; McAlister, *The Kingdom of God*; Kirkpatrick, *A Gospel for the Poor*; King, *God's Internationalists*; Kaell, *Christian Globalism at Home*; Turek, *To Bring the Good News*.

16 For a summary of the rise and fall of the (White and western) ecumenical vision for a Christian world order see: Robert, "Naming 'World Christianity.'" See also: Lindenfeld, *World Christianity*; Dunch, "Beyond Cultural Imperialism"; Sanneh, *Whose Religion Is Christianity*.

17 Weisenfeld, *New World A-Coming*. See also the articles in "Roundtable: 'Religio-Racial Identity' As Challenge and Critique," *Journal of the American Academy of Religion* 88, no. 2 (June 2020). On White supremacy, White Protestant identity, and religious studies see: Blum et al., eds., "Forum"; Gin Lum, *Heathen*; Beliso-De Jesús, "Confounded Identities"; Nye, "Race and Religion."

18 Higginbotham, *Righteous Discontent*; Giddings, *When and Where I Enter*; Gilmore, *Gender and Jim Crow*; Collier-Thomas, *Jesus, Jobs, and Justice*; Robertson, *Christian Sisterhood*; Weisenfeld, *African American Women*; Johnson, *African American Religions*.

19 Kramer, "Power and Connection."

20 Kaplan and Pease, eds., *Cultures*; Stoler, ed., *Haunted by Empire*; Chidester, *Empire of Religion*; Johnson, *African American Religions*; Wenger, *Religious Freedom*; Moran, *The Imperial Church*; Wenger and Johnson, eds., *Religion and US Empire*.

21 Conroy-Krutz, *Christian Imperialism*.

22 Chang, *Citizens of a Christian Nation*; Gin Lum, *Heathen*; Smith, "Settler Colonialism"; Brumberg, "Zenanas and Girlless Villages."

23 Renda, "Doing Everything," 374.

24 Hoganson, *Consumer's Imperium*.

25 Rosenberg, "Rescuing Women and Children"; Sasaki, *Redemption*; and Ishii, *American Women*.

26 Burton, *Burdens of History*. On the imperial feminism of British Protestant women see: Thorne, "Missionary-Imperial Feminism"; Prevost, *The Communion of Women*. Works on White American women missionaries and other female moral reformers in relation to imperialism include: Kaplan, "Manifest Domesticity"; Tyrrell, *Reforming the World*; the essays in Reeves-Ellington et al., eds., *Competing Kingdoms*; Chin, "Beneficent Imperialists." Different analyses on the legacies of White imperial feminism include: Mohanty, "Under Western Eyes: Feminist Scholarship and Colonial Discourses"; Abu-Lughod, *Do Muslim Women Need Saving*; and Grewal, *Transnational America*.
27 Chidester, *Empire of Religion*, 5.
28 Zubovich, *Before the Religious Right*.
29 Winant, *The World Is a Ghetto*; Buchanan, "Domesticating Hegemony." On civil rights and discourses of American multiculturalism in relation to US power during the Cold War see: Von Eschen, *Race against Empire*; Dudziak, *Cold War*; Melamed, *Represent and Destroy*.
30 Asad, *Formations of the Secular*; Cady and Hurd, eds., *Comparative Secularisms*; Mahmood, *Religious Difference*; Wenger and Johnson, "Introduction," *Religion and US Empire*, 10–11. On matters of feminism, race, and secularism see: Fessenden, *Culture and Redemption*, 161–180; Coviello, *Make Yourself Gods*, 33–42.
31 Lloyd, "Introduction," in *Race and Secularism in America*, ed. Kahn and Lloyd, 6.
32 On Emory Ross, colonial secularism, and religious freedom debates in the Belgian Congo see: Kenny and Wenger, "Church, State."
33 Hall, *Lived Religion*; Maffly-Kipp, Schmidt, and Valeri, eds., *Practicing Protestants*; Lofton, *Consuming Religion*; Lofton, "The Methodology of Modernists." On what constitutes "religious" practice and ritual see: Maldonado-Estrada, *Lifeblood of the Parish*; Gross, *Beyond the Synagogue*; Logan, *Awkward Rituals*. My thinking about ritualization and the power dynamics of control, resistance, and appropriation in play in these practices has been shaped by Bell, *Ritual Theory*.
34 Maldonado-Estrada, *Lifeblood of the Parish*, 12. See also: Butler, "Performative Acts."
35 Schuller, *The Biopolitics of Feeling*; Berlant, *The Female Complaint*.
36 Meyer, "Religious Sensations."
37 Adams, *Black Women's Christian Activism*, 275–276.
38 McAlister, "What Is your Heart For?," 873.
39 Nell Irving Painter, "Why White Should be Capitalized Too," *Washington Post*, July 22, 2022. My thinking on this was shaped in part by the argument of Kathryn Gin Lum.

CHAPTER 1. CHRISTIAN IMPERIAL FEMINISM AND MISSION STUDY

1 Atwater Mason, *Lux Christi*, 106–115.
2 Atwater Mason, *Little Green God*, 44–45.
3 The Central Committee on the United Study of Missions became the Central Committee on the United Study of Foreign Missions, probably to distinguish its

books from "home missions" publications from the Home Missions Council and the Missionary Education Movement. The women's boards included the (Congregationalist) Woman's Board of Missions; the (Episcopal) Woman's Auxiliary; the American Baptist Woman's Foreign Missionary Society; the Woman's Foreign Missionary Society of the Methodist-Episcopal Church; and the different regional boards that comprised the Women's Foreign Missionary Societies of the Presbyterian Church. On the institutional history of the UMS program see: Hardesty, "The Scientific Study of Missions."

4 Montgomery, *Western Women in Eastern Lands*, 206.
5 On the popularity of cosmopolitanism among American women in the late 1800s and early 1900s see: Hoganson, "Cosmopolitan Domesticity"; Kern, "Spiritual Border-Crossings"; Jain, "Subversive Spiritualities," 40–41. On liberal religion more generally see: Albanese, *Republic of Mind and Spirit*, 330–393; Schmidt, *Restless Souls*, 136–141. On a related "spiritual cosmopolitanism" in a British imperial context see: van der Veer, "Colonial Cosmopolitanism," 165–179.
6 Cott, *The Grounding of Modern Feminism*, 13. Missionary women participated in the discourse seeking to define the "New Woman" and feminism as in this article comparing "Christian feminism" to other forms of feminism: Mary S. Young, "Mothers and Daughters," *Woman's Work*, July 1915, 163–164.
7 On imperial feminism and suffrage in the United States: Sneider, *Suffragists in an Imperial Age*. On White American women missionaries and other female moral reformers in relation to imperialism include: Tyrrell, *Reforming the World*; Renda, "Doing Everything." On imperial feminism in British imperial contexts: Burton, *Burdens of History*; Thorne, "Missionary-Imperial Feminism."
8 Hill, *The World Their Household*, 159–60. For critiques and alternatives to Hill's interpretation see: Bendroth, "Women and Missions," 49–59; Robert, *American Women in Mission*, 262, 302–307; Hardesty, "The Scientific Study of Missions," 106–122. My analysis is shaped by Tracy Fessenden's work on secular feminists at this time, except here I focus on how Christian women used their own racial imperialist missionary hierarchies in their interpretation of the Bible as a feminist text. See: Fessenden, *Culture and Redemption*.
9 In addition to the UMS program, other mission study programs were put out by the Student Volunteers Movement and the Christian Endeavor program targeting children and youth. The latter included Brain, *Fuel for Missionary Fires* and Brain, *Fifty Missionary Programmes*.
10 Brumberg, "Zenanas and Girlless Villages," 352–354.
11 Mrs. M. M. Gray, "How To Interest," *Helping Hand*, Nov. 1896, 5.
12 *History of Woman Suffrage*, ed. Elizabeth Cady Stanton, Susan B. Anthony, and Matilda Joselyn Gage, 3 vols. (New York: Fowler & Wells, 1889), 1:14.
13 Ellen C. Parsons, "History of Woman's Organized Missionary Work as Promoted by American Women," in *Papers and Addresses Presented at the Woman's Congress of Missions*, ed. E. M. Wherry (New York: American Tract Society, 1894), 85, 94.
14 On the capitalist practices of missionary women see: Kaell, "Evangelist of Fragments."

15 Mrs. Moses Smith, "Woman Under the Ethnic Religions," in Wherry, *Papers and Addresses*, 20, 25.
16 *Report of the Ecumenical Conference*, 1:15.
17 Ibid., 1:144–45.
18 Ibid., 1:147.
19 In addition to Abbie Child and Lucy Peabody, the original members were Annie Ryder Gracey, who worked on the Methodist's mission study program, Presbyterian Ellen C. Parsons, and Episcopalian Mary Twing (1843–1901). Clementina Butler (1862–1913), the daughter of Methodist missionaries William and Clementina Butler, was the Central Committee's secretary and treasurer. At the time of the Central Committee's formation, Lucy Peabody had not yet married her second husband, Henry, and was then known as Lucy Waterbury.
20 "A Gigantic Mission Study Class," *Life and Light for Woman*, June 1903, 241.
21 Montgomery, *Christus Redemptor*, 1.
22 No title, *Light and Life for Woman*, July 1902, 188.
23 See advertisements at the end of Montgomery, *Western Women in Eastern Lands*.
24 Montgomery, *The How to Use: A Handbook of Suggestions to Accompany* The King's Highway, 2–3.
25 Miss Linda W. Clatworthy, "What a Librarian Thinks of 'United Study' Books," *Woman's Work for Woman*, May 1904, 113.
26 Mrs. N. M. Waterbury, "Report of the Central Committee on the United Study of Missions," *Life and Light for Woman*, Apr. 1904, 167–172.
27 Mrs. E. O. Silver, "Union Mission Study Classes," *Report of the Conference of the Federation of Woman's Boards of Foreign Missions*, Philadelphia, Feb. 28–29, 1912, 13.
28 Mobley, *Helen Barrett Montgomery*, 201–208.
29 Ibid.
30 On rethinking historical subjects as ritual theorists see: Logan, "Ritual Chores."
31 Montgomery, *How to Use: A Handbook of Suggestions to Accompany the Textbook* Western Women in Eastern Lands, 27.
32 Montgomery, *Western Women in Eastern Lands*, 18.
33 Montgomery, *How to Use for* Western Women, 6–10.
34 Ibid., 27.
35 Lofton, "The Methodology of the Modernists," 378. Emphasis added.
36 Montgomery, *How to Use for* The King's Highway, 31, 40.
37 Ibid., 51.
38 Montgomery, *How to Use* Christus Redemptor *with Outlines of Lectures*, 30.
39 Raymond, *The King's Business*, 159–160, 132.
40 *Report of the Ecumenical Conference*, 1:160–161.
41 Montgomery, *Christus Redemptor*, 116.
42 Montgomery, *How to Use for* Christus Redemptor, 13, 21.
43 Ibid., 21, 22.
44 Wenger, *Religious Freedom*, especially chapters 1–2; Kramer, *The Blood of Government*.

45 Montgomery, *How to Use for* Christus Redemptor, 11.
46 Ibid., 10.
47 Ibid., 21.
48 Ibid., 22; Katherine D. Moran, *The Imperial Church*, especially chapters 5–6.
49 Montgomery, *How to Use for* Christus Redemptor, 23. On Protestant missionary critics of Aglipay see: Wenger, *Religious Freedom*, 78–79.
50 Ibid., 13.
51 Ibid., 22.
52 Montgomery, *Christus Redemptor*, 136.
53 Chin, "Beneficent Imperialists."
54 Montgomery, *How to Use for* Christus Redemptor, 22.
55 Robert, *American Women in Mission*, 269.
56 Montgomery, *Western Women in Eastern Lands*, 44–45.
57 Ibid., 45. Brumberg's analysis of *Western Women* describes it as "missionary ethnology." Brumberg, "Zenanas and Girlless Villages." On the imperialism of other comparative religion projects see: Chidester, *Empire of Religion*; Masuzawa, *The Invention of World Religions*.
58 Montgomery, *How to Use*: Western Women, 28.
59 Ibid., 47, 46.
60 Montgomery, *Western Women in Eastern Lands*, 52, 56–57.
61 Ibid., 69, 70.
62 Ibid., 72. On antislavery hermeneutics and their connection to White feminist hermeneutics see: Oshatz, *Slavery and Sin*.
63 Montgomery, *Western Women in Eastern Lands*, 74.
64 "Women Begin Jubilee," *Washington Post*, Feb. 3, 1911, 2.
65 Montgomery, *Western Women in Eastern Lands*, 268–269.
66 "Would Free Women of the Oriental Countries," *San Francisco Chronicle*, Oct. 15, 1910, 20.
67 "Five Reasons Why Women Should Help Christianize the World," *Louisville* (KY) *Courier-Journal*, Jan. 30, 1911, 10.
68 Montgomery, *Western Women in Eastern Lands*, 205, 238. For a critical analysis of Ramabai's complicated relationship with English Anglican missionaries, see: Viswanathan, *Outside the Fold*.
69 Laura White, Address at the Tenth Interdenominational Conference, Woman's Boards of Foreign Missions, Jan. 15–16, 1915, 20, Day Missions Annual Reports Digital Collection, Yale Divinity Library.
70 Montgomery, *The King's Highway*, 146.
71 *Conference of Federation of Woman's Boards for Foreign Missions*, 1909; *Report of Federation of Woman's Boards for Foreign Missions*, 1912.
72 "Women Begin Jubilee," 2.
73 "Missionary Jubilee," *Pittsburgh Courier*, Nov. 25, 1911, 1.
74 On a similar strategy of "reconciliation" between White northerners and southerners in the WCTU, see chapter 6 of Blum, *Reforging the White Republic*.

75 Mrs. Henry W. Peabody, "Fruits of the Jubilee," and "Mrs. H. S. Prentiss Nichols, "Scientific Efficiency in Missions," in *Conference of the Federation of Woman's Boards of Foreign Missions*, Feb. 28–29, 1912, 12, 23. Day Missions Library Digital Collection, Yale Divinity Library.

CHAPTER 2. PERFORMING CHRISTIAN IMPERIAL FEMINISM IN MISSIONARY PAGEANTS

1 Helen Barrett Montgomery, "A Pageant of Missions, 1860–1910," Missionary Research Library Pamphlets Collections, Burke Library, Columbia University. Hereafter cited as MRL Pamphlets.
2 "A New Kind of Missionary Sermon," *The New Outlook*, Aug. 6, 1910, 757.
3 "The Northfield Summer School," *Life and Light for Woman*, Sept. 1910, 389.
4 Pageants were less controversial than modern dance, even though the two shared much in common. See: Wenger, "The Practice of Dance."
5 Glassberg, *American Historical Pageantry*.
6 Groeneveld, "'I felt as Never Before.'" For later ecumenical US White Protestants' enthusiasm for the Oberammergau see: Spear, "Claiming the Passion."
7 Meyer, "Religious Sensations."
8 See the contributions in Promey, ed., *Sensational Religion*. For a comprehensive study of material religion and visual culture see: Morgan, *The Thing About Religion*.
9 Meyer, "Media and the Senses," 129.
10 Kaell, *Christian Globalism at Home*, 11, 92–93.
11 On Adam Smith's discussion of the spatial limits of sympathy see Forman-Barzilai, "Sympathy in Space(s)." On the implicit hierarchies that White evangelical women's sympathy preserved see: Ryan, *The Grammar of Good Intentions*.
12 Pageantry was not only of interest to White liberal Protestants seeking to display racial diversity. On the contemporary Protestant White nationalist themed pageants to the Ku Klux Klan see: Baker, *The Gospel According to the Klan*.
13 Rogin, "Making America Home," 1052. On blackface minstrelsy see: Lott, *Love and Theft*. On pageantry in the context of US imperialism on the continent and overseas see: Laura Wexler, "The Fair Ensemble: Kate Chopin in St. Louis in 1904," in Stoler, ed., *Haunted by Empire*, 271–296, 278–284; Moran, *The Imperial Church*, 81–86; Phillips, "Performance over Policy"; Phillips, *Staging Indigeneity*.
14 Vincent W. Lloyd, "Managing Race, Managing Religion," in *Race and Secularism in America*, ed. Kahn and Lloyd, , 5.
15 In her book *Heathen*, religious studies scholar Kathryn Gin Lum provides her own account of being asked to play the part of a "Wanna Wiggle Indian" in a missionary pageant in the 1990s. Gin Lum, *Heathen*, 3–4.
16 Meyer, "Religious Sensations," 161.
17 William Chauncey Langdon, "America, Like England, has become Pageant Mad," *New York Times*, June 15, 1913, 5.
18 Davol, *Handbook*, 11–12.

19 Ibid., 37. On women as pageantry's leading enthusiasts see: Blair, *The Torchbearers*.
20 Glassberg, *American Historical Pageantry*, 161–3; Wilson, *The City Beautiful Movement*.
21 Glassberg, *American Historical Pageantry*, 160; Moran, *The Imperial Church*, 81–86.
22 Glassberg, *American Historical Pageantry*, 53–67; Rothermel, "Acting Up"; O'Donnell et al., *Greek Games*.
23 Alice Holdship Ware, "The Open Door," 1919, Box 2 Folder 21, Atlanta University Collection, Archives Division, Auburn Avenue Research Library on African-American Culture and History, Atlanta-Fulton Public Library System. http://dlg.galileo.usg.edu. For reviews of some performances of this pageant see: "Pageant of Open Door," *Hartford Courant*, March 6, 1921, 6; "Community Theatres," *The Drama*, July 1923, 320–322.
24 For example: Woolverton, *The Open Door*. See also: Mary Reed Jackson, "Building a Successful Pageant," *Home Mission Monthly*, Sept. 1916, 264.
25 Selig, *Americans All*, 81, 126, 224–225; Hoganson, *The Consumer's Imperium*, 137–145, 209–222, 236–238; White, "'The Pageant is the thing,'" 512–529.
26 Hewitt, "'Looking at One's Self Through the Eyes of Others'"; Krasner, *A Beautiful Pageant*, 81–94; Moore, "Making a Spectacle."
27 American Pageantry Association, *"Who's Who" in Pageantry*.
28 Most, *Theatrical Liberalism*.
29 Wenger, "The Practice of Dance." On White Protestant concerns about Native American dances and their comparative distaste for "jazz" see: Wenger, *We Have a Religion*, 140–143.
30 Lears, *No Place of Grace*, xv–xvi.
31 Beegle and Crawford, *Community Drama and Pageantry*, 7–8; 10, 15–16.
32 Davol, *Handbook*, 103.
33 Langdon, "Pageant Mad," 5.
34 The American Pageantry Association's *"Who's Who" in Pageantry* listed seventeen women out of its thirty-two notable pageant writers, directors, and composers.
35 Gabrielle Elliot, "Mission Pageants: Why Have them? Suggestions of Themes," *Woman's Work*, Nov. 1914, 258–259.
36 Miss Margaret Reynolds, "The Possibilities of Pageants," *Mission Studies*, Oct. 1916, 301–304.
37 YWCA, "A Second List of Plays and Pageants."
38 Miller, *Church Pageantry*, 11, 17–18, 145, 155.
39 Langdon, "Pageant Mad," 5.
40 John Oxenham and Hugh Moss, "The Pageant of Darkness and Light"; Montgomery, "Pageant of Missions." Oxenham was the pen name of William Arthur Dunkerly.
41 On the World in Boston and other missionary exhibitions, see: Hasinoff, *Faith in Objects*.
42 "World Exposition Ends," *Baltimore Sun*, Dec. 1, 1912, 5.

43 Oxenham and Moss, "Pageant of Darkness and Light," 35, 36–39.
44 "World's Fair for the Gospel," *Hartford Courant*, April 8, 1911, 20.
45 "Pageant of Darkness and Light Given in Boston," *Chicago Daily Tribune*, April 25, 1911, 6. On Baltimore's version see: "Opening a Great Success," *Baltimore Sun*, Oct. 27, 1912, 7.
46 "Opening a Great Success," 7.
47 Montgomery, "Pageant of Missions."
48 Conroy-Krutz, *Christian Imperialism*, 20–21.
49 Montgomery, "Pageant of Missions."
50 "The Northfield Summer School," *Life and Light for Woman*, Sept. 1910, 389.
51 Ibid.
52 "Missionary Pageant," *The News Journal* (Wilmington, DE), Oct. 17, 1914, 11.
53 "Young People's Missionary Society of Lincoln, Nebr., as Oriental Pilgrims." *Missionary Tidings*, July 1904, 81.
54 "The Northfield Summer School," *Life and Light for Woman*, Sept. 1910, 389.
55 "Woman's Boards in Annual Meeting, 1911," *Woman's Work*, June 1911, 138.
56 Montgomery, "Pageant of Missions"; "Big Mission Jubilee Opens Here Today," *New York Times*, March 27, 1911, 20.
57 "Jubilee Echoes Still Rolling," *Woman's Work*, August 1911, 188–189.
58 Davol, *Handbook*, 103–104.
59 Ahmed, *On Being Included*, 32.
60 Montgomery, *How to Use for* An African Trail, 19.
61 Ibid., 14.
62 Ibid.
63 Ibid., 20.
64 "There's a Way," *Church Woman*, March 1941, 33.
65 Montgomery, *How to Use for* Christus Redemptor, 31.
66 Montgomery, *How to Use for* The King's Highway, 21.
67 Montgomery, *How to Use for* Western Women in Eastern Lands, 49.
68 Montgomery, *Western Women in Eastern Lands*; Speer, *The Light of the World*.
69 A mission study that took up a similar theme was Murray, *The Apologetic*, 9–10, 38.
70 Speer, *The Light of the World*, ix. On the imperial study of comparative religions and the role of missionaries see: Chidester, *Empire of Religion*. On Speer's efforts and position in the missionary movement more generally see: Hutchison, *An Errand to the World*, 120–122, 147, 170–174.
71 Montgomery, *How to Use for* The Light of the World, 58.
72 Montgomery, *How to Use for* The King's Highway, 25–27.
73 Montgomery, *How to Use for* Western Women in Eastern Lands, 28–29; Montgomery, *How to Use for* The Light of the World, 16–18. Emphasis original.
74 Mace, "Comparative Religions."
75 Montgomery, *How to Use for* The Light of the World, 4–5, 15.
76 Ibid., 38, 37–42.

77 Ibid.
78 Ibid., 51–52.
79 Ibid.
80 Burton, *Women Workers*. Burton had first traveled to Asia with her father, Ernest, in 1908 when he headed the Oriental Investigation Commission to investigate the status of missionary colleges. Margaret Burton then became the YWCA secretary for "Missionary Interests and Oriental Students." "Margaret E. Burton of YWCA Board, 83," *New York Times*, Jan. 24, 1969, 40; "Changes in the National Staff," *The Association Monthly*, Feb. 1914, 42. See also: Sasaki, *Redemption*, 63–64. Burton's publications include: Margaret E. Burton, *The Education of Women in China* (New York: Fleming H. Revell Company, 1911); Margaret E. Burton, *Notable Women of Modern China* (New York: Fleming H. Revell Company, 1912); Margaret E. Burton, *The Education of Women in Japan* (New York: Fleming H. Revell Company, 1914); Margaret E. Burton, *Comrades in Service* (Missionary Education Movement, 1915); Margaret E. Burton, *The Assembly of the League of Nations* (Chicago: University of Chicago Press, 1941).
81 Montgomery, *How to Use Handbook for* Woman Workers of the Orient, 44.
82 Ibid., 24–30.

CHAPTER 3. LEARNING TO COOPERATE BY COOPERATING
1 Interview with Myrta Ross by Hilda Lee Dail, 1225-2-4:13, Church Women United Papers, GCAH, Drew University.
2 "Annual Report of the Executive Secretary," April 1935, Rochester Council of Church Women, Folder 6, Box 18, EIAR.
3 Handy, "The American Religious Depression."
4 Genevieve Brown, "The Wood for the Temple," *Church Woman*, Jan. 1941, 9.
5 "Brief Excerpts from Reports Presented at the Ninth Annual Conference," *Church Woman*, Sept. 1937, 5, 10.
6 Curtis, *A Consuming Faith*, 23–27.
7 Wall, "The 1930s Roots." For an instructive case study of religious liberal exclusion see: Todd, "The Temple of Religion." Other scholars have written a more celebratory analysis of ecumenical Protestants' contributions to liberal consensus: Hollinger, *Protestants Abroad*; Schultz, *Tri-Faith America*.
8 "Study Books," *Annual Report of the Federation of Woman's Boards of Foreign Missions*, 1924, 23.
9 "The Contribution of Youth," *Annual Report of the Federation of Woman's Boards of Foreign Missions*, January 1927, 13, RG 27, Folder 16, Box 4, Foreign Missions Conference of North America, Presbyterian Historical Society, Philadelphia, Pennsylvania. Cited hereafter as FMC Papers, PHS.
10 This institutional history can be found in Beaver, *All Loves Excelling*, 177–209.
11 Freedman, "Separatism as Strategy."
12 Lucy Peabody, "Report of the President of the Federation," *Annual Report of the Federation of Woman's Boards of Foreign Missions* 1922, 33.

13 William R. Hogg, *Ecumenical Foundations: A History of the Rise of the International Missionary Council and its Nineteenth-Century Background* (Eugene, OR: Wipf and Stock Publishers, 2002, originally published by Harper & Brothers, 1952), 225.
14 "Women's Organizations," *Annual Report of the Federation of Woman's Boards of Foreign Missions* 1922, 25.
15 Ibid., 26.
16 "Quadrennial Meeting, Federal Council of Churches, Atlanta, Dec. 3–9, 1924, *FCC Bulletin*, Nov.–Dec. 1924, 19–22; Minutes of the Conference of Organized Women's Work, Pittsburgh, PA, Dec. 11–12, 1924, 1221-2-1-05, CWU Papers, GCAH; Frances MacMillan Ferguson, "New Plan of Relationships with Home Missions Councils," *FCC Bulletin*, Feb. 1927, 4.
17 Florence Quinlan to Carrie Kerschner, Dec. 20, 1924, 1221-2-1-05, CWU Papers, GCAH.
18 Minutes of the Conference of Organized Women's Work, Pittsburgh, PA, Dec. 11–12, 1924, 1221-2-1-05, CWU Papers, GCAH.
19 Florence Quinlan to Carrie Kerschner, Dec. 20, 1924, 1221-2-1-05, CWU Papers, GCAH.
20 Ibid.
21 Ibid.
22 Ibid.
23 Ibid.
24 "Dr. Roy B. Guild Dies," *New York Times*, Jan. 14, 1945, 40; "Roy B. Guild Will Accept New Work," *Topeka Daily Capital*, March 15, 1915, 6. One newspaper headline speaks to how his background as an athlete factored into his identity: "Missionary Who Is Also Muscular, College Athlete to Open Campaign," *Pittsburgh Daily Post*, Jan. 8, 1912, 6. See also: Bederman, "'The Women.'"
25 Guild, *Practicing Christian Unity*, 1.
26 Ibid., 23.
27 "Church Federation to Result from World War," *Topeka Daily Capital*, Jan. 25, 1918, 10.
28 Guild, *Practicing Christian Unity*, 60.
29 "Strongly Back Federation of City Churches," *Democrat and Chronicle* (Rochester, NY), Dec. 3, 1918, 10. Guild also used metaphors of Versailles and both baseball and football teams in *Practicing Christian Unity*.
30 Minutes of the Meeting of the Woman's Council of the Rochester Federation of Churches, Jan. 10, 1922, Box 18, Folder 1, Ecumenical and Interfaith Archives of Rochester, University of Rochester. Cited hereafter as EIAR.
31 "Annual Report of Executive Secretary," Council of Church Women of Rochester and Monroe County, April 1936, Box 18, Folder 6, EIAR.
32 "Council of Church Women Honors Aide on 25-Year Task," *Democrat and Chronicle*, Oct. 7, 1950, 29; "Church Leader Dies at 85," *Democrat and Chronicle*, Sept. 7, 1968, 11.

33 National Council of Federated Church Women, Annual Conference, May 23, 1935, *Yearbook*, CWU Papers, 1221-2-1-23, GCAH.
34 Annual Report, Women's Council, Jan. 26, 1923, Box 18, Folder 1, EIAR.
35 Minutes, Council of Church Women, Jan. 25, 1924, Box 18, Folder 1, EIAR.
36 Minutes of the Meeting of the Woman's Council of the Rochester Federation of Churches, March 21, 1922, EIAR.
37 "Sects Declared Waste of Work and Inefficient," *Democrat and Chronicle*, Jan. 27, 1923, 18.
38 "Representatives of the Churches of the Woman's Council of the Rochester Federation of Churches," n.d. [1923], Box 18, Folder 1, EIAR. Mrs. R. J. Gorman represented Memorial AME Zion and Serena Dennis represented Trinity Presbyterian. Carrie Dukes, "The Neighborhood House," *Spelman Messenger*, Dec. 1917, 6. See also: Louie Davis Shivery and Hugh H. Smyth, "The Neighborhood Union: A Survey of the Beginnings of Social Welfare Movements Among Negroes in Atlanta," *Phylon* 3, no. 2 (1942): 149–162; Jacqueline A. Rouse, "The Legacy of Community Organizing: Lugenia Burns Hope and the Neighborhood Union," *Journal of Negro History* 69, no. 3/4 (1984): 114–133; Sarah H. Case, *Leaders of Their Race: Educating Black and White Women in the New South*, (Urbana: University of Illinois Press, 2017), 113–114; "'Mother' Dorsey Is Given Purse of Gold," *Democrat and Chronicle*, Aug. 3, 1922, 24; "Faculty Notes," *Spelman Messenger*, Nov. 1944, 25.
39 Minutes of the Woman's Council of the Rochester Council of Churches, Oct. 30, 1925, Folder 1, Box 18, EIAR.
40 Minutes, Women's Council of the Federation of Churches, Oct. 22, 1926, Box 18, Folder 2, EIAR.
41 Minutes, Special Meeting of the Women's Council, Nov. 5, 1926; Minutes, Executive Committee, Dec. 3, 1927, Box 18, Folder 2, EIAR.
42 Lillian Teller Snodgrass, "Weaving the Tapestry of Council Service and Fellowship: 25th Anniversary History," [1947], Box 29, Folder 6, EIAR.
43 Minutes, Exec. Com. of Women's Council, June 30, 1927 and Oct. 7, 1927, Box 18, Folder 2, EIAR.
44 "President's Message," Annual Report pamphlet, 1931–1932, Box 29, Folder 1, EIAR.
45 Mrs. Grace Hondelink Dies, Churchwoman," *Democrat and Chronicle*, Nov. 29, 1961, 16.
46 Annual Report of the Woman's Council of the Federation of Churches, Jan. 23, 1925, Box 18, Folder 1, EIAR.
47 Minutes, Meeting of the Woman's Council of the Federation of Churches, Jan. 26, 1923, Box 18, Folder 1, EIAR.
48 "Missionary Group Opens Sessions at Salem Church," and "Hadassah to Meet," *Democrat and Chronicle*, Sept. 20, 1927, 22.
49 "Missions Institute Will Open To-Day," *Democrat and Chronicle*, Sept. 23, 1924, 26.

50 Fletcher, *Maude Royden*. On Christian internationalism see: Thompson, *For God and Globe*, 15–20.
51 "Defends Smoking," *Tampa Tribune*, Jan. 9, 1928, 1; "Women Have Right to Smoke If Men Can," *Albuquerque Journal*, Jan. 9. 1928, 5; "Church Musn't Talk," *Cincinnati Enquirer*, Jan. 9, 1928, 3.
52 "Ban on Miss Royden Amuses the British," *New York Times*, Jan. 4, 1928, 2. On the religious responses to the companionate marriage debate in the 1920s see: Davis, "'Not Marriage at All.'" "Drop Maude Royden Lecture in Chicago," *Boston Globe*, Jan. 2, 1928, 10; Corinne Danforth, "Miss Royden to Have Chances Enough to Be Heard in Boston," *Boston Globe*, Jan. 8, 1928, C7; "Miss Royden Here, Defends Smoking," *New York Times*, Jan. 5, 1928, 5.
53 Minutes, Special Meeting of the Council of Church Women, Jan. 10, 1928, Box 18, Folder 2, EIAR.
54 "Banning Woman Lecturer for Smoking Held Unjust," *Democrat and Chronicle*, Jan. 8, 1928, 10.
55 "Maude Royden to Lecture at Baptist Temple," *Democrat and Chronicle*, Jan. 22, 1928, 40; Minutes, Special Meeting of the Council of Church Women, Jan. 10, 1928, Box 18, Folder 2, EIAR.
56 William Ernest Hocking, *Re-thinking Missions: A Laymen's Inquiry After One Hundred Years* (New York: Harper and Brothers, 1932); Mrs. Henry W. Peabody, "Woman's Criticism of the Laymen's Report," *Missionary Review of the World*, Jan. 1933, 39–42.
57 William H. Brackney, "The Legacy of Helen B. Montgomery and Lucy W. Peabody," *International Bulletin of Missionary Research* (Oct. 1991), 176.
58 Ernest Hocking to Georgiana Sibley, Oct. 20, 1958, Box 1, Folder 18, Papers of Georgiana Sibley, University of Rochester Library.
59 "What Do I Believe about Foreign Missions," n.d., Box 1, Folder 15, Papers of Georgiana Sibley, University of Rochester Library.
60 Katherine Silverthorn, "Report of President," *Annual Report of the Twentieth Interdenominational Conference of the Federation of Woman's Boards of Foreign Missions of North America*, Atlantic City, Jan. 9–12, 1926, 11.
61 Conference on Organized Women's Interdenominational Work, Cleveland, Ohio, June 2, 1926, CWU Papers, 1221-2-1-06, GCAH.
62 "Friends" circular, Feb. 23, 1927, 1221-2-1-07, CWU Papers, GCAH.
63 Conference Women's Organized Interdenominational Work,—Findings Committee Report—CWU Papers, 1221-2-1-07, GCAH.
64 "*All That Is Past Is Prologue*" (New York, 1944), 1244-03-02-09, CWU, GCAH. See also: Robert, *American Women in Mission*, 260–272; Kenny, "The World Day of Prayer."
65 Mary Hough, "Report of the Day of Prayer Committee," in *Annual Report of the Federation of Woman's Boards of Foreign Missions*, Jan. 1927, RG 27, Box 4, Folder 16, FMC Papers, PHS.

66 "The World Task: International, Inter-Racial, Industrial," in the *Annual Report of the FWBFM*, January 1927, 13.
67 "The Missionary Enterprise in Relation to World Peace," *Annual Report of the Twenty-Third Interdenominational Conference of the Federation of Woman's Boards of Foreign Missions of North America*, Detroit, Jan. 14–18, 1929, 13.
68 Minutes, Administrative Committee of the Federation and Council, June 13, 1928, RG 27, Box 4, Folder 14, FMC Papers, PHS.
69 National Commission of Protestant Church Women and National Council of Federated Church Women, March 1930, RG 27, Box 4, Folder 14, FMC Papers, PHS; Joint Session of the Administrative Committees of the Council, Federation, and the National Council of Federated Church Women, March 10–11, 1930, RG 27, Box 4, Folder 14, FMC Papers, PHS.
70 Lofton, "The Methodology of the Modernists."
71 Wieman, *Methods of Private Religious Living*, 101–107; Joint Session of the Administrative Committees of the Council, Federation, and the National Council of Federated Church Women, March 10–11, 1930, RG 27, Box 4, Folder 14, FMC Papers, PHS.
72 Wieman, *Methods of Private Religious Living*, 101–107; Joint Session of the Administrative Committees of the Council, Federation, and the National Council of Federated Church Women, March 10–11, 1930, RG 27, Box 4, Folder 14, FMC Papers, PHS.
73 Wieman, *Methods of Private Religious Living*, 114–115.
74 Joint Session of the Administrative Committees of the Council, Federation, and the National Council of Federated Church Women, March 10–11, 1930, RG 27, Box 4, Folder 14, FMC Papers, PHS.
75 Ibid.
76 Minutes, Joint Session of the Administrative Committees of the Council, Federation, and the National Council of Federated Church Women, March 10–11, 1930, RG 27, Box 4, Folder 14, FMC Papers, PHS.
77 National Commission of Protestant Church Women and National Council of Federated Church Women, March 1930, RG 27, Box 4, Folder 14, FMC Papers, PHS.
78 Joint Session of the Administrative Committees of the Council, Federation, and the National Council of Federated Church Women, March 10–11, 1930, RG 27, Box 4, Folder 14, FMC Papers, PHS.
79 National Commission of Protestant Church Women and National Council of Federated Church Women, March 1930, RG 27, Box 4, Folder 14, FMC Papers, PHS.

CHAPTER 4. CHRISTIAN AMERICANIZATION AND THE TRI-FAITH MOVEMENT

1 Council of Women for Home Missions, "Christian Americanization: Our National Ideals and Mission," 1918, Missionary Research Library Pamphlets, Union Theological Seminary.
2 Pruitt, *Open*, 42.

3   Ibid., 40–48. See also: Kaufman, *Horace Kallen*; Hutchison, *Religious Pluralism*; Hollinger, "Pluralism."
4   Smith, "Settler Colonialism and U.S. Home Missions".
5   Davidson, "An Evangelical Occupation," 203–228, 210.
6   Schultz, *Tri-Faith America*; Mislin, *Saving Faith*; Gaston, *Imagining Judeo-Christian America*.
7   Davidson, "An Evangelical Occupation," 203–228, 210.
8   Wenger, *We Have a Religion*; McCrary, *Sincerely Held*, 83–110. On other exclusions inherent in tri-faith pluralism see: Todd, "The Temple of Religion." On Jewish and Catholic alternatives to a Protestant (and secular) conception of religious liberty see: Greene, *Jewish Origins*; Curtis, *Production of American Religious Freedom* , 88–90.
9   For a broader overview of race and European immigration see: Matthew Frye Jacobson, *Whiteness of a Different Color: European Immigrants and the Alchemy of Race* (Cambridge, MA: Harvard University Press, 1999). On debates among Jews at the time about religious, racial, and national identity, see: Wenger, *Religious Freedom*, 145, 167–172. See also: Batnitzky, *How Judaism Became a Religion*.
10 On settlement houses and imperial logics of surveys see: Burnidge, "Imperial Intersections."
11 Ngai, *Impossible Subjects*, 18–20, 24–25.
12 On White Protestant home missionaries' generally pro-immigration views see: Chang, *Citizens of a Christian Nation*; Pruitt, *Open Hearts*, 38–40.
13 Pruitt, *Open Hearts*, 52. On the Americanization movement see: John Higham, *Strangers in the Land: Patterns of American Nativism, 1860–1925*, 2nd ed. (New Brunswick, NJ: Rutgers University Press, 2002), 234–263. For the critical role educators played in Americanization see: Selig, *Americans All*.
14 "To Americanize Foreign-Born Who Live Here," *New York Times Magazine*, Oct. 24, 1915, 8.
15 Butler, *Community Americanization*, 9, 11. Butler was the director of the Americanization Bureau of Education within the Department of the Interior.
16 There are many examples of this in women's home missionary magazines. See, for example, the suggestion that local missionary societies make a "living newspaper" called "The Americanization Herald: Negro Edition." Estella Sutton Aitchison, "Missionary Dynamics," *Missions*, March 1919, 206. It was used in reference to Native Americans as well: *Co-operation for Indians: A Conference of Christian Workers Among Indians* (New York: Home Missions Council, 1919).
17 Giles, *Adventures in Brotherhood*, 172. Giles was an editor at *McCall's* Magazine and had no formal position with a missionary society.
18 Brooks, *Christian Americanization*, 11, 16.
19 Gin Lum, *Heathen*, 129–130.
20 For some examples see: Butler, *Community Americanization*, and several books compiled in Talbot, ed., *Americanization*.

21 Brooks, *Christian Americanization*, 2.
22 Ibid., 16.
23 Ibid.
24 Seebach, *Land of All Nations*, v–vi.
25 Ibid., vi.
26 Brooks, *Christian Americanization*, 31.
27 Ibid., 103, 102.
28 "Side-Lights," *Missions*, April 1919, 293.
29 Giles, *Adventures in Brotherhood*, 141.
30 "Committee on New Americans," *Report of the Sixteenth Annual Meeting of the Home Missions Council and Council fo Women for Home Missions* (New York, 1923), 179.
31 Greene and Gould, eds., *Handbook-Bibliography*, 7–8.
32 Speer, *Of One Blood*, 13; Giles, *Adventures in Brotherhood*, 11.
33 Miller, *Peasant Pioneers*, 12. Miller cited William Z. Ripley's *The Races of Europe* (1899). Miller was a Presbyterian minister who spent time in Bohemia after graduating from Union Theological Seminary. He later worked for the Presbyterian Board of Home Missions on Americanization work and at the Jan Hus Neighborhood House.
34 Edith Mae Bell, "Suggestions to Leaders on 'Adventures in Brotherhood,'" *Woman's Home Missions*, Nov. 1924, 8.
35 Speer, *Of One Blood*, 227.
36 Eva Clark Waid, "Suggestions on the Use of the Home Study Books," *Women and Missions*, Oct. 1924, 272.
37 Korelitz, "'A Magnificent Piece of Work'"; Zeien-Stuckman, "Creating New Citizens"; McGuinness, "Body and Soul"; Cosson, "Catholic Gatekeepers."
38 Giles, *Adventures in Brotherhood*, 140.
39 Proceedings of the Americanization Conference, May 1919, Washington, DC: Government Printing Office, 373.
40 "Thirty-First Annual Convention of the Central Conference of American Rabbis, Address of the President," *The Jewish Voice* (St. Louis, MO), July 9, 1920, 5–6; "Grant Request of Rabbis," *New York Times*, March 29, 1920, 6.
41 Wenger, *Religious Freedom*, 167–172.
42 Spear, "Claiming the Passion," 834–835.
43 See for example: John Stuart Conning, "Israel on Trek," *Women and Missions*, March 1928, 447–449. Conning was the Superintendent of Jewish Evangelization for the Presbyterian Board of Missions. Citing Hebrew schools and synagogues as well as the Zionist movement, he wrote that Jewish leaders' "appeal is racial rather than religious" and that this indicated the "failure of Judaism" as a religion and presented Christians with an opportunity to create Jewish Christians.
44 Harkness, *The Church and the Immigrant*, 26.
45 Joint Administrative Committee Report, *Report of the Fifteenth Annual Meeting of the Home Missions Council and Council of Women for Home Missions* (New York, 1922), 116.

46 Applegarth, 28–29, 31–32.
47 Jakobsen and Pellegrini, *Love the Sin*, 49.
48 See for example: Gordon, *The Mormon Question*.
49 Brooks, *Christian Americanization*, 125–126.
50 Tisa Wenger, "Indian Dances and the Politics of Religious Freedom, 1870–1930," *Journal of the Academic of American Religion* 79, no. 4 (Dec. 2011): 850–878; Evans, *The Burden of Black Religion*, 115–139; Gin Lum, *Heathenism*.
51 Henry P. Judd, "Report of the Hawaiian Evangelical Association," *Report of the Fifteenth Annual Meeting of the Home Missions Council and Council of Women for Home Missions* (New York, 1922), 203–204.
52 Miller, *Peasant Pioneers*, 37.
53 Ibid., 152.
54 "Foreign-Born Poorly Led By Film, She Says," *Democrat and Chronicle*, May 22, 1926, 28.
55 Giles, *Adventures in Brotherhood*, 135.
56 Ibid., 133.
57 Curtis, *Production of American Religious Freedom*, 89–90.
58 "Chips from Our Reconstruction Chisel," *Missions*, Feb. 1919, 130–131.
59 Report of the Committee on City, Immigrant, and Industrial Work, *Report of the Thirteenth Annual Meeting of the Home Missions Council* (New York, 1920), 104.
60 Boris Mikolji, "Ethnic Groups in America: the Italians of Rochester," *Il Politico* 34, no. 4 (Dec. 1971): 660–682, 664.
61 "Seminary Will Merge Italian, English Work," *Democrat and Chronicle*, Feb. 9, 1931, 14; Edwin P. Farham, "Rev. Mangano," *Baptist Home Mission Monthly*, Sept. 1907, 315–316; "Bequest of $30,000 Comes to Preacher," *Brooklyn Eagle*, May 2, 1915, 69; "Divinity School Here Announces Addition of Italian Department," *Democrat and Chronicle*, Sept. 25, 1928, 15; "Church Calls Back Seminary Faculty Man," *Democrat and Chronicle*, Feb. 5, 1931, 17; Esther Coster, "A Dream Comes True for Italian Baptists," *Brooklyn Daily Eagle*, June 29, 1940, 8. One of the Manganos' three sons, Philip, shared his mother's interest in foreign relations. He worked for the Office of Strategic Services during the Second World War and was a career officer in the State Department. Philip Mangano, "Foreign Service Officer and Annapolis Professor," *Washington Post*, Oct. 3, 1980.
62 Blake McKelvey, "The Italians of Rochester: An Historical Review," *Rochester History* 22, no. 4 (Oct. 1960). www.libraryweb.org.
63 "Sects Declared Waste of Work," *Democrat and Chronicle*, Jan. 27, 1923, 18.
64 Minutes, Woman's Council of the [Rochester] Federation of Churches, Jan. 26, 1923, Folder 1, Box 18, EIAR.
65 "Americanization: A Program of Action and Service for the Churches," New York: Home Missions Council, 1919. https://iiif.lib.harvard.edu.
66 Helen Young, "A Report of the Christian Americanization Work of the Women's Council of the Federation of Churches," Rochester Council of Church Women, Jan. 1923, Box 18, Folder 1, EIAR.

67 Butler, *Community Americanization*, 37.
68 "Americanization: A Program of Action and Service for the Churches," New York: Home Missions Council, 1919. https://iiif.lib.harvard.edu.
69 "A Report of the Christian Americanization Work of the Women's Council of the Federation of Churches," Jan. 1923, Box 18, Folder 1, EIAR.
70 "Foreign-Born Poorly Led by Film, She Says," *Democrat and Chronicle*, May 22, 1926, 28.
71 Laura E. Dixon, "The Immigrant Woman in the New World," *Women and Missions*, March 1926, 449–451.
72 "Americanization Pageant Is Given by Baptist Group," *Ithaca Journal*, March 27, 1924, 7.
73 Helen Young, Americanization Committee Report, Annual Meeting of the Woman's Council of the Federation of Churches of Rochester and Monroe County, January 28, 1927, Box 29, Folder 1, EIAR.
74 "Americanization: A Program of Action and Service for the Churches."
75 "Americanization Work Told in Letters," *Woman's Home Missions*, April 1923, 22.
76 Ruswick, *Almost Worthy*, 71.
77 Laura E. Dixon, "The Immigrant Woman in the New World," *Women and Missions*, March 1926, 449–451.
78 "The March Meeting," *Woman's Home Missions*, Feb. 1920, 17.
79 Pruitt, *Open Hearts*, 25–34.
80 On the settlement house movement see: Gal, *The Settlement House Movement*. On the training of Protestant women settlement workers see: William P. Shriver, "Give Us Leaders," *Women and Missions*, March 1928, 456–457.
81 Anson Phelps Stokes, *The Early History of Lowell House* (New Haven, Published for Farnum-Neighborhood House, 1946), 2.
82 Davis, *Spearheads*; Carson, *Settlement Folk*; Crocker, *Social Work and Social Order*.
83 "One Thousand Facts," *Missions*, June 1925, 342; "Home Mission Trails to Seattle," *Missions*, July 1925, 388.
84 "Neighbors to All," *Woman's Home Missions*, March 1924, 5–6. For a much longer analysis of this and other settlement houses in Indiana, including a Catholic project, see: Crocker, *Social Work and Social Order*.
85 Stanley B. Hazzard, "Greater New York as a Mission Field," *Missions*, Jan. 1924, 21–22.
86 Brooks, *Christian Americanization*, 32.
87 For the insider's perspective of an Italian Catholic neighborhood see Orsi, *The Madonna of 115th Street*.
88 Miller, *Peasant Pioneers*, 165.
89 "Race Relations in America," *Missions*, Sept. 1924, 431–433.
90 "Vacation Bible Schools Expect 7,000 Children," *Democrat and Chronicle*, June 29, 1924, 28. For some background on the Daily Vacation Bible School and outlines of the lessons, see: Bovine and Merrill, eds., *Manual of Graded Bible Courses*.

91 "A Gleam," *Women's Home Missions*, August 1926, 12.
92 Speer, *Of One Blood*, 94–95.
93 The Commission's name would be changed to the Department of Race Relations in the 1930s.
94 Minutes, Rochester Council of Church Women, Jan. 8, 1932, Box 18, Folder 4, EIAR.
95 Minutes, Executive Committee of Rochester Council of Church Women, March 4, 1932, Box 18, Folder 4, EIAR.
96 Mrs. L. Michelson, Summary Race Relations Conference, Rochester Council of Church Women, Oct. 20, 1932, Box 18, Folder 4, EIAR.
97 Minutes, Executive Committee, Rochester Council of Church Women, Dec. 2, 1932, Box 18, Folder 4, EIAR.
98 Minutes, Executive Committee, Rochester Council of Church Women, Feb. 2, 1933, Box 18, Folder 4, EIAR; "Lincoln's Birthday Meeting Scheduled at Y.W. Sunday," *Democrat and Chronicle*, Feb. 5, 1933, 34.
99 Gaston, *Imagining Judeo-Christian America*, 63–71.
100 Schultz, *Tri-Faith America*, 194.
101 Mrs. John Ferguson (Frances Macmillan) and Mrs. E. Tallmadge Root (Georgiana M. Root), 1931, CWU Papers, 1221.2.1.16, GCAH.
102 "Women of 3 Faiths to Hold Miniature Institute Thursday," *New York Herald Tribune*, May 3, 1936, D8; "Women Urged to Lead Fight on Intolerance," *New York Herald Tribune*, Feb. 27, 1937, 12. Bader's husband, Jesse, a Disciples of Christ minister, headed the Federal Council's Department of Evangelism.
103 Mrs. Jesse M. Bader, "Conferences of Jews and Christians," *Church Woman*, Feb. 1938, 5.
104 Mrs. Stephen S. Wise, "How does the Jew Feel in the World Today," *Church Woman*, Feb. 1938, 7–8.
105 "Church Women Aid Santa With Dolls at Toy Depot," *Democrat and Chronicle*, Nov. 28, 1937; "Clerics, Rabbi, Will Address Holiday Rite," *Democrat and Chronicle*, Nov. 16, 1939, 18.
106 Zeiger, "Finding a Cure for War."
107 Minutes, Rochester Council of Church Women, Feb. 21, 1930, Box 18, Folder 3, EIAR.
108 Annual Report of the International Relations Department, Rochester Council of Church Women, April 1935, Box 18, Folder 6, EIAR.
109 "Interfaith Women's Council Hears Plea for Tolerance," *Democrat and Chronicle*, Nov. 24, 1937, 17.
110 Minutes, Council of Church Women, Sept. 23, 1938, Box 18, Folder 8, EIAR.
111 Elinor K. Purvis, "The Church Woman in the Peace Movement," *Church Woman*, Jan. 1938, 18–19. Notably, Purvis would later become the chairwoman of the Federal Council's Department of International Justice and Good Will. She also testified before the House Committee on Immigration and Naturalization on behalf of lifting immigration and citizenship restrictions against Indians in the mid-1940s.

112 Minutes of the Special Called Meeting of the Board of Directors of the National Council of Federated Church Women, Indianapolis, May 27–28, 1937, 1221-2-1-24, CWU Papers, GCAH.
113 Purvis, "The Church Woman in the Peace Movement," 18–19.
114 Minutes of Council of Church Women, March 6, 1931, Box 18, Folder 3, EIAR.
115 Meeting Minutes, Council of Church Women, Rochester, NY, Dec. 2, 1938, Box 18, Folder 8, EIAR.
116 Mrs. Edwin Allen Stebbins, "Growing Together Through Richer Experience in Worship," *Church Woman*, Dec. 1938, 10–12.
117 Minutes, Rochester Council of Church Women, Nov. 6, 1942, Box 18, Folder 10, EIAR.
118 Sears, *Refuge Must Be Given*, chapter 2.
119 Minutes, CWCRR, March 27, 1939, Folder 12, Box 56, FCC Papers, PHS.
120 Minutes, CWCRR, May 15, 1939, Folder 12, Box 56, FCC Papers, PHS.

CHAPTER 5. THE SPIRITUAL FEELINGS AND RELIGIOUS POLITICS OF INTERRACIAL COOPERATION

1 "Summary of Discussion on Objective," March 1934, FCC Papers, RG 18, Box 56, Folder 12, PHS.
2 Jacobs, ed., *Black Americans*; Sarah L. Silkey, *Black Woman Reformer: Ida B. Wells, Lynching, and Transatlantic Reform* (Athens: University of Georgia Press, 2015); Gin Lum, *Heathens*, 137–149. Foundational and more recent scholarship focused on Black women's activism in the early 1900s includes: Higginbotham, *Righteous Discontent*; Collier-Thomas, *Jesus, Jobs, and Justice*; Cooper, *Beyond Respectability*; Jones, *Vanguard*.
3 Weisenfeld, *African American Women*, 35. See also: Robertson, *Christian Sisterhood*; Collier-Thomas, *Jesus, Jobs, and Justice*; Mary E. Frederickson, "'Each One is Dependent on the Other': Southern Churchwomen, Racial Reform, and the Process of Transformation, 1880–1940," *Visible Women: New Essays on American Activism* (Urbana and Chicago: University of Illinois Press, 1993).
4 The CWCRR's planning ewas evident in denominational women's organizations' work such as CWCRR member Thelma Stevens's work within the northern Methodist Church. On Stevens's civil rights interpretation of the World Order Movement see: Zubovich, *Before the Religious Right*, 99–104.
5 Haynes, *The Negro at Work*; Haynes, *Negro Newcomers in Detroit*.
6 Wilson, *The Segregated Scholars*, 61–66, 109–14, 205–208; Weisenfeld, *African American Women*, 10–14; 116–117; Robertson, *Christian Sisterhood*, 55–56; Carlton-LaNey, "Elizabeth Ross Haynes."
7 S.M.C. [Samuel McCrea Cavert], "The Race Problem Presses to the Fore," *FCC Bulletin*, Sept.–Oct. 1924, 31; W. E. Weatherford, *The Negro from Africa to America* (New York: George H. Doran , 1924).
8 On southern interracialism see: Ellis, *Race Harmony*; Gilmore, *Gender and Jim Crow*, 177–202; Hall, *Revolt Against Chivalry*; Brooks, *The Uplift Generation*. On

the development of interracial cooperation among elite Blacks and Whites after the 1906 racist violence in Atlanta, see David Fort Godshalk, *Veiled Visions: The 1906 Atlanta Race Riot and the Reshaping of American Race Relations* (Chapel Hill: University of North Carolina Press, 2005).

9 On the founding of the NAACP see: Langston Hughes, *Fight for Freedom: The Story of the NAACP* (New York: Norton, 1962); Carolyn Wedin, *Inheritors of the Spirit: Mary White Ovington and the Founding of the NAACP* (New York: Wiley, 1998); Berg, *The Ticket to Freedom*. On the Urban League see: Moore, *A Search for Equality*.

10 Roberts, *Crucible for a Vision*, PhD diss., 1975, Columbia University.

11 Formed in 1921 as the Commission was the Commission on the Negro Church and Race Relations, "Negro" was dropped in 1922, and in 1932, it was renamed the Department of Race Relations.

12 "Coming to Grips with the Racial Problem," *FCC Bulletin*, Aug.–Sept. 1922, 100. The same statement was affirmed by the Home Missions Council and Council of Women for Home Missions' Committee on Negro Americans. Home Missions Council, *Annual Report*, 1922, 177–178.

13 Edith H. Allen, Report of the Committee on Study Courses and Literature," *Report of the Sixteenth Annual Meeting of the Home Missions Council and Council of Women for Home Missions* (New York, 1923). 91.

14 Haynes, *The Trend of the Races*, v.

15 Ibid., 21.

16 Ibid., 168, 182, emphasis in original.

17 Adams, *Black Women's Christian Activism*, 17–30. On Black women workers in this period see: Frederickson, *Sisterhood and Solidarity*, 75–106; Phyllis Palmer, *Domesticity and Dirt: Housewives and Domestic Servants in the United States, 1920–1945* (Philadelphia: Temple University Press, 1989), 111–133. For an overview of Black women's work see Tera W. Hunter, *To 'Joy My Freedom: Southern Black Women's Lives and Labors After the Civil War* (Cambridge, MA: Harvard University Press, 1997) and Elizabeth Clark-Lewis, *Living In, Living Out: African American Domestics in Washington DC, 1910–1940* (Washington, DC: Smithsonian Institution Press, 1994).

18 Haynes, *Trend of the Races*, 172. He also cites Elizabeth Ross Haynes, "Three Million of Negro Women at Work," *Southern Workman*, Feb. 1921.

19 Haynes, *Trend of the Races*, 171–72.

20 Ibid., 19, emphasis in original.

21 Ibid., 19–20.

22 Edith H. Allen, Report of the Committee on Study Courses and Literature," *Report of the Sixteenth Annual Meeting of the Home Missions Council and Council of Women for Home Missions* (New York, 1923), 91.

23 Hammond, *Vanguard of a Race*. On Hammond see: Robertson, *Christian Sisterhood*, 45–46.

24 Hammond, *Vanguard of a Race*, xii.

25 Ben Wright, *Bonds of Salvation: How Christianity Inspired and Limited American Abolitionists* (Baton Rouge: Louisiana State University Press, 2020).
26 Hammond, *Vanguard of a Race*, xiii.
27 "Negro Americans—an Asset or a Liability," *The Missionary Review of the World*, June 1922, 421–422.
28 Pascoe, *What Comes Naturally*. See especially chapter 6. Dailey, "Sex, Segregation, and the Sacred after *Brown*."
29 Minutes, Meeting of the Women's Council of the Federation of Churches, Nov. 24, 1922, Box 18, Folder 1, EIAR; "Democracy Sham If Lynchings Persist," *Democrat and Chronicle*, Nov. 25, 1922, 21. On other mission study classes for 1922–23 see for example: "Buffalo Baptists Women to Conduct Mission Institute," *Buffalo Morning Express*, Sept. 11, 1922, 9; "Edna David Society to Hold Meeting," *Greenville (SC) News*, Sept. 26, 1922, 6; "Church Folk to Meet in Wilton," *The Muscatine (Iowa) Journal*, Sept. 27, 1922, 4; "5 Week Study of Home Missions," *Lima (OH) Republican-Gazette*, Oct. 8, 1922, 5; "Nashvillians to Attend Race Relations Meeting," *Nashville Tennessean*, Dec. 4, 1922, 10; "Methodist Meeting on Social Service," *Atlanta Constitution*, Dec. 5, 1922, 16; "Mission Study School Session to End Tonight," *Baltimore Sun*, Nov. 3, 1922, 4; "Mission School at City Temple Ends," *Dallas Morning News*, Oct. 1, 1922, 8; Mrs. John (Frances) Ferguson, "Schools of Missions," Annual Report of the Home Missions Council and Council of Women for Home Missions, 93; "Chautauqua," Annual Report of the Home Missions Council, 95–97.
30 Robertson, *Christian Sisterhood*, 126.
31 Robertson, *Christian Sisterhood*, and Weisenfeld, *African American Women*; Collier-Thomas, *Jesus, Jobs, and Justice*, 338–360; Adams, *Black Women's Christian Activism*; Denomme, "To End This Day of Strife."
32 Minutes, Woman's Continuation Committee, Nov. 1, 1926, RG 18, Box 56, Folder 11, FCC Papers, PHS.
33 "Services for Social Worker Set Tomorrow," *The Record* (Hackensack, NJ), June 16, 1958, 10.
34 Katherine Gardner, "Church Women At Work on the Race Problem," *Church School Herald*, Feb. 1929, 7–8.
35 "Church Women At Work on the Race Problem," Nov. 1928, RG 18, Box 56, Folder 11, FCC Papers, PHS; *For a Clearer Vision of the Race Problem*, Feb. 1928, RG 18, Box 56, Folder 11, FCC Papers, PHS.
36 "Church Women At Work on the Race Problem," Nov. 1928, RG 18, Box 56, Folder 11, FCC Papers, PHS.
37 "Church Women in Interracial Conference," *Federal Council Bulletin*, Oct. 1928, 13–14.
38 Minutes, CWCRR, Oct. 8, 1928, RG 18, Box 56, Folder 11, FCC Papers, PHS.
39 Collier-Thomas, *Jesus, Jobs, and Justice*, 332–333.
40 Minutes, CWCRR, Oct. 8, 1928, RG 18, Box 56, Folder 11, FCC Papers, PHS.
41 Minutes of Council of Colored Work, Oct. 8, 1926, YWCA/NB, cited in Robertson, *Christian Sisterhood*, 126.

42 Minutes, CWCRR, Oct. 8, 1928, RG 18, Box 56, Folder 11, FCC Papers, PHS.
43 Alice Dunbar-Nelson, "As in a Looking Glass," 28 Sept. 1928, in *Works of Alice Dunbar-Nelson*, ed. Gloria T. Hull (New York: Oxford University Press, 1988), 3: 232–233; Diary: *Give Us Each Day*, 264, cited in Robertson, *Christian Sisterhood*, 127.
44 "Church Women At Work on the Race Problem," Nov. 1928, RG 18, Box 56, Folder 11, FCC Papers, PHS.
45 Ibid.
46 Ibid.
47 Katherine Gardner, "Church Women At Work on the Race Problem," *Church School Herald* Feb. 1929, in FCC Papers, RG 18, Box 58, Folder 2, PHS.
48 Minutes, Executive Committee of Rochester Council of Church Women, March 2, 1928, Box 18, Folder 2, EIAR; "Council of Church Women Sponsors Mass Meeting to Mark Inter-Racial Sunday," *Democrat and Chronicle*, Feb. 5, 1928, 44.
49 Arthur Patrick Farren, "All Kinds of People: Estelle Fitzgerald," *Democrat and Chronicle Sunday Magazine*, Jan. 15, 1939, 6.
50 "Race Harmony Will Be Found in Tolerance," *Democrat and Chronicle*, Feb. 11, 1929, 7.
51 Ibid.
52 "Racial Groups to Present Programs at Church Fete," *Democrat and Chronicle*, Feb. 10, 1938, 19.
53 "Suggestions for Interracial Gatherings," Jan. 1933, RG 18, Box 56, Folder 12, FCC Papers, PHS; Invitation to the CWCRR tea, Nov. 15, 1932, RG 18, Box 56, Folder 12, FCC Papers, PHS.
54 Minutes, CWCRR, March 25, 1934, RG 18, Box 56, Folder 12, FCC Papers, PHS.
55 Elenore Kellogg, "African Negro Art Attracts Throng in New York," *Democrat and Chronicle*, April 7, 1935, 62.
56 Isabel C. Herdle, "African Negro Art Opens Gallery's April Exhibit," *Democrat and Chronicle*, April 5, 1936, 63.
57 Annual Report of Race Relations Department, 1935–1936, Rochester Council of Church Women, Box 18, Folder 6, EIAR.
58 "Children of Churches Invited to Gallery Thursday for Exhibit of African Art," *Democrat and Chronicle*, April 12, 1936, 53.
59 Suggestions for Interracial Gatherings, Jan. 1933, RG 18, Box 56, Folder 12, FCC Papers, PHS.
60 On Lester see: Koven, *The Match Girl and the Heiress*. Lester had just published her autobiography in the United States at the time of her visit for these two conferences: Muriel Lester, *It Occurred to Me* (New York: Harper, 1937).
61 "Dean Augustus Trowbridge," *Princeton Alumni Weekly*, March 23, 1934, 552.
62 Sarah Esther Trowbridge, "Asbury Park Inter-Racial Conference," *The Church Woman*, Feb. 1938, 17–19.
63 Ibid.

64 Katherine Gardner, "Church Women Meet to Plan the Next Chapter in Racial Understanding," *Church Woman*, Feb. 1938, 9–11.
65 Minutes, CWCRR, April 28, 1930, RG 18, Box 56, Folder 11, FCC Papers, PHS.
66 Minutes, CWCRR, Sept. 29, 1930, RG 18, Box 56, Folder 11, FCC Papers, PHS.
67 Minutes, CWCRR, March 30, 1931, RG 18, Box 56, Folder 11, FCC Papers, PHS.
68 Minutes, Nov. 25, 1935 and Jan. 27, 1936, CWCRR, RG 18, Box 56, Folder 12, FCC Papers, PHS.
69 Minutes, CWCRR, Jan. 29, 1940, RG 18, Box 56, Folder 12, FCC Papers, PHS; Cuthbert, *Juliette Derricotte*; Minutes, CWCRR, Jan. 25, 1932, RG 18, Box 56, Folder 12, FCC Papers, PHS.
70 Minutes, CWCRR, March 30, 1936, RG 18, Box 56, Folder 12, FCC Papers, PHS.
71 Minutes, CWCRR, Jan. 25, 1937, RG 18, Box 56, Folder 12, FCC Papers, PHS.
72 "Group Fights Hospital Pact," *Democrat and Chronicle*, Dec. 11, 1937, 15; Minutes, Executive Committee, Rochester Council of Church Women, Dec. 17, 1937, Box 18, Folder 7, EIAR.
73 Beasley was a journalist who wrote for a Black Catholic newspaper, the *American Catholic Tribune*, before moving to California in the early 1910s. She authored a history of Black migrants to the state in addition to her work as a columnist for the *Oakland Tribune*. Lena M. Wysinger, "In Memoriam-Miss Delilah L. Beasley," *Oakland Tribune*, Oct. 14, 1934, 55. For more on Beasley see: Lorraine Jacobs Crochet, *Delilah Leontium Beasley: Oakland's Crusading Journalist* (El Cerrito, CA: Downey Place Publishing House, 1990); Harris, "We Did What We Had to Do," 84–103.
74 Letter from the Oakland Council of Church Women, *Oakland Tribune*, Dec. 28, 1935, 5.
75 "Council of Church Women Accomplishes Varied Tasks," *Oakland Tribune*, Oct. 13, 1928, 6; Beasley, "Activities Among Negroes," *Oakland Tribune*, Dec. 1, 1929, B4.
76 Beasley, "Activities Among Negroes," *Oakland Tribune*, Dec. 1, 1929, B4.
77 Beasley, "Activities Among Negroes," *Oakland Tribune*, April 20, 1930, M4.
78 Beasley, "Activities Among Negroes," *Oakland Tribune*, Feb. 4, 1934, B4.
79 Beasley, "Activities Among the Negroes," *Oakland Tribune*, Nov. 30, 1930, O12.
80 Beasley, "Activities Among Negroes," *Oakland Tribune*, Jan. 18, 1931, 8. On the racial makeup of the Council of Church Women, see the organizers and attendees listed in: "Council of Church Women Plan All-Day Conference," *Oakland Tribune*, Oct. 31, 1931, 8.
81 Beasley, "Activities Among Negroes," *Oakland Tribune*, Feb. 4, 1934, B4.
82 "A Statement from the Church Women's Committee," 1933, RG 18, Box 56, Folder 12, FCC Papers, PHS. See also: Mary Jane Brown, *Eradicating This Evil: Women in the American Anti-Lynching Movement, 1892–1940* (New York: Routledge, 2000); Hall, *Revolt Against Chivalry*.

83 George C. Rable, "The South and the Politics of Antilynching Legislation, 1920–1940," *Journal of Southern History* 51, no. 2 (May 1985): 201–220.
84 Baker, "Domestication of Politics," 640–643.
85 Minutes, CWCRR, May 13, 1935, RG 18, Box 56, Folder 12, FCC Papers, PHS.
86 Ibid.
87 Minutes, CWCRR, May 13, 1935, Box 56, Folder 12, FCC Papers, PHS.
88 "Anti-Lynching Bill," *Church Woman*, Dec. 1937, 12.
89 "Department of Government," *Church Woman*, Oct. 1937, 16.
90 Minutes, CWCRR, Oct. 6, 1942, Folder 12, Box 56, FCC Papers, PHS.
91 "A High Point in the Assembly," *Church Woman*, Feb. 1942, 29.
92 "Continuation of the Assembly Meeting," Dec. 5, 1942, IV, 1223-2-2:01, CWU, GCAH.
93 Gardner, "Church Women Meet," 9.

CHAPTER 6. CHRISTIAN CITIZENS, WORLD CITIZENS

1 Mabel Jordan Hudelson, "A Christian Woman's Citizenship," *Church Woman*, Sept. 1944, 11; George Gallup, "Women to Be a Big Factor in '44," *Atlanta Constitution*, Jan. 16, 1944, 5B.
2 Millicent S. Foster, "Church Women and the Coming Election," *Church Woman*, Nov. 1944, 17.
3 Igo, *The Averaged American*. Protestant women tried to tabulate their own constituency in their Ecumenical Register in the early 1950s. Mrs. Harper Sibley, "Ecumenical Registration," *Church Woman*, Dec. 1949, 5.
4 Foster, "Church Women and the Coming Election," 19.
5 Christian citizenship derives from White evangelicals' Christian republicanism, as described in Noll, *America's God*. Iterations of White women's Christian citizenship can be traced back to the revolutionary era: Kerber, *Women of the Republic*; Kaplan, "Manifest Domesticity"; Dumenil, "Women's Reform Organizations." For a primary source elaborating on the topic see: Mary E. Craigie, *Christian Citizenship* (New York: National American Woman Suffrage Association, 1912).
6 Evans, *Do Everything*, 138–145; Newman, *White Women's Rights*; Sneider, *Suffragists in an Imperial Age*.
7 Adams, *Black Women's Christian Activism*.
8 Zubovich, *Before the Religious Right*, 78. On the broader enthusiasm for a postwar world order with American leadership see: Buchanan, "Domesticating Hegemony."
9 Berlant, *The Female Complaint*, 5. Protestant women's Christian citizenship writings resemble the citizenship manuals Berlant discusses in the chapter "Uncle Sam Needs a Wife," but Protestant women's unflagging focus on "the world" was deeply "ambivalent" about "the national" as they proposed a Christian World Order in critique of the nation. Berlant, 158.
10 "World Order and Peace," *Church Woman*, Dec. 1944, 30.

11 "Peace Pageants in Every Town," *New York Times*, June 27, 1915; Early, *A World Without War*. On the role of Black women in the peace movement see: Plastas, *A Band of Noble Women*. On the dynamics between Christian and Jewish women at international women's conferences see: Rupp, *Worlds of Women*, 15–37, 55–58.
12 Thompson, *For God and Globe*, 3–4.
13 On the NCCCW in comparison to other post–WWI women's peace organizations see: Zeiger, "Finding a Cure for War." On American pacifists more generally see: Michael Kazin, *War Against War: The American Fight for Peace, 1914–1918* (New York: Simon & Schuster, 2017).
14 Minutes, Executive Committee of Council of Church Women, Dec. 3, 1927, Box 18, Folder 2, EIAR; Minutes, Council of Church Women, Dec. 6, 1928, Box 18, Folder 3, EIAR; Minutes, Council of Church Women, Dec. 7, 1928, Box 18, Folder 2, EIAR; Minutes, Council of Church Women, Dec. 3, 1937, Box 18, Folder 7, EIAR. Committee on World Friendship Among Children, *Dolls of Friendship*. For more on the Japanese side of the exchange as well, see: Kohiuama, "The 1927 Exchange of Friendship Dolls."
15 "Legislative Department," Annual Report, Rochester Council of Church Women, April 27, 1928, Box 18, Folder 2, EIAR.
16 Zeiger, "Finding a Cure for War."
17 Edwin P. Farnham, "Rev. Antonio Mangano," *Baptist Home Mission Monthly*, Sept. 1907, 315–318; "Bequest of $30,000 Comes to Preacher," *Brooklyn Daily Eagle*, May 2, 1915, 9; "Ida Hersh Post, 97, Dies Was Pioneer Peace Activist," *Democrat and Chronicle*, Sept. 19, 1984, 1B.
18 North, *The Kingdom and the Nations*, 18–19, 197, 224–225.
19 "Legislative Department," Annual Report, Rochester Council of Church Women, April 27, 1928, Box 18, Folder 2, EIAR.
20 "Helps for Local Groups to Develop Program of Committee on International Relations," National Council of Federated Church Women, Oct. 21, 1931, 1221-2-1-16, CWU Papers, GCAH.
21 Minutes, Special Meeting of the Council of Church Women, Feb. 7, 1928, Box 18, Folder 2, EIAR.
22 "Coolidge Insists Only on Cruisers, Britten Reports," *New York Times*, Feb. 15, 1928, 1; "Churchmen Assail Bill for Big Navy, Provoking Storm," *New York Times*, Feb. 16, 1928, 1.
23 "Cutting the Naval Program," *New York Times*, Feb. 24, 1928, 13.
24 Annual Report of the Department of International Relations, Rochester Council of Church Women, April 1932, Box 18, Folder 4, EIAR.
25 Annual Report of Legislative Department, Rochester Council of Church Women, April 1936, Box 18, Folder 6, EIAR.
26 Mrs. Jean Beaven Abernethy, "Is Personal Faith Outmoded?" *Church Woman*, Jan. 1939, 11–13.
27 Minutes, National Council of Church Women, Jan. 19, 1939, 1221-2-1-27, CWU Papers, GCAH.

28 "Imperatives for Church Women in Time of War," *Church Woman*, Nov. 1939, 6–7.
29 Zubovich, *Before the Religious Right*, 69–74; Andrew Preston, *Sword of the Spirit, Shield of Faith: Religion in American War and Diplomacy* (New York: Knopf Doubleday, 2012), 292–296.
30 H.H.D., "A Moratorium on Christianity?" *Church Woman*, Nov. 1940, 5.
31 Muriel Lester, "Speed the Food Ships," *Church Woman*, Nov. 1940, 7–9. For a biography of Lester see: Koven, *The Match Girl and the Heiress*.
32 Henry P. Van Dusen, "Food or Freedom," *Church Woman*, Nov. 1940, 10–12.
33 Susannah Crowe to Mrs. Abram LeGrand, June 18, 1948, 1223-5-2:02, CWU Papers, GCAH.
34 *Church Woman*, Dec. 1940, 35.
35 Katherine Willard Eddy, "'If Ye Love Not Your Brother,'" *Church Woman*, Oct. 1939, 7–9, 24; Lynn Zimmerman, "Scattergood Hostel," *Church Woman*, Sept. 1940, 16–18.
36 Donald M. Sterling, "Toward Christian-Jewish Understanding," *Church Woman*, Feb. 1941, 14–17; Toru Matsumoto, "Issei, Nisei, and America," *Church Woman*, June 1941, 7–9; Earl E. Speicher, "Intolerance," *Church Woman*, Sept. 1941, 16–21; William W. Biddle, "Can You Believe What You Read?," *Church Woman*, Oct. 1941, 11.
37 Annual Report of the Committee on International Relations, Jan. 17–19, 1940, 1221-2-1-28, CWU Papers, GCAH.
38 Elinor K. Purves, "The Churches and the International Situation," *Church Woman*, April 1940, 17–19.
39 Elinor K. Purves, "Conference on Cause and Cure of War," *Church Woman*, Jan. 1941, 29.
40 "Church Women in the Emergency," Box 69, Folder 1, FCC Papers, PHS.
41 Agenda, "The Place of Church Women in the Emergency," Oct. 6, 1941, Box 69, Folder 1, FCC Papers, PHS.
42 Amy Welcher, "History Weighs the Intangibles," *Church Woman*, Jan. 1942, 5.
43 See for example: "Report of Findings of the All Day Meeting of Church Women to Consider the Place of Church Women in the Emergency," Oct. 6, 1941, Box 69, Folder 1, FCC, PHS.
44 For more see: Kenny, "The World Day of Prayer."
45 Margaret Applegarth, "The World This Year Is Unusually Round," *Church Woman*, Feb. 1944, 88.
46 Applegarth, "Standing in the Need of Prayer: Being an Account of the 1943 Observances of the World Day of Prayer," 1225-6-1:04, CWU, GCAH.
47 Applegarth, "I Was Glad When they Said Unto Me: 'Let us Go . . . ,'" *Church Woman*, March 1943, 10.
48 Jean Beaven Abernethy, "How, Not Why, Do I Pray?" *Church Woman*, Apr. 1939, 9. Emphasis in the original.
49 Margaret Applegarth, "The World Day of Prayer," *Church Woman*, May 1946, 17.

50 "Rural Radio Broadcast," *Handbook: Suggestions for the Leader of a World Day of Prayer Service*, 1942, 20–21, MRL, UTS.
51 Minutes of the WDP Committee, Apr. 23, 1940, 1225-6-1:03, CWU, GCAH.
52 Margaret Applegarth, "Standing in the Need of Prayer," *Radio Review of Women's National Radio Committee*, Feb. 1944, 9, 1226-6-1:04, CWU, GCAH.
53 Applegarth, "The World This Year is Unusually Round," Feb. 1944, 1225-6-1:04, CWU, GCAH.
54 *Handbook: Suggestions for the Leader*, WDP, Mar. 8, 1946, 17, 1225-6-2:20, CWU, GCAH.
55 Applegarth, *While Earth Rolls Onward Into Light*, Account of the 1944 Observances of the WDP, 1225-6-1:04, CWU, GCAH.
56 "World Day of Prayer: Early Reports," *Church Woman*, Apr. 1945, 32.
57 Florence Tyler, "The East and the West Are One," *Church Woman*, Feb. 1938, 13.
58 Letitia Knight Mintz, "The Church, a World Fellowship," *Church Woman*, November 1938, 15; a similar account of Chinese war refugees in Canton praying for the Japanese people appeared in the "Account of Observances" from 1943, 1225-6-1:04, CWU, GCAH.
59 Georgia Harkness, "Writing the Service for the World Day of Prayer," *Church Woman*, Mar. 1943, 9.
60 Minutes of the WDP Committee, May 16, 1941, CWU, GCAH.
61 *Handbook: Suggestions for the Leader*, WDP Program, Feb. 20, 1942, 3, 8; "I am the Way," WDP service, Feb. 20, 1942, MRL, UTS.
62 "I Am the Way," WDP service, Feb. 20, 1942, MRL, UTS.
63 Program of the Second Biennial Assembly, Nov., 1944, 1223-2-2-02, CWU Papers, GCAH.
64 Christine S. Smith, "Post-War Plans," *Church Woman*, Jan. 1944, 11–12.
65 Myrta Ross, "Our Responsibility in Our World-Wide Christian Fellowship," *Church Woman*, Nov. 1944, 5–7.
66 Program of the Third Biennial Assembly, Nov. 1946, 1223-2-2-03, CWU Papers, GCAH.
67 *Mothers of the World: A Christmas Play*, Ginling College, Box 129, Folder 2642, United Board Christian Higher Education in Asia Records, (RG 11) Special Collections, Yale Divinity School Library. URL: http://divinity-adhoc.library.yale.edu. This four-page English summary of the pageant was likely made by Ginling professor Eva Dykes Spicer.
68 Amelia Joseph Elmore, *Mothers of the World: A Christmas Play*, United Board (RG 11), Box 129, Folder 2642. http://divinity-adhoc.library.yale.edu. Elmore added a prologue, and her version has a complete script with lines for each character.
69 Elmore, *Mothers of the World*, 10–11.
70 Elmore, *Mothers of the World*.
71 Margaret T. Applegarth, "The World Day of Prayer," *Church Woman*, May 1945, 24–27.

72 Resolution for Action on San Francisco Charter, Adopted by Exec. Com., May 25–26, 1945, FCC Papers, RG 18.40.19, PHS.
73 Report of the Executive and Associate Secretaries, 1941–1946, CWU Papers, 1223-2-3-03, GCAH.
74 Joy Hume Falk, "A New Way to Be Christian," *Church Woman*, May 1946, 20.
75 "Resolutions of the Assembly," *Church Woman*, December 1948, 28–39.
76 Ibid.
77 UCCW, Discussion Guide for the Fifth National Assembly: New Patterns for Christian Women in the American Community, in the International Outreach, Nov. 1950, 1223-2-2-05, CWU Papers, GCAH.
78 The public-facing religious activism of organized Protestant women shows how churchwomen defied the privatization of both religion and women that Joan Scott identifies as the effects of secularization. Scott, *Sex and Secularism*. On prophetic religion and the civil rights movement see for example: James Cone, *Malcolm & Martin & America* (Maryknoll, NY: Orbis Books, 1991); David L. Chappell, *A Stone of Hope: Prophetic Religion and the Death of Jim Crow* (Chapel Hill: University of North Carolina Press, 2004). The UCCW and its affiliates speak to the organizational influence of suburban women around liberal politics, a phenomenon that was structurally similar to the rise of conservatism in suburbia: Lisa McGirr, *Suburban Warriors: The Origins of the New American Right* (Princeton, NJ: Princeton University Press, 2001).
79 "A Service of Worship for World Community Day," Nov. 2, 1956, UTS Pamphlets.
80 Cohen, *In War's Wake*, 5–6.
81 Tichenor, *Dividing Lines*, 176–179; Resolution, "Concerning the Immigration of Displaced People to the United States," Record Group 18, Box 7, Folder 24, FCC Papers. The 1948 law only applied to DPs who had entered the American zones in Germany and Austria before December 22, 1945, which excluded most of the Jewish Poles who had fled persecution in 1946. When Truman signed this stricter version, he wrote, "The bill is a pattern of discrimination and intolerance wholly inconsistent with the American sense of justice. It mocks the American tradition of fair play and discriminates in callous fashion against persons of the Jewish faith. It also excludes many Catholics who deserve admission." See: "Displaced Persons," *CQ Almanac 1948*, 4th ed. (Washington, DC: Congressional Quarterly, 1949), 193–195. http://library.cqpress.com.
82 George Dugan, "Churchwomen Ask Protestant DP AID," *New York Times*, Nov. 18, 1948, 6.
83 Hazel G. Ormsbee to Dr. Julius Bodensieck, Feb. 13, 1947, enclosure with previous letter, Ormsbee to Cavert. Record Group 18, Box 7, Folder 24, FCC Papers, PHS.
84 Editorial, "Being a Good Neighbor to DPs," *Federal Council Bulletin*, March 1947. Copy in Record Group 18, Box 7, Folder 24, FCC Papers, PHS. "Contrary to a widespread impression, only a small percentage of these displaced persons are Jews. Approximately three-quarters of them are Christians-Protestant, Roman Catholic, Eastern Orthodox."

85 Lily Wendel to FCC Bulletin, March 30, 1947, Record Group 18, Box 7, Folder 24, FCC Papers, PHS.
86 Cavert to Lily Wendel, April 8, 1947, RG 18, Box 7, Folder 24, FCC Papers, PHS.
87 Wendel to Cavert, April 13, 1947, RG 18, Box 7, Folder 24, FCC Papers, PHS.
88 U.S. Congress, House, Committee on the Judiciary, *Permitting Admission of 400,000 Displaced Persons into the United States: Hearings Before Subcommittee on Immigration and Naturalization*, 80th Cong., 1st sess., 1947, 635–637.
89 A list of the UCCW and later Church Women United resolutions can be found in a document they compiled in 2004: "Church Women United Social Policies, 1941–2004" and available on their website: www.churchwomenunited.net. Last accessed September 5, 2022. On liberal Protestant support for family planning and abortion rights see: Mehta, "Family Planning Is a Christian Duty," 152–169; Frank, *Making Choice Sacred*.
90 "Catching Up with the News For and About Women," *Church Woman*, June 1949, 3–4.
91 "Catching Up with the News For and About Women," *Church Woman*, March 1950, 4.

CONCLUSION

1 David Stout, "A Nation Challenged: The First Lady," *New York Times*, Nov. 18, 2001.
2 See for example: Rosenberg, "Rescuing Women and Children"; Elora Shehabuddin, "Gender and the Figure of the 'Moderate Muslim,'" 102–142; Abu-Lughod, *Do Muslim Women Need Saving?*; Mahmood, *The Politics of Piety*.
3 "Progress," *Church Woman*, Nov. 1948, 4.
4 In his recent book, Gene Zubovich also makes the case that "the story of 'mainline' decline is misleading partly because it misses the political work ecumenical Protestants have done—and continue to do—that shapes our world today." Zubovich, *Before the Religious Right*, 310. For the standard statistics used to discuss "mainline decline" see: "Mainline Protestants," Religious Landscape Study, Pew Research Center, www.pewresearch.org, accessed Sept. 6, 2022.
5 See for example: Griffith, *Moral Combat*; Gillian Frank, Bethany Moreton, and Heather R. White, eds., *Devotions and Desires*; Jakobsen and Pellegrini, eds., *Secularisms*; McGarry, *Ghosts of Futures Past*.
6 Church Women United, "Social Justice," www.churchwomenunited.net/blog/social-justice, accessed Sept. 8, 2022.

BIBLIOGRAPHY

MANUSCRIPT COLLECTIONS

Church Women United Records, United Methodist Church, GCAH, Madison, New Jersey

Missionary Research Library, Burke Library, Union Theological Seminary, Columbia University, New York City, New York

Papers of the Rochester Council of Church Women, Ecumenical and Interfaith Archives of Rochester, Rare Books, Special Collections, and Preservation, River Campus Libraries, University of Rochester, Rochester, New York

Presbyterian Historical Society, Philadelphia, Pennsylvania
    Federal Council of Churches of Christ in America Records
    Foreign Missions Conference Records

PERIODICALS

The Church Woman
Democrat and Chronicle (Rochester, NY)
Federal Council Bulletin
Helping Hand
Home Mission Monthly
Life and Light for Heathen Women / Life and Light for Woman
Missions
Missionary Review of the World
Missionary Tidings
The New Outlook
New York Times
Oakland Tribune
Washington Post
Woman's Home Missions
Woman's Work for Heathen Woman / Woman's Work for Woman / Woman's Work
Women in Missions

OTHER PUBLISHED SOURCES

American Pageantry Association. *"Who's Who" in Pageantry* (Boston, 1914).

Applegarth, Margaret. *Color Blind: A Missionary Play in Three Acts* (New York: G.H. Doran, 1923).

Beegle, Mary Porter and Jack Randall Crawford. *Community Drama and Pageantry* (New Haven, CT: Yale University Press, 1916).

Bovine Robert G. and Jenny B. Merrill, eds. *Manual of Graded Bible Courses* and *Habit, Health and First-Aid Outline* (New York: The Century Co., 1917).

Brain, Belle M. *Fuel for Missionary Fires: Some Programmes and Plans for Use in Young People's Societies* (Boston, MA: United Society of Christian Endeavor, 1894).

———. *Fifty Missionary Programmes* (Boston and Chicago: United Society of Christian Endeavor, 1901).

Brooks, Charles Alvin. *Christian Americanization: A Task for the Churches* (New York: Council of Women for Home Missions and Missionary Education Movement, 1919).

Burton, Margaret E. *Women Workers of the Orient* (West Medford, MA: Central Committee for the United Study of Foreign Missions, 1918).

Butler, Fred Clayton. *Community Americanization: A Handbook for Workers* (Washington, DC: Government Printing Office, 1920).

Committee on World Friendship Among Children. *Dolls of Friendship: The Story of a Goodwill Project between the Children of America and Japan* (New York: Friendship Press, 1929).

Council of Women for Home Missions. *Americanization: A Program of Action and Service for the Churches* (New York: Home Missions Council, 1919).

Cuthbert, Marion V. *Juliette Derricotte* (New York: The Womans Press, 1933).

Davol, Ralph. *A Handbook of American Pageantry* (Taunton, MA: Davol Publishing Company, 1914).

Giles, Dorothy. *Adventures in Brotherhood* (Council of Women for Home Missions and Missionary Education Movement, 1924).

Greene, Amy Blanche and Frederic A. Gould, eds. *Handbook-Bibliography on Foreign Language Groups in the United States and Canada* (Council of Women for Home Missions and Missionary Education Movement, 1925).

Guild, Roy B. *Practicing Christian Unity* (International Committee of the Young Men's Christian Association, 1919).

Hammond, Lily Hardy. *In the Vanguard of a Race* (New York: Council of Women for Home Missions and Missionary Education Movement, 1922).

Harkness, Georgia. *The Church and the Immigrant* (New York: G.H. Doran, 1921).

Haynes, George E. *The Negro at Work in New York City* (New York: Columbia University Press, 1912).

———. *Negro Newcomers in Detroit* (New York: Home Missions Council, 1918).

———. *The Trend of the Races* (New York: Council of Women for Home Missions and Missionary Education Movement, 1922).

Mason, Caroline Atwater Mason. *Lux Christi: An Outline Study of India, a Twilight Land* (New York: Macmillan, 1902).
———. *Little Green God* (New York: Fleming H. Revell Company, 1902).
Miller, Kenneth D. *Peasant Pioneers: An Interpretation of the Slavic Peoples in the United States* (Council of Women for Home Missions and Missionary Education Movement, 1925).
Miller, Madeline Sweeny. *Church Pageantry* (New York and Cincinnati: The Methodist Book Concern, 1924).
Montgomery, Helen Barrett. *Christus Redemptor* (New York: Macmillan, 1906).
———. *How to Use* Christus Redemptor *with Outlines of Lectures* (West Medford, MA: Central Committee on the United Study of Missions, 1906).
———. *Western Women in Eastern Lands* (New York: Macmillan, 1910).
———. *How to Use: A Handbook of Suggestions to Accompany the Textbook* Western Women in Eastern Lands (West Medford, MA: Central Committee on the United Study of Foreign Missions, 1910).
———. *How to Use: A Handbook of Suggestions to Accompany* The Light of the World (West Medford, MA: Central Committee on the United Study of Foreign Missions, 1911).
———. *The King's Highway* (West Medford, MA: Central Committee for the United Study of Missions, 1915).
———. *How to Use: A Handbook of Suggestions to Accompany* The King's Highway (West Medford, MA: Central Committee for the United Study of Foreign Missions, 1915).
———. *How to Use for* An African Trail (West Medford, MA: Central Committee for the United Study of Foreign Missions, 1917).
———. *How to Use Handbook for* Woman Workers of the Orient (West Medford, MA: Central Committee for the United Study of Foreign Missions, 1918).
Murray, J. Lovell. *The Apologetic of Modern Missions: Eight Outline Studies* (Student Volunteer Movement, 1909).
North, Eric. *The Kingdom and the Nations* (West Medford, MA: Central Committee for the United Study of Foreign Missions, 1921).
O'Donnell, Mary Patricia, et al. *Greek Games: An Organization for Festivals* (New York: A.S. Barnes and Company, 1932).
Oxenham, John and Hugh Moss. "The Pageant of Darkness and Light" (New York: Young People's Missionary Movement of the United States and Canada, 1911).
Proceedings of the Americanization Conference, May 1919 (Washington, DC: Government Printing Office, 1919).
Raymond, Mary Maud. *The King's Business: A Study of Increased Efficiency for Women's Missionary Societies* (West Medford, MA: Central Committee for the United Study of Foreign Missions, 1913).
Report of the Ecumenical Conference on Foreign Missions (New York: American Tract Society, 1900).
Reports of the Annual Meetings of the Home Missions Council and Council of Women for Home Missions. Vols. 13–19, New York, 1920–1926.

Reports of the Interdenominational Conference of the Federation of Woman's Boards of Foreign Missions. Vols. 8–27. New York, 1909–1933.

Seebach, Margaret R. *Land of All Nations* (New York: Council of Women for Home Missions and Missionary Education Movement, 1924).

Speer, Robert E. *The Light of the World: A Brief Comparative Study of Christianity and Non-Christian Religions* (West Medford, MA: Central Committee on the United Study of Missions, 1911).

———. *Of One Blood: A Short History of the Race Problem* (New York: Council of Women for Home Missions and Missionary Education Movement, 1924).

Talbot, Winthrop, ed. *Americanization: The Principles of Americanism, Essentials of Americanization, Technic of Race-Assimilation* (New York: H.W. Wilson Company, 1920).

Ware, Alice Holdship. "The Open Door," 1919, Box 2 Folder 21, Atlanta University Collection, Archives Division, Auburn Avenue Research Library on African-American Culture and History, Atlanta-Fulton Public Library System. http://dlg.galileo.usg.edu/aaed/do:aarl89.017-002-021

Wherry, E. M., ed. *Papers and Addresses Presented at the Woman's Congress of Missions* (New York: American Tract Society, 1894).

Wieman, Henry Nelson. *Methods of Private Religious Living* (New York: Macmillan, 1928).

Woolverton, Dorothy. *The Open Door: A Home Missions Pageant* (New York: Woman's Board of Home Missions of the Presbyterian Church in the USA, 1921).

YWCA. "A Second List of Plays and Pageants" (New York: The Woman's Press, 1921).

SECONDARY SOURCES

Abu-Lughod, Lila. *Do Muslim Women Need Saving* (Cambridge, MA: Harvard University Press, 2013).

Adams, Betty Livingston. *Black Women's Christian Activism: Seeking Social Justice in a Northern Suburb* (New York: New York University Press, 2016).

Ahmed, Sara. *On Being Included: Racism and Diversity in Institutional Life* (Durham, NC: Duke University Press, 2012).

Albanese, Catherine. *Republic of Mind and Spirit: A Cultural History of American Metaphysical Religion* (New Haven, CT: Yale University Press, 2007).

Asad, Talal. *Formations of the Secular: Christianity, Islam, Modernity* (Stanford, CA: Stanford University Press, 2003).

Baker, Kelly J. *The Gospel According to the Klan: The KKK's Appeal to Protestant America, 1915–1930* (Lawrence: University Press of Kansas, 2017).

Baker, Paula. "The Domestication of Politics: Women and American Political Society, 1780–1920." *American Historical Review* 89, no. 3 (June 1984): 620–647.

Batnitzky, Leora. *How Judaism Became a Religion: An Introduction to Modern Jewish Thought* (Princeton, NJ: Princeton University Press, 2011).

Beaver, R. Pierce. *All Loves Excelling: Protestant Women in World Mission* (Grand Rapids, MI: William B. Eerdmans, 1968).

Bederman, Gail. "'The Women Have Had Charge of the Church Work Long Enough': The Men and Religion Forward Movement of 1911–1912." *American Quarterly* 41, no. 3 (September 1989): 432–465.

Beliso-De Jesús, Aisha M. "Confounded Identities: A Meditation on Race, Feminism, and Religious Studies in Times of White Supremacy." *Journal of the American Academy of Religion* 86, no. 1 (June 2018): 307–340.

Bell, Catherine. *Ritual Theory, Ritual Practice* (New York: Oxford University Press, 1992).

Bendroth, Margaret. "Women and Missions: Conflict and Changing Roles in the Presbyterian Church in the USA, 1870–1935." *American Presbyterian* 65 (Spring 1987): 49–59.

———. *Good and Mad: Mainline Protestant Churchwomen, 1920–1980* (New York: Oxford University Press, 2022).

Berg, Manfred. *The Ticket to Freedom: The NAACP and the Struggle for Black Political Integration* (Gainesville: University Press of Florida, 2005).

Berlant, Lauren. *The Female Complaint: The Unfinished Business of Sentimentality in American Culture* (Durham, NC: Duke University Press, 2008).

Blair, Karen J. *The Torchbearers: Women and Their Amateur Arts Associations in America, 1890–1920* (Bloomington: Indiana University Press, 1994).

Blum, Edward J. *Reforging the White Republic: Race, Religion, and American Nationalism, 1865–1898* (Baton Rouge: Louisiana State University Press, 2005).

Blum, Edward J., Tracy Fessenden, Prema Kurien, and Judith Weisenfeld, eds. "Forum: American Religion and 'Whiteness.'" *Religion and American Culture* 19, no. 1 (Winter 2009): 1–35.

Borja, Melissa. *Follow the New Way: American Refugee Resettlement Policy and Hmong Religious Change* (Cambridge, MA: Harvard University Press, 2023).

Braude, Ann. "Women's History *Is* American Religious History." In *Retelling U.S. Religious History*, ed. Thomas Tweed (Berkeley: University of California Press, 1997), 87–107.

Brereton, Virginia Lieson. "United and Slighted: Women as Subordinated Insiders." In *Between the Times: The Travail of the Protestant Establishment in America, 1900–1960*, ed. William R. Hutchinson (Cambridge: Cambridge University Press, 1989).

Brereton, Virginia Lieson and Margaret Lamberts Bendroth. "Secularization and Gender: An Historical Approach to Women and Religion in the Twentieth Century." *Method and Theory in the Study of Religion* 13, no. 2 (2001): 209–233.

Brooks, Clayton McClure. *The Uplift Generation: Cooperation Across the Colorline in Twentieth-Century Virginia* (Charlottesville: University of Virginia Press, 2017).

Brumberg, Joan Jacobs. "Zenanas and Girlless Villages: The Ethnology of American Evangelical Women, 1870–1910." *Journal of American History* 69, no. 2 (1982): 347–371.

Buchanan, Andrew. "Domesticating Hegemony: Creating a Globalist Public, 1941–1943." *Diplomatic History* 45, no. 2 (2021): 301–329.

Burnidge, Cara Lea. "Imperial Intersections: Social Surveys, Sentimental Biopolitics, and Religion at Hull House." In *Religion and US Empire: Critical New Histories,* ed. Tisa Wenger and Sylvester A. Johnson (New York: New York University Press, 2022), 101–123.

Burton, Antoinette. *Burdens of History: British Feminists, Indian Women, and Imperial Culture, 1865–1915* (Chapel Hill: University of North Carolina Press, 1995).

Butler, Judith. "Performative Acts and Gendered Constitution: An Essay in Phenomenology and Feminist Theory." *Theatre Journal* 40, no. 4 (December 1988): 519–531.

Cady, Linell and Elizabeth Shakman Hurd, eds. *Comparative Secularisms in a Global Age* (New York: Palgrave MacMillan, 2010).

Carlton-LaNey, Iris. "Elizabeth Ross Haynes: An African American Reformer of Womanist Consciousness, 1908–1940." *Social Work* 42, no. 6 (November 1997): 573–583.

Carson, Mina. *Settlement Folk: Social Thought and the American Settlement Movement, 1885–1930* (Chicago: University of Chicago Press, 1990).

Chang, Derek. *Citizens of a Christian Nation: Evangelical Missions and the Problem of Race in the Nineteenth Century* (Philadelphia: University of Pennsylvania Press, 2010).

Chidester, David. *Empire of Religion: Imperialism and Comparative Religion* (Chicago: University of Chicago Press, 2014).

Chin, Carol. "Beneficent Imperialists: American Women Missionaries in China at the Turn of the Twentieth Century." *Diplomatic History* 27, no. 3 (June 2003): 327–352.

Coffman, Elesha J. *The Christian Century and the Rise of the Protestant Mainline* (New York: Oxford University Press, 2013).

Cohen, G. Daniel. *In War's Wake: Europe's Displaced Persons in the Interwar Era* (New York: Oxford University Press, 2012).

Collier-Thomas, Bettye. *Jesus, Jobs, and Justice* (Philadelphia: Temple University Press, 2010).

Conroy-Krutz, Emily. *Christian Imperialism: Converting the World in the Early American Republic* (Ithaca, NY: Cornell University Press, 2015).

Cooper, Brittney C. *Beyond Respectability: The Intellectual Thought of Race Women* (Urbana: University of Illinois Press, 2017).

Cosson, William S. "Catholic Gatekeepers: The Church and Immigration Reform in the Gilded Age and Progressive Era." *U.S. Catholic Historian* 34, no. 3 (Summer 2016): 1–23.

Cott, Nancy F. *The Grounding of Modern Feminism* (New Haven, CT: Yale University Press, 1989).

Coviello, Peter. *Make Yourself Gods: Mormons and the Unfinished Business of American Secularism* (Chicago: University of Chicago Press, 2019).

Crocker, Ruth Hutchinson. *Social Work and Social Order: The Settlement Movement in Two Industrial Cities, 1889–1930* (Urbana: University of Illinois Press, 1991).

Curtis, Finbarr. *The Production of American Religious Freedom* (New York: New York University Press, 2016).

Curtis, Heather D. *Holy Humanitarians: American Evangelicals and Global Aid* (Cambridge, MA: Harvard University Press, 2018).

Curtis, Susan. *A Consuming Faith: The Social Gospel and Modern American Culture* (Columbia: University of Missouri Press, 1992).

Dailey, Jane. "Sex, Segregation, and the Sacred after *Brown*." *Journal of American History* 91, no. 1 (June 2004): 119–144.

Davidson, Christina C. "An Evangelical Occupation: The Racial and Imperial Politics of US Protestant Missions in the Dominican Republic." In *Religion and US Empire: Critical New Histories*, ed. Tisa Wenger and Sylvester A. Johnson (New York: New York University Press, 2022), 203–228.

Davis, Allen F. *Spearheads for Reform: The Social Settlements and the Progressive Movement, 1890–1914* (New York: Oxford University Press, 1967).

Davis, Rebecca. "'Not Marriage at All, but Simple Harlotry': The Companionate Marriage Controversy." *Journal of American History* (March 2008): 1137–1163.

Denomme, Janine Marie. "'To End This Day of Strife': Churchwomen and the Campaign for Integration, 1920–1970." PhD diss., University of Pennsylvania, 2001.

Du Mez, Kristin Kobes. *Jesus and John Wayne: How White Evangelicals Corrupted a Faith and Fractured a Nation* (New York: Liveright, 2020).

Dudziak, Mary L. *Cold War, Civil Rights: Race and the Image of American Democracy* (Princeton, NJ: Princeton University Press, 2000).

Dumenil, Lynn. "Women's Reform Organizations and Wartime Mobilization in World War I–Era Los Angeles." *Journal of the Gilded Age and Progressive Era* 10, no. 2 (April 2011): 213–245.

Du Mez, Kristin Kobes. *Jesus and John Wayne: How White Evangelicals Corrupted a Faith and Fractured a Nation* (New York: Liveright, 2020).

Dunch, Ryan. "Beyond Cultural Imperialism: Cultural Theory, Christian Missions, and Global Modernity." *History and Theory* 41, no. 3 (2002): 301–325.

Early, Frances H. *A World Without War: How U.S. Feminists and Pacifists Resisted World War I* (Syracuse, NY: Syracuse University Press, 1997).

Ellis, Mark. *Race Harmony and Black Progress: Jack Woofter and the Interracial Cooperation Movement* (Bloomington: Indiana University Press, 2013).

Evans, Christopher H. *Do Everything: The Biography of Frances Willard* (New York: Oxford University Press, 2022).

Evans, Curtis J. *The Burden of Black Religion* (New York: Oxford University Press, 2008).

Fessenden, Tracy. *Culture and Redemption: Religion, the Secular, and American Literature* (Princeton, NJ: Princeton University Press, 2007).

———. "Religious Liberalism and the Liberal Geopolitics of Religion." In *American Religious Liberalism*, ed. Leigh E. Schmidt and Sally M. Promey (Bloomington: Indiana University Press, 2012), 359–373.

Fletcher, Sheila. *Maude Royden: A Life* (Cambridge, MA: Basil Blackwell, 1989).

Forman-Barzilai, Fonna. "Sympathy in Space(s): Adam Smith on Proximity." *Political Theory* 33, no. 2 (April 2005): 189–217.

Frank, Gillian. *Making Choice Sacred: Liberal Religion and Reproductive Rights Before Roe v. Wade* (Chapel Hill: University of North Carolina Press, forthcoming).

Frederickson, Mary. *Sisterhood and Solidarity: Workers' Education for Women, 1914–1984* (Philadelphia: Temple University Press, 1984).
Freedman, Estelle. "Separatism as Strategy: Female Institution Building and American Feminism, 1870–1930." *Feminist Studies* 5, no. 3 (Autumn 1979): 512–529.
Gal, John. *The Settlement House Movement Revisited: A Transnational History* (Bristol: Policy Press, 2021).
Gaston, K. Healon. *Imagining Judeo-Christian America: Religion, Secularism, and the Redefinition of Democracy* (Chicago: University of Chicago Press, 2019).
Giddings, Paula. *When and Where I Enter: The Impact of Black Women on Race and Sex in America* (New York: William Morrow, 1996).
Gilmore, Glenda. *Gender and Jim Crow: Women and the Politics of White Supremacy in North Carolina, 1896–1920* (Chapel Hill: University of North Carolina Press, 1996).
Gin Lum, Kathryn. *Heathen: Religion and Race in American History* (Cambridge, MA: Harvard University Press, 2022).
Glassberg, David. *American Historical Pageantry: The Uses of Tradition in the Early Twentieth Century* (Chapel Hill: University of North Carolina Press, 1990).
Gloege, Timothy E. W. *Guaranteed Pure: The Moody Bible Institute and the Making of Modern Evangelicalism* (Chapel Hill: University of North Carolina Press, 2015).
Gordon, Sarah Barringer. *The Mormon Question: Polygamy and Constitutional Conflict in Nineteenth-Century America* (Chapel Hill: University of North Carolina Press, 2002).
Greene, Daniel. *The Jewish Origins of Cultural Pluralism: The Menorah Association and American Diversity* (Bloomington: Indiana University Press, 2011).
Grewal, Inderpal. *Transnational America: Feminisms, Diasporas, Neoliberalisms* (Durham, NC: Duke University Press, 2005).
Griffith, R. Marie. *Moral Combat: How Sex Divided American Christians and Fractured American Politics* (New York: Basic Books, 2017).
Groeneveld, Leanne. "'I Felt as Never Before, Under Any Sermon That I Ever Heard Preached': Word, Image, and the Oberammergau Passion Play, 1840–1900." *Nineteenth Century Theatre and Film* 43, no. 2 (November 2016): 131–159.
Gross, Rachel. *Beyond the Synagogue: Jewish Nostalgia as Religious Practice* (New York: New York University Press, 2021).
Hall, David. *Lived Religion in America: Toward a History of Practice* (Princeton, NJ: Princeton University Press, 1997).
Hall, Jacqueline Dowd. *Revolt Against Chivalry: Jessie Daniel Ames and the Women's Campaign Against Lynching* (New York: Columbia University Press, 1993).
Handy, Robert T. "The American Religious Depression, 1925–1935." *Church History* 29, no. 1 (March 1960): 3–16.
Hardesty, Nancy A. "The Scientific Study of Missions: Textbooks of the Central Committee on the United Study of Foreign Missions." In *The Foreign Missionary Enterprise at Home: Explorations in North American Cultural History*, ed. Daniel H. Bays and Grant Wacker (Tuscaloosa and London: University of Alabama Press, 2003), 106–122.

Harris, Jessica Christina. "We Did What We Had to Do: Black Women and the Struggle for Civil Rights in Oakland, California, 1900–1940." PhD diss., Cornell University, 2011.

Harvey, Paul and Kathryn Gin Lum, eds. *The Oxford Handbook of Religion and Race in America* (New York: Oxford University Press, 2018).

Hasinoff, Erin. *Faith in Objects: American Missionary Expositions in the Early Twentieth Century* (New York: Palgrave Macmillan, 2011).

Hawkins, J. Russell. *The Bible Told Them So: How Southern Evangelicals Fought to Preserve White Supremacy* (New York: Oxford University Press, 2021).

Hedstrom, Matthew. *The Rise of Liberal Religion: Book Culture and American Spirituality in the Twentieth Century* (New York: Oxford University Press, 2015).

Hewitt, Rebecca. "'Looking at One's Self Through the Eyes of Others': Representations of the Progressive Era Middle Class in W.E.B. Du Bois's *The Star of Ethiopia*." *Theater History Studies* 30 (2010): 187–201.

Higginbotham, Evelyn Brooks. *Righteous Discontent: The Women's Movement in the Black Baptist Church, 1880–1920* (Cambridge, MA: Harvard University Press, 1993).

Hill, Patricia R. *The World Their Household: The American Woman's Foreign Mission Movement and Cultural Transformation, 1870–1920* (Ann Arbor: University of Michigan Press, 1985).

Hoganson, Kristin L. *Consumer's Imperium: The Global Production of American Domesticity, 1865–1920* (Chapel Hill: University of North Carolina Press, 2007).

———. "Cosmopolitan Domesticity: Importing the American Dream, 1865–1920." *American Historical Review* 107, no. 1 (February 2002): 55–83.

Hollinger, David A. "Pluralism, Cosmopolitanism, and the Diversification of Diversity." In *Postethnic America: Beyond Multiculturalism*, 10th anniversary edition. New York: Basic Books, 2000.

———. *Protestants Abroad: How Missionaries Tried to Change the World but Changed America* (Princeton, NJ: Princeton University Press, 2017).

Hutchison, William R., ed. *Between the Times: The Travail of the Protestant Establishment in America, 1900–1960* (New York: Cambridge University Press, 1989).

Hutchison, William R. *An Errand to the World: American Protestant Thought and Foreign Missions* (Chicago: University of Chicago Press, 1987).

———. *Religious Pluralism in America: The Contentious History of a Founding Ideal* (New Haven, CT: Yale University Press, 2003).

Igo, Sarah. *The Averaged American: Surveys, Citizens, and the Making of a Mass Public* (Cambridge, MA: Harvard University Press, 2008).

Ishii, Noriko. *American Women Missionaries at Kobe College, 1873–1909* (New York: Routledge, 2004).

Jacobs, Sylvia, ed. *Black Americans and the Missionary Movement in Africa* (Westport, CT: Greenwood Press, 1982).

Jain, Andrea. "Subversive Spiritualities: Yoga's Complex Role in the Narrative of Sex and Religion in the Twentieth-Century United States." In *Devotions and Desires: Histories of Sexuality and Religion in the Twentieth-Century United States*, ed. Gillian Frank, Bethany Moreton, and Heather R. White (Chapel Hill: University of North Carolina Press, 2018).

Jakobsen, Janet R. and Ann Pellegrini, eds. *Love the Sin: Sexual Regulation and the Limits of Religious Tolerance* (New York: New York University Press, 2003).

———. *Secularisms* (Durham, NC: Duke University Press, 2008).

Johnson, Melinda Marie. "Building Bridges: Church Women United and Social Reform Work Across the Mid-Twentieth Century." PhD diss., University of Kentucky, 2015.

Johnson, Sylvester. *African American Religions, 1500–2000* (New York: Cambridge University Press, 2015).

Jones, Martha S. *Vanguard: How Black Women Broke Barriers, Won the Vote, and Insisted on Equality for All* (New York: Basic Books, 2020).

Kaell, Hillary. "Evangelist of Fragments: Doing Mite-Box Capitalism in the Late Nineteenth Century." *Church History* 86, no. 1 (March 2017): 86–119.

———. *Christian Globalism at Home: Child Sponsorship in the United States* (Princeton, NJ: Princeton University Press, 2020).

Kahn, Jonathan S. and Vincent W. Lloyd, eds. *Race and Secularism in America* (New York: Columbia University Press, 2016).

Kaplan, Amy. "Manifest Domesticity." *American Literature* 70, no. 3 (September 1998): 581–606.

Kaplan, Amy and Donald E. Pease, eds. *Cultures of United States Imperialism* (Durham, NC: Duke University Press, 1994).

Kaufman, Matthew J. *Horace Kallen Confronts America: Jewish Identity, Science, and Secularism* (Syracuse, NY: Syracuse University Press, 2019).

Kenny, Gale L. "The World Day of Prayer: Liberal Churchwomen and Christian Cosmopolitanism, 1920–1946." *Journal of Religion and American Culture*, 27, no. 2 (Summer 2017): 43–75.

Kenny, Gale and Tisa Wenger. "Church, State, and 'Native Liberty' in the Belgium Congo." *Comparative Studies in Society and History* 62, no. 1 (January 2020): 156–185.

Kerber, Linda. *Women of the Republic: Intellect and Ideology in Revolutionary America* (Chapel Hill: University of North Carolina Press, 1980).

Kern, Kathi. "Spiritual Border-Crossings in the U.S. Women's Rights Movement." In *American Religious Liberalism*, ed. Leigh E. Schmidt and Sally M. Promey (Bloomington: Indiana University Press, 2012), 162–180.

King, David. *God's Internationalists: World Vision and the Age of Evangelical Humanitarianism* (Philadelphia: University of Pennsylvania Press, 2019).

Kirkpatrick, David. *A Gospel for the Poor: Global Social Christianity and the Latin American Left* (Philadelphia: University of Pennsylvania Press, 2019).

Kohiyama, Rui. "The 1927 Exchange of Friendship Dolls: U.S.-Japan Cultural Diplomacy in the Inter-War Years." *Diplomatic History* 43, no. 2 (April 2019): 282–304.

Korelitz, Seth. "'A Magnificent Piece of Work': The Americanization Work of the National Council of Jewish Women." *American Jewish History* 83, no. 2 (June 1995): 177–203.

Koven, Seth. *The Match Girl and the Heiress* (Princeton, NJ: Princeton University Press, 2014).
Kramer, Paul. "Power and Connection: Imperial Histories of the United States in the World." *American Historical Review* 116, no. 5 (December 2011): 1348–1391.
———. *The Blood of Government: Race, Empire, the United States, and the Philippines* (Chapel Hill: University of North Carolina Press 2006).
Krasner, David. *A Beautiful Pageant: African American Theater, Drama, and Performance in the Harlem Renaissance* (New York: Palgrave, 2002).
Lears, T. Jackson. *No Place of Grace: Antimodernism and the Transformation of American Culture, 1880–1920* (Chicago: University of Chicago Press, 1981).
Lindenfeld, David. *World Christianity and Indigenous Experience: A Global History, 1500–2000* (New York: Cambridge University Press, 2021).
Lofton, Kathryn. "The Methodology of Modernists: Process in American Protestantism." *Church History* 75, no. 2 (June 2006): 374–402.
———. *Consuming Religion* (Chicago: University of Chicago Press, 2017).
Logan, Dana. "Ritual Chores: Catharine Beecher's Domesticity." *Journal of the American Academy of Religion* 89, no. 3 (September 2021): 1074–1099.
———. *Awkward Rituals: Sensations of Governance in Protestant America* (Chicago: University of Chicago Press, 2022).
Lott, Eric. *Love and Theft: Blackface Minstrelsy and the American Working Class* (New York: Oxford University Press, 1993).
Mace, Emily. "Comparative Religions and the Practice of Eclecticism: Intersections in Nineteenth-Century Liberal Religious Congregations." *Journal of Religion* 94, no. 1 (January 2014): 74–96.
Maffly-Kipp, Laurie F., Leigh E. Schmidt, and Mark Valeri, eds. *Practicing Protestants: Histories of Christian Life in America, 1630–1965* (Baltimore, MD: Johns Hopkins University Press, 2006).
Mahmood, Saba. *The Politics of Piety* (Princeton, NJ: Princeton University Press, 2011).
———. *Religious Difference in a Secular Age: A Minority Report* (Princeton, NJ: Princeton University Press, 2015).
Maldonado-Estrada, Alyssa. *Lifeblood of the Parish: Men and Catholic Devotion in Williamsburg, Brooklyn* (New York: New York University Press, 2020).
Masuzawa, Tomoko. *The Invention of World Religions: Or, How European Universalism Was Preserved in the Language of Pluralism* (Chicago: University of Chicago Press, 2005).
McAlister, Melani. "'What Is Your Heart For?' Affect and Internationalism in the Evangelical Public Sphere." *American Literary History* 20, no. 4 (December 2008): 873.
———. *The Kingdom of God Has No Borders: A Global History of American Evangelicals* (New York: Oxford University Press, 2018).
McCrary, Charles. *Sincerely Held: American Secularism and Its Believers* (Chicago: University of Chicago Press, 2022).
McGarry, Molly. *Ghosts of Futures Past: Spiritualism and the Cultural Nineteenth-Century America* (Berkeley: University of California Press, 2008).

McGuinness, Margaret M. "Body and Soul: Catholic Social Settlements and Immigration." *U.S. Catholic Historian* 13, no. 3 (Summer 1995): 63–75.

McKelvey, Blake. "The Italians of Rochester: An Historical Review." *Rochester History* 22, no. 4 (October 1960): 1–24.

Mehta, Samira. "Family Planning Is a Christian Duty: Religion, Population Control, and the Pill in the 1960s." In *Devotions and Desires: Histories of Sexuality and Religion in the Twentieth-Century United States*, ed. Gillian Frank, Bethany Moreton, and Heather R. White (Chapel Hill: University of North Carolina Press, 2018), 152–169.

Melamed, Jodi. *Represent and Destroy: Rationalizing Violence in the New Racial Capitalism* (Minneapolis: University of Minnesota Press, 2011).

Meyer, Birgit. "Media and the Senses in the Making of Religious Experience: An Introduction." *Material Religion* 4, no. 2 (July 2008): 124–134.

——. "Religious Sensations: Media, Aesthetics, and the Study of Contemporary Religion." In *Religion, Media, and Culture: A Reader*, ed. Gordon Lynch and Joylon Mitchell (London: Routledge, 2012), 159–170.

Mislin, David. *Saving Faith: Making Religious Pluralism an American Value at the Dawn of the Secular Age* (Ithaca, NY: Cornell University Press, 2015).

Mobley, Kendal P. *Helen Barrett Montgomery: The Global Mission of Domestic Feminism* (Waco, TX: Baylor Press, 2009).

Mohanty, Chandra Talpade. "Under Western Eyes: Feminist Scholarship and Colonial Discourses." In *Third World Women and the Politics of Feminism*, ed. Chandra Talpade Mohanty, Ann Russo, and Lourdes Torres (Bloomington: Indiana University Press, 1991), 51–80.

Moore, Jesse Thomas. *A Search for Equality: The National Urban League, 1910–1961* (University Park: Penn State University Press, 1981).

Moore, Sarah. "Making a Spectacle of Suffrage: The National Woman Suffrage Pageant, 1913," *Journal of American Culture* 20, no. 1 (1997): 89–103.

Moran, Katherine. *The Imperial Church: Catholic Founding Fathers and United States Empire* (Ithaca, NY: Cornell University Press, 2020).

Morgan, David. *The Thing About Religion: An Introduction to the Material Study of Religion* (Chapel Hill: University of North Carolina Press, 2021).

Most, Andrea. *Theatrical Liberalism: Jews and Popular Entertainment in America* (New York: New York University Press, 2013).

Newman, Louise Michele. *White Women's Rights: The Racial Origins of Feminism in the United States* (New York: Oxford University Press, 1999).

Ngai, Mae. *Impossible Subjects: Illegal Aliens and the Making of Modern America* (Princeton, NJ: Princeton University Press, 2004).

Noll, Mark A. *America's God: From Jonathan Edwards to Abraham Lincoln* (New York: Oxford University Press, 2002).

Nye, Malory. "Race and Religion: Postcolonial Formations of Power and Whiteness." *Method and Theory in the Study of Religion* 31, no. 3 (June 2019): 210–237.

Orsi, Robert. *The Madonna of 115th Street: Faith and Community in Italian Harlem, 1880–1950*, 3rd edition (New Haven, CT: Yale University Press, 2010).
Oshatz, Molly. *Slavery and Sin: The Fight Against Slavery and the Rise of Liberal Protestantism* (New York: Oxford University Press, 2012).
Painter, Nell Irving. "Why White Should Be Capitalized Too." *Washington Post*, July 22, 2022.
Pascoe, Peggy. *Relations of Rescue: The Search for Female Moral Authority in the American West, 1874–1939* (New York: Oxford University Press, 1993).
———. *What Comes Naturally: Miscegenation Law and the Making of Race in America* (New York: Oxford University Press, 2009).
Phillips, Katrina. "Performance over Policy: Promoting Indianness in Twentieth-Century Wisconsin Tourism." *Radical History Review* 129 (October 2017): 34–50.
———. *Staging Indigeneity: Salvage Tourism and the Performance of Native American History* (Chapel Hill: University of North Carolina Press, 2021).
Plastas, Melinda. *A Band of Noble Women: Racial Politics in the Women's Peace Movement* (Syracuse, NY: Syracuse University Press, 2011).
Preston, Andrew. *Sword of the Spirit, Shield of Faith: Religion in American War and Diplomacy* (New York: Knopf Doubleday, 2012).
———. "The Limits of Brotherhood: Race, Religion, and World Order in American Ecumenical Protestantism." *American Historical Review* 127, no. 3 (September 2022): 1222–1251.
Prevost, Elizabeth. *The Communion of Women: Missions and Gender in Colonial Africa and the British Metropole* (New York: Oxford University Press, 2010).
Promey, Sally, ed. *Sensational Religion: Sensory Cultures in Material Practice* (New Haven, CT: Yale University Press, 2014).
Pruitt, Nicholas. *Open Hearts, Closed Doors: Immigration Reform and the Waning of Mainline Protestantism* (New York: New York University Press, 2021).
Rable, George C. "The South and the Politics of Antilynching Legislation, 1920–1940." *Journal of Southern History* 51, no. 2 (May 1985): 201–220.
Reeves-Ellington, Barbara, Kathryn Kish Sklar, and Connie A. Shemo, eds. *Competing Kingdoms: Women, Mission, Nation, and the American Protestant Empire, 1812–1960* (Durham, NC: Duke University Press, 2010).
Renda, Mary. "Doing Everything: Religion, Race, and Empire in the U.S. Protestant Women's Missionary Enterprise, 1812–1960." In *Competing Kingdoms: Women, Mission, Nation, and the American Protestant Empire, 1812–1960*, ed. Barbara Reeves-Ellington, Kathryn Kish Sklar, and Connie A. Shemo (Durham, NC: Duke University Press, 2010).
Robert, Dana L. *American Women in Mission: A Social History of Their Thought and Practice* (Mercer, GA: Mercer University Press, 1992).
———. "Naming 'World Christianity': Historical and Personal Perspectives on the Yale-Edinburgh Conference in World Christianity and Mission History." *International Bulletin of Mission Research* 44, no. 2 (April 2020): 111–128.

Roberts, Samuel K. "Crucible for a Vision: The Work of George Edmund Haynes and the Commission on Race Relations, 1922–1947." PhD diss., Columbia University, 1975.

Robertson, Nancy Marie. *Christian Sisterhood, Race Relations and the YWCA, 1906–46* (Urbana: University of Illinois Press, 2007).

Rogin, Michael. "Making America Home: Racial Masquerade and Ethnic Assimilation in the Transition to Talking Pictures." *Journal of American History* 79 no. 3 (December 1992): 1050–1077.

Rosenberg, Emily S. "Rescuing Women and Children." *Journal of American History* 89, no. 2 (September 2002): 456–465.

Rothermel, Beth Ann. "Acting Up: Drama and the Rhetorical Education of Progressive-Era Teachers at Three Massachusetts State Normal Schools." *Advances in the History of Rhetoric* 8 (2005): 105–112.

Rouse, Jacqueline A. "The Legacy of Community Organizing: Lugenia Burns Hope and the Neighborhood Union." *Journal of Negro History* 69, no. 3/4 (1984): 114–133.

Rupp, Leila. *Worlds of Women: The Making of an International Women's Movement* (Princeton, NJ: Princeton University Press, 1997).

Ruswick, Brent. *Almost Worthy: The Poor, Paupers, and the Science of Charity in America, 1877–1917* (Bloomington: Indiana University Press, 2012).

Ryan, Susan M. *The Grammar of Good Intentions: Race and the Antebellum Culture of Benevolence* (Ithaca, NY: Cornell University Press, 2003).

Sanneh, Lamin. *Whose Religion Is Christianity?: The Gospel beyond the West* (Grand Rapids, MI: Eerdmans, 2003).

Sasaki, Motoe. *Redemption and Revolution: American and Chinese New Women in the Early Twentieth Century* (Ithaca, NY: Cornell University Press, 2016).

Schmidt, Leigh Eric. *Restless Souls: The Making of American Spirituality* (Berkeley: University of California Press, 2012).

Schuller, Kyla. *The Biopolitics of Feeling: Race, Sex, and Science in the Nineteenth Century* (Durham, NC: Duke University Press, 2017).

Schultz, Kevin M. *Tri-Faith America: How Catholics and Jews Held Postwar America to Its Protestant Promise* (New York: Oxford University Press, 2011).

Scott, Joan Wallach. *Sex and Secularism* (Princeton, NJ: Princeton University Press, 2018).

Sears, John F. *Refuge Must Be Given: Eleanor Roosevelt, the Jewish Plight, and the Founding of Israel* (Indianapolis, IN: Purdue University Press, 2021).

Sehat, David. *The Myth of American Religious Freedom* (New York: Oxford University Press, 2010).

Selig, Diana. *Americans All: The Cultural Gifts Movement* (Cambridge, MA: Harvard University Press, 2008).

Shehabuddin, Elora. "Gender and the Figure of the 'Moderate Muslim': Feminism in the Twenty-First Century." In *The Question of Gender: Joan W. Scott's Critical Feminism*, ed. Judith Butler and Elizabeth Weed (Bloomington: Indiana University Press, 2011), 102–142.

Smith, Matthew J. "Settler Colonialism and U.S. Home Missions." *Oxford Research Encyclopedia of Religion*, February 2018. DOI: 10.1093/acrefore/9780199340378.013.392.

Sneider, Allison L. *Suffragists in an Imperial Age: U.S. Expansion and the Woman Question, 1870–1929* (New York: Oxford University Press, 2008).
Spear, Sonja E. "Claiming the Passion: American Fantasies of the Oberammergau Passion Play, 1023–1947." *Church History* 80, no. 4 (December 2011): 832–862.
Stoler, Ann Laura, ed. *Haunted by Empire: Geographies of Intimacy in North American History* (Durham, NC: Duke University Press, 2006).
Thompson, Michael G. *For God and Globe: Christian Internationalism in the United States between the Great War and the Cold War* (Ithaca, NY: Cornell University Press, 2015).
Thorne, Susan. "Missionary-Imperial Feminism." In *Gendered Missions: Women and Men in Missionary Discourse*, ed. Mary Taylor Huber and Nancy Lutkehaus (Ann Arbor: University of Michigan Press, 1999).
Tichenor, Daniel J. *Dividing Lines: The Politics of Immigration Control in America* (Princeton, NJ: Princeton University Press, 2002).
Todd, J. Terry. "The Temple of Religion and the Politics of Religious Pluralism: Judeo-Christian America at the 1939–1940 New York World's Fair." In *After Pluralism: Reimagining Religious Engagement*, ed. Courtney Bender and Pamela E. Klassen (New York: Columbia University Press, 2010).
Turek, Lauren. *To Bring the Good News to All Nations: Evangelical Influence on Human Rights and US Foreign Relations* (Ithaca, NY: Cornell University Press, 2020).
Tyrrell, Ian. *Reforming the World: The Creation of America's Moral Empire* (Princeton, NJ: Princeton University Press, 2010).
Vaca, Daniel. *Evangelicals Incorporated: Books and the Business of Religion in America* (Cambridge, MA: Harvard University Press, 2019).
Van der Veer, Peter. "Colonial Cosmopolitanism." In *Conceiving Cosmopolitanism: Theory, Context, and Practice*, ed. Steven Vertovec and Robin Cohen (New York: Oxford University Press, 2002), 165–179.
Viswanathan, Gauri. *Outside the Fold: Conversion, Modernity, and Belief* (Princeton, NJ: Princeton University Press, 1998).
Von Eschen, Penny M. *Race against Empire: Black Americans and Anticolonialism, 1937–1957* (Ithaca, NY: Cornell University Press, 1997).
Wall, Wendy L. "The 1930s Roots of the Postwar 'Consensus.'" In *The Liberal Consensus Reconsidered: American Politics and Society in the Postwar Era*, ed. Robert Mason and Iwan Morgan (Gainesville: University of Florida Press, 2017).
Warren, Heather A. *Theologians of a New World Order: Reinhold, Niebuhr and the Christian Realists, 1920–1948* (New York: Oxford University Press, 1997).
Watt, David Harrington. *Anti-Fundamentalism in Modern America* (Ithaca, NY: Cornell University Press, 2017).
Weisenfeld, Judith. *African American Women and Christian Activism: New York's Black YWCA, 1905–1945* (Cambridge, MA: Harvard University Press, 1997).
———. *New World A-Coming: Black Religion and Racial Identity during the Great Migration* (New York: New York University Press, 2016).
———. "Roundtable: 'Religio-Racial Identity' As Challenge and Critique." *Journal of the American Academy of Religion* 88, no. 2 (June 2020): 299–459.

Wenger, Tisa. "The Practice of Dance for the Future of Christianity: 'Eurythmic Worship' in New York's Roaring Twenties." In *Practicing Protestants: Histories of Christian Life in America*, ed. Laurie Maffly-Kipp, Leigh Schmidt, and Mark Valeri (Baltimore, MD: Johns Hopkins University Press, 2006), 222–249.

———. *We Have a Religion: The 1920s Pueblo Indian Dance Controversy and American Religious Freedom* (Chapel Hill: University of North Carolina Press, 2009).

———. *Religious Freedom: The Contested History of an American Ideal* (Chapel Hill: University of North Carolina Press, 2017).

Wenger, Tisa and Sylvester A. Johnson, eds. *Religion and US Empire: Critical New Histories* (New York: New York University Press, 2022).

White, Heather. *Reforming Sodom: Protestants and the Rise of Gay Rights* (Chapel Hill: University of North Carolina Press, 2015).

White, Kate. "'The Pageant Is the Thing': The Contradictions of Women's Clubs and Civic Education during the Americanization Era." *College English* 77, no. 6 (July 2015): 512–529.

Wiggins, Martha Lee. "United Church Women: 'A Constant Drip of Water Will Wear a Hole in Iron': The Ecumenical Struggle of Church Women to Unite Across Race and Shape the Civil Rights Century." PhD diss., Union Theological Seminary, 2006.

Wilson, Francine Rusan. *The Segregated Scholars: Black Social Scientists and the Creation of Black Labor Studies, 1890–1950* (Charlottesville: University of Virginia Press, 2006).

Wilson, William H. *The City Beautiful Movement* (Baltimore, MD: Johns Hopkins University Press, 1989).

Winant, Howard. *The World Is a Ghetto: Race and Democracy since World War II* (New York: Basic Books, 2001).

Worthen, Molly. *Apostles of Reason: The Crisis of Authority in American Evangelicalism* (New York: Oxford University Press, 2014).

Wright, Ben. *Bonds of Salvation: How Christianity Inspired and Limited American Abolitionists* (Baton Rouge: Louisiana State University Press, 2020).

Yohn, Susan M. "'Let Christian Women Set the Example in Their Own Gifts': The 'Business' of Protestant Women's Organizations." In *Women and Twentieth-Century Protestantism*, ed. Margaret Lamberts Bendroth and Virginia Lieson Brereton (Urbana: University of Illinois Press, 2002).

Yukich, Grace and Penny Edgell, eds. *Religion Is Raced: Understanding American Religion in the Twenty-First Century* (New York: New York University Press, 2020).

Zeien-Stuckman, Emily. "Creating New Citizens: The National Council of Jewish Women's Work at Neighborhood House in Portland, 1896–1912." *Oregon Historical Quarterly* 113, no. 3 (Fall 2012): 312–333.

Zeiger, Susan. "Finding a Cure for War: Women's Politics and the Peace Movement in the 1920s." *Journal of Social History* 24, no. 1 (Autumn 1990): 69–86.

Zubovich, Gene. *Before the Religious Right: Liberal Protestants, Human Rights, and the Polarization of the United States* (Philadelphia: University of Pennsylvania Press, 2022).

INDEX

Abbott, Helen Probst, 93–94, 153
Abernethy, Jean Beaven, 176, 182–83
abolition/abolitionists, 43, 45–46, 48, 85–86
abortion, 5, 196
activism, 39, 83, 91–92, 152, 159, 168, 178, 201; by Black Protestant women, 48–49; Christian citizenship and, 170–76; civil rights, 160–63; CWHM on, 87, 144
Adams, Betty Livingston, 14
Addams, Jane, 124
An Adventure in Brotherhood (Giles), 109–10, 113
Afghanistan, 199–200, 202–3
Africa, 11, 64–65, 156–57
Aghetto, Vittorio, 153
Aglipay, Gregorio, 38
Ahmed, Sara, 66–67
Alexander, Will W., 141–42
Allen, Edith, 142
Americanization, 105–6, 108–11, 120–21, 133–34. *See also* Christian Americanization
Americanization Committee, Rochester Council of Church Women, 120–21, 127–28, 150
American Pageantry Association, 57–58
American Society of Church History, 80
Ames, Jessie Daniel, 141, 163
AME Zion church, 141–42, 153–54
anti-Black racism, 67, 106, 127, 140, 155
anti-lynching laws/efforts, 67, 127, 163–65
anti-militarism, 170, 175
anti-racism/anti-racist, 167, 203

antisemitism, 106, 131, 134–37, 178, 194–95
anti-war, 173, 189
Applegarth, Margaret, 181–82, 184–85, 191
Arai, Tsuru, 65
artists, Black, 156–57, 162
assimilation, immigrant, 15, 56, 108, 111; in Christian Americanization, 104, 119, 122
Association of Southern Women for the Prevention of Lynching, 141, 163
audiences, 15, 25, 47, 59, 62, 86, 88, 166; of missionary pageants, 52, 54, 61, 65
authenticity, 65–67

Bader, Golda, 130–31, 132
Baker, Ella J., 161
Baptists, 4, 81, 91, 95
Beasley, Delilah L., 161–63, 232n73
Beegle, Mary, 57
Belcher, May B., 149–50
Bennett, Katherine, 100–101, 105
Berlant, Lauren, 170
Berman, Jeremiah, 154
Bible, 24, 30, 42–44, 49, 62, 65
Black/African Americans, 1, 18, 56, 109, 127–28, 142; children, 65–66, 162; Great migration of, 6, 139, 141; men, 78, 141–42, 169
blackface, 53–54, 64–65, 67–68
Black Protestant women/churchwomen, 2–3, 6–7, 144, 159–60, 187, 197, 201; as Christian citizens, 169–70; on CW-CRR, 146–47, 149–51, 159–61; interracial cooperation and, 13–14, 16–17, 67, 139, 166–67

Black women, 45–49, 91, 144–45, 146–47, 149–51, 159, 201–2, 234n11
Boas, Franz, 150
Bowles, Eva, 140, 147, 150–51
Brimson, Alice, 122
Brooks, Charles Alvin, 109–11, 125
Brumberg, Joan Jacobs, 8
Buddhism, 42, 96, 112
budgets, 83, 92, 102, 172
Bulletin (FCC publication), 194–95
bureaucracy, 80, 81–82, 100, 103
Bureau of Education, US Department of Interior, 105–6
Burks, Ernestine, 153
Burroughs, Nannie, 47, 145
Burton, Margaret, 75–77, 218n80
Bush, Laura, 199, 203–4

Catholic Church/Catholics, 12–13, 82, 90, 106, 119–21, 209n4; Americanization by, 129; "immigrant colonies," 125; immigrants, 107, 114, 201; missionaries, 55–56; Montgomery on, 34; in the Philippines, 37; prayers, 30; refugees, 193–94; rituals, 52, 57; on temperance, 169; in tri-faith movement, 129–37; voting by, 268
Catt, Carrie Chapman, 132
Cavert, Samuel McCrea, 194–95
Central Committee on the United Study of Foreign Missions, UMS, 20, 23–29, 81, 83, 211n3, 213n19
Central Conference of American Rabbis, 114, 129
Chang, Derek, 8
Chapin, Caroline, 160
Chiang Kai-shek (Madame), 26
Chidester, David, 9
Child, Abbie, 24–26, 213n19
children, 70, 99, 128, 156–57, 177–78, 186, 190, 195; Americanization and, 132–34; Black, 65–66, 162; Christian internationalism and, 172–73; in missionary pageants, 64–66

Chin, Carol, 39
China/Chinese people, 62, 64, 71, 108, 189, 199; in dramatic skits, 73–75, 77; Japanese invasion of, 176; Montgomery on, 42, 46–47
Chinese Protestant women, 170–71, 180, 189–91
Christian Americanization, 5, 10, 66, 105–6, 152, 200, 202; "friendly visits" in, 107, 119–28; in mission study, 15–16; neighborhood houses in, 107, 119–28; in tri-faith movement, 129–37; Vacation Bible School programs in, 107, 126
Christian Americanization (Brooks), 110
Christian citizens/citizenship, 168–69, 180, 188–89, 195, 233n5, 233n9; Rochester Council of Church Women on, 173–75; voting and, 168, 192; world citizenship as, 197–98
Christian cosmopolitanism, 11–14, 82, 94–95, 110–11, 181, 197, 209n4; Christian Americanization in, 106, 125–26; of foreign missions, 39–40; immigration and, 200–201; of missionary pageants, 53, 60, 64–69, 152, 154–55; in mission study, 21, 32; neighborhood houses in, 107, 124–25
"Christian home," 22, 26–27, 193
Christian imperial feminism, 2–4, 9, 53, 78, 83, 100–101, 145, 147, 193, 209n4; Christian Americanization and, 107, 126–27; Christian citizenship and, 17, 180; comparative religion and, 40–50; emancipation of women in, 176, 187–88; on "ethnic religions," 120, 136; interracial cooperation impacted by, 16, 151–52; "scientific" emphasis in, 25, 45, 112–13. *See also* Christian cosmopolitanism
Christian internationalism, 5, 77, 94, 171–73, 175–76, 197
Christianization, 15, 44, 81, 94, 100, 176, 193, 197

Christian Social Relations department, UCCW, 137, 166
Christian World Order, 5–6, 84, 172, 187, 197, 200, 233n9; postwar, 167, 169; World War II and, 179–81
Christus Redemptor (Montgomery), 33, 35–37, 69–70
Church Pageantry (Miller, M.), 59
Church Woman (magazine), 11, 134, 166, 168, 176, 191, 196–97, 199; on antilynching law, 165; on civil rights, 187–88; on CWCRR national conferences, 158; on NCCJ, 130–31; on prayer, 182–83; on UCCW National Assemblies, 187; on World War II, 178–79
Church Woman's Committee on Race Relations (CWCRR), 146–52, 155, 161, 166, 228n4; on antisemitism, 136–37; civil rights focus of, 138–40, 169; national conferences, 16, 140, 149–51, 157–60
Church Women at Work on the Race Problem (CWCRR pamphlet), 151–52
"churchwomen" identity, 82, 93, 97–104
Church Women United, 196, 203, 209n4
CIC. *See* Commission on Interracial Cooperation
citizenship, 17, 114, 227n111. *See also* Christian citizens/citizenship
civil rights, 5, 10, 147, 160, 187–88, 193, 196, 200–201; activism, 161–63; UCCW supporting, 169–70
Civil War, US, 4, 48, 153
class, 123–24; race and, 147, 158–59. *See also* middle-class
A Clearer Vision of the Race Problem (CWRR pamphlet), 148–49
Clement, George C., 141–42
Cleveland, Ohio, 187
Clinton, Hillary, 199
Cold War, 167
colleges, Protestant women's in Asia, 40, 99
colonialism, 34, 56, 157–58, 192; settler, 7, 51–52, 58, 68, 77–78, 108

Commission on International Justice and Goodwill, FCC, 127, 162, 172, 179
Commission on Interracial Cooperation (CIC), 141–42
Commission on the Church and Race Relations, FCC, 127, 140–42
communism, 129, 167, 193
"Community Americanization," 108–9
comparative religions, 21–22, 24–25, 40–50, 70–72, 78
Conference on the Churches and International Situation (1940), 179
Congress, US, 108, 164, 192–93
Conning, John Stuart, 224n43
Conroy-Krutz, Emily, 7–8
conservatism/conservative, 4–5, 77–78, 96–97, 195, 200; gender ideologies, 201, 203
Constitution, US, 144, 171
conversion/converts, 36, 52, 100, 114–16, 130, 145; in dramatic skits, 72–73; in missionary pageants, 61–63
cooperation, 15, 81–82, 90, 94–95, 97, 136; interreligious, 16, 131–32; pageant participation as, 58–59, 78–79. *See also* interracial cooperation
Costigan, Edward, 153
Costigan-Wagner bill, 163–65
costumes, dramatic skit, 69–70, 76–77
costumes, missionary pageants, 51, 75–76, 76, 154–55; Orientalism of, 56, 62, 64–65, 65
Council of Church Women, Rochester, 68–69, 82, 87–97, 107, 115; Americanization Committee, 120–21, 127–28, 150; Executive Committee, 94, 161; founding of, 89–90; International Relations Department, 132, 173–74; Legislative Department, 172–74, 175; Missions Department, 127, 172–73; pageant by, 154; protestant interracialism at, 152–59; tri-faith movement in, 131–32

Council of Jewish Women, 114, 131–32, 134, 175
Council of Social Agencies, 131–32
Council of Women for Home Missions (CWHM), 4, 83–85, 87, 105, 112, 141, 171; approach to cooperation of, 80–81; mission study textbooks, 109–10; reorganization of, 97–103; *The Trend of the Races* studied by, 142–45
Crawford, Jack, 57
Crowe, Susannah, 178
Cullen, Countee, 155–57
cultural pluralism, 106, 127, 136
CWCRR. *See* Church Woman's Committee on Race Relations
CWHM. *See* Council of Women for Home Missions

Davidson, Christina C., 107
Davol, Ralph, 57–58, 66
Day of Prayer for Missions, 99, 181
deaths, 61, 96, 161–62, 195
Declaration of Human Rights, UN, 192–93
democracy/democratic values, 57, 110–11, 146, 165, 167, 168–69, 195; Bible and, 43–44; Christian, 177; cooperation as, 82; interreligious cooperation and, 131–32; religious freedom and, 129
Democrat and Chronicle (newspaper), 146, 153, 155, 156
DeMond, Abraham Lincoln, 47
Department of Christian World Relations, UCCW, 137, 191
Department of Interior, US, 105–6, 114
Department of Labor, US, 139–40
Department on Race Relations, FCC, 135, 138, 156, 227n93, 229n11
Derricotte, Juliette, 161
Dett, Nathaniel, 156–57
devolution, 73, 78–79
Dickerson, Addie W., 150
disarmament, 163, 173, 175

Disciples of Christ, 1, 4, 64, 81, 91
discrimination, 152, 237n81; racial, 127, 143, 160–61, 177
displaced persons, 193–96, 237n81
diversity, 15, 108–14, 140, 184–85; cosmopolitan, 124–25; racial, 155, 181, 200–201, 215n12; religious, 77, 135–36
Dixon, Laura, 122–23
domestic policy, US, 173, 192, 198
domestic workers, Black, 140–41, 143–44
Dorsey Home for Dependent Colored Children, 91
Du Bois, W. E. B., 56
Dunbar-Nelson, Alice, 151
Dyer Anti-Lynching Act, 146

Eagles Mere, Pennsylvania, 146, 149, 151
ecumenical Protestantism, 3–7, 12, 81–83, 87–97, 158, 172, 209n4; Christian Americanization programs by, 106–7, 109, 125, 129; gendered organizations in, 80, 83–88; on immigrant labor, 108; liberalism of, 200–201; Missionary Education Movement, 59; against nativism, 106; in tri-faith movement, 129–37. *See also* Council of Church Women, Rochester; men/male, ecumenical Protestant
education/educational programs, 29–32, 78, 85–86, 124, 144, 180, 196; for Christian Americanization programs, 120, 122–23; English language, 105–6, 125; for immigrants, 123, 128; interracial cooperation and, 139, 142–43; missionary pageants and, 51–52, 63; religious, 14, 88–89, 102; at Vacation Bible School programs, 107, 126. *See also* mission study
Elliot, Gabrielle, 58–59
Ellis Island, 114
Elmore, Amelia Joseph, 190
Elzy, Ruby, 155–56
emancipation, 56, 143, 151

emancipation of women, 8–9, 23, 44, 46, 48–49, 176, 187–89, 197; conversion equated with, 53; in missionary pageants, 63; via foreign missions, 51
Emerick, J. W., 162
empire/imperialism, British, 8–9, 171–72
empire/imperialism, US, 7–11, 20, 33–40, 171–72. *See also* Christian imperial feminism
English (language), 105–6, 125, 189–90
English Arts and Crafts movement, 51–52, 55
Episcopalians, 4, 81
Equal Rights Amendment, 196–97
"ethnic" costumes, 154–55
"ethnic religions," 23–24, 41, 120, 125, 136, 202; depicted in missionary pageants, 53–54; Protestant Christianity as, 36; racialization of, 6, 9; UMS on, 20–21
Europe/European, refugees, 193–94. *See also* immigrants
evangelism, 2–5, 21, 68–69, 200
Evanston, Illinois, 157m 159

Federal Council of Churches (FCC), 81, 84–87, 109, 114, 138, 141, 147–48, 193; Administrative Committee, 160; Commission on International Justice and Goodwill, 162, 172, 179; Commission on the Church and Race Relations, 127, 140–42; Committee on Religious Drama, 59; Department on Race Relations, 135, 138, 156, 227n93, 229n11; on displaced persons, 194–95; on immigration policies, 193; reorganization of, 97–103; segregation opposed by, 139; UCCW and, 194; Women's Cooperating Commission, 179; YWCA and, 146–47
Federation of Woman's Boards of Foreign Missions (FWBFM), 4, 47–48, 80–81, 83–85, 92, 171

feminism, 14, 21, 43–45, 70, 74–78, 76, 199, 212n6; second-wave, 10, 196, 202. *See also* Christian imperial feminism
Ferguson, Frances, 101–2, 130
Findings Committee, FWBFM, 86–97, 98, 100
Fitzgerald, Estelle, 128, 153
Foreign Missions Conference and Federation of Woman's Boards of Foreign Missions (FWBFM), 102, 141
foreign policy, US, 5, 13, 40, 103, 170–74
Foster, Millicent, 168
France, 56, 146
"friendship"/"friendly visits," 16, 107, 114–17, 119–28, 134, 136, 147
Fundamentalism, 95–97
fundraising, 40, 54, 56, 102
FWBFM. *See* Federation of Woman's Boards of Foreign Missions; Foreign Missions Conference and Federation of Woman's Boards of Foreign Missions

Gannett, Mary L., 153
Gannett, William C., 153
Gardner, Katherine, 15, 148–49, 152, 158–59, 161, 164–65
Gary, Indiana, 124–25
gender/gendered constructs, 6–7, 9, 192–93, 195, 238n4; conservative, 77–78, 201; in ecumenical organizations, 80, 83–87; norms, 13, 78, 107; White Protestant women on, 2, 21–22
Gentleman's Agreement (1907), US, 108
Germany/Germans, 135, 176, 189–90, 193; Nazi regime, 131, 134, 177, 194–95
Gianfranceschi, Marietta, 121
Giles, Dorothy, 109–10, 112, 113, 125
Gin Lum, Kathryn, 8, 109
Glassberg, David, 51, 55
goodwill, 1, 106–7, 123, 172, 201
Gracey, Annie Ryder, 25

Grand Rapids, Michigan, 187, 191
Great Depression, US, 83, 102, 162
Great migration (Black southerners), 6, 139, 141
Guerry, William A., 47
Guild, Roy B., 87–88, 93, 219n24
Gulick, Sidney, 93, 172

Hammond, Lily, 144–45
Handbook of American Pageantry (Davol), 66
Handy, Robert, 80
Harkness, Georgia, 179, 185–86
Harmon Foundation, 152, 156
Hawaii, 33, 35, 39, 117
Haynes, Elizabeth Ross, 139–40, 143, 147, 150–51
Haynes, George E., 16, 87, 127, 135, 139–46, 147–48, 162
Head, Mabel, 191
"heathenism," 8, 20, 30, 62, 70, 109, 112, 139
Hedgeman, Anna Arnold, 11
Heilbrunn, Madeleine, 132
hierarchies, 7–9, 42, 62, 73; missionary, 53, 129, 170; racial, 38, 106–7, 202. *See also* power
Hinduism, 19–20, 22, 41–42, 49, 64–65, 71–73
Hocking, William Ernest, 96
Home Missions Council, 112, 119, 141, 211n3
home missions/missionary societies, 106, 108, 136, 141; Black Americans in, 127; foreign missions vs, 4, 80–81; segregated, 147
homes, 58, 123, 143, 145, 188; "Christian," 22, 26–27, 193
Hondelink, Grace, 92
Hoover, Herbert, 177
Hope, Lugenia Burns, 91
Hough, Mary, 99
housewives, 144, 191–92

How to Use handbooks, UMS textbooks, 12, 29–32, 37, 41, 49, 59, 69–77, 76; for *An African Trail*, 67–68; for *Christus Redemptor*, 35
Hudelson, Mabel Jordan, 168
Hü King Eng, 46
Hull House, 124
human rights, 169–70, 192–93, 199
Hunt, Mathilda, 93
Hunton, Addie W., 153

I Believe in God (Royden), 94
identity, 10, 106, 130, 133, 169, 187, 197, 203; "churchwomen," 82, 93, 97–104; gender, 6–7; "missionary woman," 82, 86, 93, 97–104; national, 107, 201; racial, 1, 5, 107, 111–12, 125, 132, 147; religious, 5, 107, 116, 195; shared, 25, 169, 188; White Protestant women, 3, 11–12, 200
"immigrant colonies," 109, 125, 141, 201
immigrants/immigration policies, 105–6, 108, 177, 201, 227n111; Christian Americanization targeting, 105, 107, 121–22; displaced people and, 195–96; European, 6, 109, 110, 120, 128, 152, 154, 237n81; racialized, 56, 169; Truman on, 193–94. *See also* assimilation, immigrant
Immigration Act (1924), US, 172
imperialism. *See* empire/imperialism
inclusion, racial, 6, 107, 114–19, 139
India, 19–20, 41–42, 46, 77, 84, 158; in missionary pageants, 62, 64
integration, racial, 48–49, 149, 160–61, 166; ecumenical Protestants on, 201
Interdenominational Woman's Foreign Missions Conference, 51
interfaith/interreligious programs, 16, 75–76, 76, 182, 196, 201; Christian Americanization and, 107, 127. *See also* tri-faith movement
International Relations Department, Rochester Council of Church Women, 132, 173–74

International Review of Missions (publication), 84
interracial conferences, 16, 140, 142, 146
interracial cooperation, 1–2, 66–67, 87, 103, 127, 165–66, 187, 200–202; Black-White, 128, 140, 142, 152; Haynes, G., on, 142–45; interfaith programs in, 182, 201; mission study and, 141–46
interracial marriage, 111, 145
interwar period, 10, 79, 140, 173, 188–89, 192
In the Vanguard of a Race (Hammond), 144–45
"intimate public," 13, 170
Islam/Muslims, 23, 37, 63, 71, 209n8
Italian (language), 119–20

Jacobstein, Meyer, 93
Japan/Japanese, 71, 77, 93, 96, 176, 178, 189; doll exchange program with, 172; immigration, 108; in missionary pageants, 62, 64–65
Jim Crow laws, 78, 139
Johnson, Halla, 101
Johnson-Reed Immigration Act, US, 108
Judaism/Jewish people, 82, 106, 112, 125–26, 154, 168, 224n43; Council of Jewish Women, 114, 131–32, 134, 175; immigrants, 107, 113–14, 201; in National Urban League, 141; Nazi persecution of, 134–35; in NCCJ, 115, 129–35, 167; refugees, 134–35, 193–95; in tri-faith movement, 129–38

Kaell, Hillary, 53
Kagawa, Toyohito, 185
Kallen, Horace, 106
Kansas City, Missouri, 126
Kellogg-Briand Pact, 173
Kerschner, Carrie, 85, 86
Kester, Howard, 151, 161
Kim, Helen, 181
The Kingdom and the Nations (North), 174

The King's Highway (Montgomery), 46
Kohiuama, Rui, 172
Kramer, Paul, 7
Ku Klux Klan, 106
Kyles, Josephine, 149–50, 187

labor, 108, 126
Land of All Nations (Seebach), 110
Langdon, William Chauncey, 55, 58
language/s, 66, 183; English, 105–6, 125, 189–90; Italian, 119–20; translation, 40, 189–90
Laymen's Inquiry Report, 95–96
Leadership Training Workshops, UCCW, 192
League of Nations, 132, 170, 173, 176
League of Women Voters, 133, 196–97
Lee, Anna, 153
Lee, John, 153
Legislative Department, Rochester Council of Church Women, 172–74, 175
Lester, Muriel, 157–58, 177–78
letter-writing campaigns, 7, 39, 99–100, 164–65, 174–75, 178, 191, 194
liberalism, 169, 198, 200–201; racial, 3, 9–10, 17, 67, 78, 145, 152–53, 166–67
liberty, religious, 16, 107, 114–18, 202
Life and Light for Women (publication), 24, 63
The Light of the World (Speer), 70, 72
The Little Green God (Mason), 19–20, 22
Lofton, Kathryn, 31
London, 60–61, 94, 124
Louderbaugh, Ellen, 135
Lucy Webb Hayes National Training School, 123
Lux Christi (Mason), 19–20
lynchings, 78, 141, 146, 163

MacFarlane, Adeline, 150
MacLaurin, Ella, 85
magazines, missionary, 12, 22, 126–27
Maldonado-Estrada, Alyssa, 12–13

Mandarin (language), 189
Mangano, Antonio, 173
Mangano, Mabel, 133–34, 173–74, 225n8
marriage, 11–12, 18, 74, 91; interracial, 111, 145
Mason, Caroline Atwater, 19–20
maternalist/maternalism, 189–91, 195, 200
McAlister, Melani, 15
McGowan, Clelia, 150
McQueen, Donald B., 91
men, Black, 78, 141–42, 169
Men and Religion Forward Movement, 88
men/male, ecumenical Protestant, 44, 102–3, 170, 177–78; gendered organizations and, 80, 83–89
Methodists, 4, 81, 91
Methods of Private Religious Living (Wieman), 100–101
Mexico, 172–73
Meyer, Birgit, 13, 15, 52
Michelson, Nellie, 127–28
middle-class, 36–37, 55, 57–58, 91, 126, 144, 159, 165; domesticity, 121–22
Miller, Kenneth D., 110, 113, 125, 224n33
Miller, Madeline, 59–60
minstrel shows, 57, 66–68
Missionary Education Movement, 59, 211n3
"missionary ethnology," 2, 8, 49, 208n3, 214n57
"missionary intelligence," 21, 33, 49
missionary movement, White women's foreign, 14, 17, 23–24, 107, 136, 172, 197, 200–201; Christian Americanization and, 106, 126–27; home missions vs., 4, 80–81; immigration and, 108; interracial cooperation as departure from, 147–50; pageants influenced by, 190; panoramic pageants as, 53–54, 60–69; prayer services in, 181–82; racial hierarchy in, 107; reorganization of, 2, 80–87, 92–93, 97–104; Rochester Council of Church Women and,

92–93. *See also* costumes, missionary pageants
Missionary Review of the World (publication), 145
"missionary woman" identity, 82, 86, 93, 97–104
Missions Department, Rochester Council of Church Women, 127, 172–73
mission study, 9, 15–16, 33–40, 99; dramatic skits in, 54, 69; on "friendly visits," 123–24; interracial cooperation and, 141–46
mission study textbooks/literature, 13, 112–13, 125, 140, 173–74; Christian Americanization in, 107, 109–10
modernization, 76–77, 83
Montgomery, Helen Barrett, 78, 90, 95–96, 99, 119–20, 197; on the Bible, 42–44, 49; Christian feminism defined by, 14–15; *Pageant of Missions* by, 60–61; *Western Women in Eastern Lands*, 40–41, 45, 51, 62, 70, 84. *See also How to Use* handbooks
moral authority, 3, 5–6, 9, 49–50, 81, 100, 122
Moran, Katherine, 37–38, 56
"Mothers of the World" (pageant), 189–91
movies/films, 55, 121
multiculturalism, 4, 66

NAACP. *See* National Association for the Advancement of Colored People
National Assemblies, UCCW, 180–81, 187–89, 191–92
National Association for the Advancement of Colored People (NAACP), 141, 153, 160–63, 165
National Association of Colored Women, 166
National Commission of Protestant Church Women, 98, 100
National Committee of Church Women, 176, 178–79

National Conference of Christians and Jews (NCCJ), 115, 129–35, 167
National Conference on the Cause and Cure of War (NCCCW), 132–34, 171, 174, 176, 179
National Council of Churches, 200
National Council of Federated Church Women, 130, 133, 157, 174, 175
National Geographic, 113–14
national identity, 107, 201
nationalism, 105, 110, 171, 191, 201
nationality, 107; racial identity and, 1, 111, 125, 132
National Urban League, 141, 160
National Women's Party, 196–97
Native Americans, 52, 57, 99, 109, 153–54, 182
nativism, 106, 108–9, 136
Nazi regime, 131, 134, 177, 194–95
NCCCW. *See* National Conference on the Cause and Cure of War
NCCJ. *See* National Conference of Christians and Jews
neighborhood houses/settlement houses, 16, 129, 139, 201; in Christian Americanization programs, 107, 119–28
New Deal, US, 5, 130
New Jersey, 148, 157, 159, 189
"New Women of the Orient," 21, 48, 72, 74–75, 212n6
New York, 80, 94, 147, 155–56, 159–63, 179. *See also* Rochester, New York
New York Times Magazine, 55, 58
New Zealand, 183
Ngai, Mae, 108
Niebuhr, Reinhold, 176
Normandie, USS, 134
norms, gendered, 13, 78, 107
North, Eric, 174
Northern Baptist Convention, 96
Northfield interdenominational conference, 51, 60–61

Oakland, California, 16, 45, 161–62, 165
Oakland Tribune (newspaper), 161–62
Oberammergau (passion play), 52, 61
Of One Blood (Speer), 110, 113, 127
"Old World," 112, 129
"The Open Door" (pageant), 56
oppression, 23, 56, 120
ordination of women, 170, 196
Orientalism, 8, 41, 56, 62–65, 65, 69
Orthodox Christians, 201, 209n4
"Other Foreign Women" (pageant), 122
Oxenham, John, 60–61, 77–78

pacifism, 176–77; in pageants, 189–90
Pageant and Masque of St. Louis (Glassberg), 55
The Pageant of Darkness and Light (pageant), 60–61, 77–78
Pageant of Missions (Montgomery), 51, 60–61, 64, 70, 75, 77–78
pageantry, 51–52, 55–60
pageants, missionary, 15, 49, 94, 152, 184, 215n4; authenticity in, 65–67; by Chinese Protestant women, 170–71, 180, 189–91; embodiment in, 52–54; panoramic, 53, 60–69, 71, 74–75, 77–78. *See also* costumes, missionary pageants
Pandit, Vijaya Lakshmi, 196
panoramic pageants, 53, 54, 60–69, 71, 74–75, 77–78
Parker, Arthur C., 154
Parkes Cadman, S., 175
Parsons, Ellen C., 23–25, 49, 213n19
patriarchy/patriarchal, 42, 70, 202
Peabody, Lucy, 40, 47–49, 84, 95–96, 99, 171, 172, 213n19
peace movement, women's, 169, 173, 234n11
Peasant Pioneers (Miller, K.), 110
people of color, 46, 53–54, 65–68, 72, 75, 78
performers/cast, dramatic skits, 71–78

performers/cast, missionary pageant, 51–52, 61–62; White women as, 53–54, 65–66
Philippines, 33, 35–39, 95–96, 172
Pittsburgh, Pennsylvania, 83–87
pluralism, 57–58, 129, 133, 136
Pomeroy, Helen, 153
Post, Ida, 92, 132–33, 173–74, 192
postwar era, 9–10, 17, 167, 169–70
power/power dynamics, 8–9, 44, 95, 106–7, 131, 143–44, 163; class and, 123; gendered, 88; of the home, 188; missionary, 170; US, 5, 7, 167, 198, 201; of women, 45, 202
Practicing Christian Unity (Guild), 88
prayer, 12, 30, 112, 153, 166, 176, 181–87, 193. *See also* World Day of Prayer
Presbyterians, 4, 64, 81, 91
Price, Orlo, 89
Princeton University, 83
Prohibition, 13, 91–92, 171, 197
prostitution, 19–20, 41–42
"Protestant globalism," 170
Protestant Interracialism, 16, 152–59
Protestantism. *See specific topics*
Protestant Reformation, 57
Pruitt, Nicholas, 105–6
publications, Protestant, 11–14, 211n3
"public conscience," 142
public opinion, 99–100, 103, 135–36, 152–53, 191–92; CWHM on, 105; Guild on, 88–89; power of, 144
Purvis, Elinor K., 133, 178, 227n111

Quaker, 186
Quinlan, Florence, 85–87, 98, 100
Quinn, Beulah, 123

"race problem," 110, 112, 128, 148–49, 151, 154
race/racialization, 15–16, 82, 152; in Christian Americanization, 107, 111, 125; class and, 147, 158–59; discrimination by, 127, 143, 160–61, 177; diversity, 155, 181, 200–201, 215n12; hierarchies, 38, 106–7, 202; identity, 1, 5, 107, 111–12, 125, 132, 147; of immigrants, 56, 169; inclusion, 6, 107, 114–19; Jewish people and, 113–14, 134–35; scientific, 25, 45, 112–13; shared identity and, 187–88; stereotypes, 62, 64–65; in UMS textbooks, 20. *See also* integration, racial
"race relations," 106–7, 140, 141–42, 148, 152–53, 155, 155–57; Black children impacted by, 162; Haynes, G., on, 127–28; Jewish persecution in, 134–35; in UMS textbooks, 103
Race Relations Sunday, 68, 127–28, 142, 149, 153
racial inclusion, 6, 107, 114–19
racialized religion, 49, 199–201. *See also* "ethnic religions"
racial justice, 47–48, 159–67
racial liberalism, 3, 9–10, 17, 67, 78, 145, 152–53, 166–67
"racial science," 25, 36, 112–14
racism, 1–2, 8, 16, 108, 140, 143, 191; of Christian imperial feminism, 38, 49, 145, 166
radio programming, 183–84, 192
Ramabai, Pandita, 46
Randolph, Florence Sterling, 149–51, 158
Raymond, Maud Mary, 32–33
Red Cross, 77, 90, 146
Reformed Church's Woman's Missionary Society, 85
refugees, 134–35, 176–77; World War II, 178, 193–95
relief aid, World War II, 177
Religious Census, US, 112
religious difference, 112, 125, 127
religious freedom, 129–30, 193, 199, 201
"religious liberty," 202
religious pluralism, 200
religious tolerance, 77, 129, 182
Renda, Mary, 8

representation, racial, 47, 155; in dramatic skits, 70–72; in missionary pageants, 53–54, 56, 62, 64–68, 65, 75–76, 76
respectability, 57, 144, 159
responsibilities, 33, 35, 83, 102; of Christian citizens, 17, 175, 193; Christianization, 94, 100; for displaced people, 194–95; UCCW, 187, 191; of White Protestant women, 5, 21, 23–24, 168, 200
Reynolds, Margaret, 59
rights, 4, 23, 74–75, 131, 163; human, 169–70, 192–93, 199; voting, 106–297. *See also* civil rights; women's rights
Rincón, Felisa, 196
rituals, 186; Catholic, 52, 57
Rochester, New York, 90–93; Christian Americanization in, 119–20; World Friendship projects, 172–73. *See also* Council of Church Women, Rochester
Rochester's Women's Missionary Union, 92–94
Roosevelt, Eleanor, 194, 196–97
Roosevelt, Theodore, 163–64
Rose, Carrie, 91, 146, 153, 157
Rose, James E., 93, 146, 153
Rose, William Wallace, 93
Ross, Emory, 11
Ross, Myrta, 11, 80, 183–84, 188
Rothenburger, Leila Avery, 1–3
Royden, Maude, 94–96

San Francisco Chronicle (newspaper), 45
Savage, Cornelius, 90
"savage," 37, 41, 57, 109
schools, 56, 152
science, "racial," 25, 36, 45, 112–14
second-wave feminism, 10, 196, 202
secular/secularism, 82, 97, 124, 129, 183, 203, 237n78; Americanization, 120–21; defined, 10; feminists, 199–200; pageants and, 57, 59; pluralism and, 133, 136; in settlement houses, 125–27; in UMS textbooks, 49–50

Seebach, Margaret, 110–11
segregation, racial, 47, 67, 114, 138, 147, 152, 172, 190; Jim Crow laws causing, 78, 139
Seneca Nation, 153–54, 182
"sensational forms," 12, 15, 52
September 11, 2001 attacks, 199
settlement houses. *See* neighborhood houses/settlement houses
settler-colonialism, 7, 51–52, 58, 68, 77–78, 108
shared identity, 25, 169, 188
Sheffield Neighborhood Center, 126
Sibley, Georgiana, 91, 95–96, 97, 130, 132, 134, 195–96, 198
Silverthorn, Katherine, 97–98
Singh, Lilavati, 46
skits, dramatic/"impersonations," 50, 53–54, 59, 69–79, 184
slavery/enslaved people, US, 56, 145
Slowe, Lucy D., 128
Slutes, Edna, 150
Smith, Christine, 166, 169, 187–88
Smith, Emily White, 24
Social Creed of the Churches, FCC, 138
"Social fellowship," 145
socialism, 94, 176
"the South," US, 1, 47–49, 141, 150, 201
Spain/Spanish missionaries, 37–38, 56
Spanish-American War, 34
Speer, Robert E., 70, 110, 113–14, 127
"The Star of Ethiopia" (pageant), 56
Stebbins, Elizabeth, 134
stereotypes/tropes, 8, 51, 62, 64–65, 65
Stratton Bill, US, 194, 195
suburbs, 147, 237n78
suffrage movement/suffragists, 21, 45, 144, 169, 171; Black women as, 153; Montgomery in, 39
Suggestions for Interracial Gatherings (CWCRR pamphlet), 155, 157
sympathy, 13, 53, 122, 134, 145, 152, 183
synagogues, 134, 224n43

tableaux/living pictures, pageant, 59–69, 75
Talbert, Mary Burnett, 146
Taylor, James Claire, 153–54
telegrams, 146, 163, 175
temperance, 29, 94, 163–64, 169, 171, 173
"temple girls/prostitution," 19–20, 41–42
territorial colonies, US, 7, 33–35, 39, 173
textbooks, UMS, 14–15, 21–22, 25–26, 49, 58, 93, 102; *Christus Redemptor*, 33, 69–70; *The Kingdom and the Nations* (North), 174; *Lux Christi*, 19–20; *Western Women in Eastern Lands*, 51, 62. See also *How to Use* handbooks
Theosophy, 72–73
Thompson, Blanche Jennings, 132–33
Thompson, Michael, 171
Tonga, 36–37
Topeka, Kansas, 87–88
totalitarianism, 129, 195–96
tourism, 56, 70–71
Toynbee Hall (London), 124
translation, 40, 189–90
The Trend of the Races (Haynes, G.), 16, 87, 142–46
tri-faith movement, 16, 129–37, 201
Trowbridge, Sarah, 158–59
Truman, Harry S., 191, 193, 237n81
Tubman, Harriet, 45–46
Turkey, 23, 63–64, 77
Tyler, Florence, 102–3, 185
Tyler, Samuel, 89

UCCW. See United Council of Church Women
UMS. See United Mission Study
Underhill, Muriel, 84
United Council of Church Women (UCCW), 2–3, 11, 82, 176, 195, 198; on Christian citizenship, 169–71; Christian Social Relations department, 137, 166; Department of Christian World Relations, 137, 191; FCC and, 194; formation of, 17, 180, 197; on immigration policies, 193; Leadership Training Workshops, 192; National Assemblies, 180–81, 187–89, 191–92; postwar, 192; World Community Day, 193. See also Council of Church Women, Rochester
United Mission Study (UMS), 12, 14, 19–20, 22–33, 174; Central Committee on the United Study of Foreign Missions, 20, 23–29, 81, 83, 211n3, 213n19. See also textbooks, UMS
United Nations, 170, 173, 191–93, 199
United States (US), 11, 60–61; Civil War, 4, 48, 153; Congress, 108, 164, 192–93; Constitution, 144, 171; Department of Interior, 105–6, 114; domestic policy, 173, 192, 198; foreign policy, 5, 13, 40, 103, 170–74; Great Depression, 83, 102, 162; Great migration, 6, 139, 141; power, 5, 7, 167, 198, 201. See also empire/imperialism; home missions
unity, Christian, 82, 186–87
universalism, 36, 54, 89, 107, 136, 171, 209n4
Universal Military Training (draft), 192
University of Rochester, 161
unmarried women, 11–12, 18, 81, 91
US. See United States

Vacation Bible School programs, 107, 126
Van Dusen, Henry P., 177
Van Nuys, Frederick, 165
vaudeville, 55, 57
vespers services, 128, 153–54
veterans, 194–95
volunteers, 18, 119–20, 122–24, 128
voting/voters, 163, 168; Christian citizens as, 175, 192; White Protestant women, 169, 177

Wagner, Robert F., 163, 165
Wagner-Steagall Housing Bill, 165
Waid, Eva Clark, 113–14
Walden, P. J., 33

Walker, Alice, 89, 134, 153
Walker, Maggie L., 145
Washington, Booker T., 145
"The Way of Love" (Harkness), 186
WDP. *See* World Day of Prayer
Weisenfeld, Judith, 139
Welcher, Amy, 166, 180
welfare programs, US, 124, 128
Wendel, Lily, 194–95
Westbrook, Mary, 149, 151
Western Women in Eastern Lands (Montgomery), 40–41, 45, 51, 62, 70, 84
"What Our Minister Told Dorothy" (dramatic skit), 70
White liberal Protestants, 109, 200, 209n6, 215n12
White people/Whiteness, 1, 6, 18, 34–37, 107, 141–42, 144
White Protestant women, 1–3, 21–22, 107, 158–59, 177, 197, 200; activism of, 91, 174; as Christian citizens, 169–70; Christian internationalism and, 172; on CWCRR, 138, 149–51, 159–61; identity, 3, 11–12, 200; interracial cooperation and, 13–14, 16–17, 139, 148–49, 156, 165–66, 201–2; on male-led organizations, 83–84; "race" studied by, 111–14; responsibilities of, 5, 21, 23–24, 168, 200; *The Trend of the Races* studied by, 146. *See also* Christian cosmopolitanism; Christian imperial feminism; missionary movement, White women's foreign
White supremacy, 3, 8, 10, 143–44, 154, 172
Wieman, Henry Nelson, 100–101
Wilkins, Roy, 160
Winant, John G., 161
Wise, Louise, 131
womanhood, Protestant, 12–13, 44, 78, 95, 121–22, 130, 181
Woman's Home Missions (magazine), 113
Woman's International League for Peace and Freedom, 171
Woman's Missionary Congress, World's Columbian Exposition, 23
Woman's Peace Party, 171
Woman's Work (magazine), 23, 27
Women and Missions (magazine), 113
women of color, 53–54, 65–68, 72
Women's Committee of National Defense, 146
Women's Foreign Missionary Societies of the Presbyterian Church, 211n3
Women's National Missionary Association, Universalist, 89
women's rights, 3–4, 19, 169, 196, 199, 201–2, 209n8; the Bible and, 43–44; racial progress and, 121; secular, 200
Women's Work (magazine), 58
"women's wrongs," 19, 21–22, 24, 42, 45, 51, 70
Women Workers of the Orient (Burton), 75
world citizenship, 197–98
"world-consciousness," 32–33
World Day of Prayer (WDP), 12, 17, 68, 99, 170–71, 180–87, 197
"world friendship," 172–73
World's Columbian Exposition, 23
World's Parliament of Religions, 24
World War I, 73, 77–78, 88, 105, 108, 110–11, 197
World War II, 146, 170–71, 176–77, 193
Wysinger, Lena, 162

YMCA. *See* Young Men's Christian Association
Young, Helen A., 120–21, 127
Young, Louise, 169
Young Men's Christian Association (YMCA), 4, 88
Young Women's Christian Association (YWCA), 4, 75, 150, 155; Black women active in, 7, 138–40; Board of Pageantry and Drama, 59; Committee on Colored Work, 151; FCC and, 146–47

Zubovich, Gene, 5, 170, 238n4

ABOUT THE AUTHOR

GALE L. KENNY is Assistant Professor in the Department of Religion at Barnard College in New York City, where she teaches courses in American religion. She is the author of *Contentious Liberties: American Abolitionists in Post-emancipation Jamaica, 1837–1866*.

www.ingramcontent.com/pod-product-compliance
Lightning Source LLC
Chambersburg PA
CBHW020358080526
44584CB00014B/1078